Constraint-Based Grammar Formalisms

Constraint-Based Grammar Formalisms
Parsing and Type Inference for
Natural and Computer Languages

Stuart M. Shieber

A Bradford Book
The MIT Press
Cambridge, Massachusetts
London, England

This book was typeset with Donald E. Knuth's TEX and Leslie Lamport's LATEX.

Printed and bound in the United States of America.

Library of Congress Cataloging-in-Publication Data

Shieber, Stuart M.
    Constraint-based grammar formalisms : parsing and type inference for natural and computer languages / Stuart M. Shieber.
        p.   cm.
    "A Bradford book."
    Includes bibliographical references and index.
    ISBN 0-262-19324-8
    1. Computational linguistics. 2. Grammar, Comparative and general—Data processing. 3. Programming languages (Electronic computers)—Syntax. 4. Parsing (Computer grammar). I. Title.
P98.S54 1992
410'.285—dc20   92-7820
                                                                      CIP

To Linda Ann Sarnoff (1959–1988)
Strength. Wisdom. Beauty.

Contents

Preface

A wise man once said, "Fine words butter no parsnips." I didn't make this up; you can check in Bartlett's. I don't pretend to know what that means, but I have a sneaking suspicion that it applies to this document. Worse, I fear, as all writers of technical material must, that people will have the same quizzical reaction to this book that I have to the proverb. In any case, insofar as the ideas presented herein have any currency and consequence—butter any parsnips, I suppose—I owe a debt to a great many people.

The present volume is a revised version of a Ph.D. dissertation submitted in March, 1989 to the Computer Science Department at Stanford University. It has endured a long gestation period since Stan Rosenschein first introduced me to the design of natural-language grammar formalisms. Thereafter, an increasingly large number of individuals and institutions have participated in its etiology.

Barbara Grosz persuaded me, against my better judgment at the time, to return to school; Stan Rosenschein and Fernando Pereira applied significant pressure as well. At that point, the die was cast.

SRI International allowed me to undertake the responsibilities of a student while maintaining my job; Artificial Intelligence Center directors Nils Nilsson, Stan Rosenschein, and Ray Perrault have been primarily responsible for this enlightened policy. The Center for the Study of Language and Information, under the thoughtful guidance of, variously, John Perry, Jon Barwise, Tom Wasow, and Stanley Peters, made facilities of various sorts—including computers, office space, and time—available to me. These two institutions have provided a work environment unparalleled with respect to quantity and quality of resources and ideas, academic freedom, personal camaraderie, and good humor.

The most important enabling force, however, has been the minds I have had the privilege of working with over the years. From the original work on PATR with Stan Rosenschein to the brainstorming sessions designing PATR-II with the early PATR group (comprising at various times John Bear, Lauri Karttunen, Fernando Pereira, Jane Robinson, Stan Rosenschein, Susan Stucky, Mabry Tyson, and Hans Uszkoreit) to the later consolidation of results through the aegis of the Foundations of

Grammar group at CSLI (Mark Johnson, Ron Kaplan, Lauri Karttunen, Bob Kasper, Martin Kay, Fernando Pereira, Carl Pollard, Bill Rounds, Ivan Sag, Annie Zaenen, and numerous others), many people have directly influenced my ideas on the topic of this dissertation and have kept the study of the area exciting and fast-paced.

I have also benefited from the many insights of the members of the natural-language group in the AIC (Susan Hirsh, Jerry Hobbs, Paul Martin, Bob Moore, Barney Pell, and Martha Pollack, in addition to those mentioned elsewhere in the preface) and the users of early and recent PATR versions, including Jane Robinson, Kent Wittenburg, and Mary Dalrymple. Others who deserve thanks, though they may not realize why, include Leslie Kaelbling, Dikran Karagueuzian, Peter Ludlow, Stan Reifel, Hilary Sachs, Brian Smith, Sandy Wells, and the host and frequenters of Richard Waldinger's coffees.

However, the single person with the foremost impact on this dissertation, technically and otherwise, must be Fernando Pereira, who has throughout the ordeal acted as technical source, adviser, and friend. His invaluable guidance through innumerable well-placed suggestions and comments was a determining factor in any coherence this work enjoys, and his friendship allowed me to keep the effort in its proper perspective.

I am also obliged to all of my reading committee members, Terry Winograd, Fernando Pereira, Vaughan Pratt, and Gordon Plotkin, for seeing me through draft after draft with a minimum of angst. Their comments were much appreciated and gratefully incorporated. Terry Winograd, my principal advisor, made good on that designation through his counsel on the proper negotiation of departmental and university rules and practices. Fernando Pereira spent an extraordinary amount of time assiduously examining all of the proofs, thereby maintaining my integrity at a level far above its natural station. A debt of thanks is also owed the additional members of my oral-defense committee: Nils Nilsson and Stanley Peters, committee chair.

Savel Kliachko must, once again, be thanked for exemplary editing of the final version of the thesis. He agreed (none too reluctantly) to be dragged from his bucolic retirement to perform this one last editing task for me. My heartfelt appreciation goes to him.

The research reported herein was supported in part under contract with the Nippon Telegraph and Telephone Company and in part by a grant from the System Development Foundation to the Center for the

Study of Language and Information. I am indebted to the principal investigators of these two projects—Phil Cohen and Doug Appelt for the former, David Israel for the latter—for making these funds available. Final editing of the manuscript was supported in part by a Presidential Young Investigator award IRI-9157996 from the National Science Foundation.

The genesis of a dissertation reveals to the author the deep influences in his life. I am profoundly grateful to my family—to my parents for instilling in me an appreciation of the beauty of science, the power and limits of rational thought, and the importance of competence in all undertakings; to my brothers for providing exemplars thereof.

The predominant influence on my life over the seven-year genesis of this work as a Ph.D. dissertation, and for many years before, was Linda Sarnoff. After her tragic death in 1989, I was doubtful that the present work would ever be completed. The memory of her strength in the face of incomparable adversities provided the inspiration to finish. I will love her always.

1 Introduction

Over the last few years a new subfield of computational linguistics has emerged, as subfields do, spontaneously and with surprising speed. The rapidity with which work progresses in the initial stages of a field often leaves little time for careful foundational research. Such is the case with the approaches to computational linguistics that have been referred to as unification-based, information-based, or constraint-based.

Grammar formalisms from within this general approach have been proposed independently in linguistics, computational linguistics, and artificial-intelligence research as alternatives to previous formalisms in use in the respective areas. By utilizing declarative constructs that emphasize the modularization of information and its manipulation in the face of partiality, many technical problems in language description and computer manipulation of language can be solved.[1]

Intuition suggests that these various efforts from a broad range of disciplines form a natural methodological class; still, there is no general foundation on which to ground this impression. This book comprises an attempt to build some of the foundational understanding of this class of formalisms—from both a mathematical and a computational perspective. We address the following questions:

1. What are constraint-based grammar formalisms? How are they alike and how do they differ from other formalisms?

2. What are their general properties, computational and mathematical?

3. How can they be applied to the task of describing aspects of natural and computer languages? What do they tell us about the similarities and differences between the two language classes?

We characterize the class of formalisms by focusing on their particular use of *information* and *constraints* thereon as an organizing basis. (The formalisms are thus more aptly referred to as information- or constraint-based rather than unification-based, and we will do so here.) We define the underlying conception of information implicit in previous work by examining its desired properties. Primary among these are modularity, partiality, and equationality; these are codified in a class of logics of information, each of which bears syntactic reflexes of the important

---

[1] An overview of these results can be found in earlier work (Shieber, 1985b).

semantic intuitions. A specific instance of this class of logics, $\mathcal{L}_{L,C}$, is described.

In order to provide a concrete grounding for such logics, we consider appropriate semantics. By defining a set of properties of logical systems (that is, logic plus class of models together with an appropriate relation of satisfaction), we can compare the advantages and disadvantages of various choices of models, both existing and new. These properties have not only logical but also computational ramifications. The development of the logics including $\mathcal{L}_{L,C}$ and an examination of the properties of appropriate classes of models comprise Chapter 2.

Given a logical system with the requisite properties, we can define a grammar formalism based on logical constraints over information associated with phrases. The definition is quite abstract: any logical system of sufficient expressiveness satisfying the properties outlined in Chapter 2 will serve to define a formalism. It is this abstraction that justifies considering these methods as characterizing constraint-based formalisms in general, rather than an individual formalism.

Furthermore, so long as the models of the logic have some further quite strong computational properties, a general algorithm can be defined for parsing phrases with respect to a grammar in the constraint-based formalism. The construction of the algorithm and a proof of its correctness are given independently of the details of the logic upon which the formalism is based. A further abstraction in the definition of the algorithm makes the algorithm and its correctness proof independent of the control regime employed. Thus, at one stroke, a wide range of parsing algorithms are proved correct for any constraint-based formalism. Particular instances of the algorithm, including an incarnation as an extended Earley's algorithm and a simulation of LR parsing, are discussed. The latter is especially important because of its ties to psycholinguistic effects. The definition of grammar formalisms and their parsing algorithms takes up Chapter 3.

In Chapter 4 we return to the topic of appropriate classes of models for the constraint logics, and develop a series of possible classes of models for the logic $\mathcal{L}_{L,C}$, with an eye toward their utility for logical and computational purposes.

Finally, we turn to a more speculative topic: the relation between these techniques and those devised for characterizing computer languages. In so doing, we attempt to bring out more clearly the similarities and differences between the two classes of languages.

As a concrete example of the techniques described in Chapters 2 and 3, and as an application of those techniques to both natural and computer languages, we define a more expressive logic than $\mathcal{L}_{L,C}$, extending the equational constraints of $\mathcal{L}_{L,C}$ to encompass inequations; we provide a class of models for the logic and algorithms for computing with the models on the basis of the foundations built up in Chapter 4. The existence of the logic and its model structure with appropriate properties immediately gives rise to algorithms for interpreting grammars in the formalism constructed around the logic. Chapter 5 discusses the connections to computer languages and the inequality logic.

This work can be seen as an attempt to characterize the abstract notion of a constraint-based grammar formalism. The abstraction occurs along several dimensions. First, the constraint types on which such formalisms are built are characterized generally, as logics satisfying certain properties. Second, the models for the logics are characterized by their properties rather than by direct construction. Finally, the algorithms for manipulating phrases according to a grammar are characterized independently of the specifics of the formalism and of the choice of control regime. This abstract view of constraint-based grammar formalisms engenders a rigorous understanding not just of one attempt to characterize a particular natural language from a particular perspective, but rather of a broad class of techniques applicable to both natural and computer languages from both mathematical and computational perspectives.

2 Constraint Logics for Linguistic Information

We define the underlying conception of information implicit in previous work on constraint-based formalisms by examining its desired properties. Primary among these are modularity, partiality, and equationality; these are codified in a class of logics of information, each of which bears syntactic reflexes of the important semantic intuitions. A specific instance of this class of logics, $\mathcal{L}_{L,C}$, is described.

In order to provide a concrete grounding for such logics, we consider appropriate semantics. By defining a set of properties of logical systems (that is, logic plus class of models together with an appropriate relation of satisfaction), we can compare the advantages and disadvantages of various choices of models, both existing and new. These properties have not only logical but computational ramifications. The development of the logics including $\mathcal{L}_{L,C}$ and an examination of the properties of appropriate classes of models comprise this chapter.

2.1 The Structure of Grammatical Information

The description of languages can be performed in many ways. The methodology most used within formal language theory—and inherited during the genesis of generative linguistics—is to characterize a language as a set of strings (or, more commonly in the linguistics literature, an assignment of asterisks to strings—the set's characteristic function). Perhaps the clearest example of a tool for describing languages in this way is the finite automaton with its accepting and rejecting states. But, independently of any formal limitations of finite automata, this binary distinction of well- versus ill-formed has proved in practice to present too coarse a grain of string classification for the purposes of efficiently describing languages.

In fact, even a broadening of the classificatory power of the formalism to allow for a finite set of primitive expression types, as in context-free grammars, unduly constrains writers of natural-language grammars. Primary among the reasons for the inadequacy of pure context-free grammars is that the distribution of expressions of a language does not depend exclusively on a single kind of information. Certain aspects of a

phrase's distribution might depend on morphological-agreement mark-
ings like the '-s'[1] ending that marks English nouns as plural. Other
distributional constraints depend on phonological restrictions. For instance, the cooccurrence of a noun with the determiner 'a' or 'an' depends on the phonological form of the noun. Selectional restrictions on
distribution depend on factors of a phrase's meaning. The distribution
of reflexives depends on the semantic properties of the pronoun and the
subject of its embedding clause. Distribution of the word 'I' depends
on pragmatic, contextual factors—that is, the identity of the utterer.
Describing a phrase by placing it in one of a finite number of categories
is inherently unwieldy because we are required to characterize all of the
phrase's distributional properties at once. In short, the structure of the
information as allowably stated in the formalism does not match the
natural structure of linguistic information.

This type of consideration leads to a view of grammatical description
under which a language is thought of as a relation between individual
strings and information about them, rather than as a function from
strings to well-formedness judgments, or a classification of strings into
a finite set of classes. Although these latter two views can be seen
as vestigial instances of the more general perspective, they prejudge
certain issues that are more profitably left open-ended, namely, issues
concerning the appropriate structure of the information. For instance,
considerations such as those in the previous paragraph argue for treating
the information associated with phrases of a language as entities with a
modular, hierarchical structure, rather than as atomic nonterminals or
grammaticality judgments.

Another problematic assumption inherent in the view of information
found in the context-free formalism is one of completeness. In order
to define the relation between strings and nonterminals inductively in
a context-free grammar, each stage in the induction must possess full
information about the constituent phrases. A phrase must be specified
as singular or plural, animate or inanimate, referring to the speaker
or not, regardless of the motivation for making the distinction. In a
context in which information about a phrase might arise from a variety

---

[1]In this work, we will follow the typographical convention that words and phrases
that are being mentioned, as opposed to being used, will be surrounded by single
quotes. Since the exact specification of such strings is critical in a work on grammars
and parsing, we eschew the convention of shifting following punctuation within quote
marks.

of sources, such a requirement that information be complete at all times might be too strict. Preferable would be a system in which only the information available at each inductive step is noted.[2] Since phrases may be underdetermined with respect to certain classificatory criteria, the modeling system should allow such underdetermination as a first-class notion. In essence, information is to be viewed as being partial.

A final property of the relation between strings and their associated information concerns the source of that relation. Rarely is information about a phrase given directly, as when a noun is explicitly marked for number. In general, phrasal information is determined by a system of interacting constraints that mean little separately, but that together place strong limits on the distribution of a phrase.

In fact, we can go further. A cursory examination of a few such constraints reveals interesting commonalities. For instance, consider the following constraints on English phrases:

- A subject noun and the corresponding verb *agree* with respect to certain concord features (number, gender, and person).
- The word 'I' requires that its referent be *the same as* the speaker of the utterance.
- Reflexives are in many respects (both syntactic and semantic) *identical to* the subject of the embedding clause.
- The object of a raising verb *plays the role of* the subject of the embedded infinitival clause.

All of these constraints share a reliance on the *identity* of information as the method of constraint. This reliance on identity is not coincidence; experience in linguistics has demonstrated that a wide variety of linguistic constraints can be most directly expressed as equations of some sort; rare are cases that require nonidentity or more complex relations. Consequently, the stating of such equations will play a fundamental role in the rest of this work.

In summary, information about phrases of a natural language is best regarded as possessing at least three properties: modular structure, partiality, and equationality. These properties will form the basis for the formalisms discussed in this and succeeding chapters.

---

[2]This way of seeing the need for partiality as arising from the information differentially available in the inductive construction of phrases was inspired by some informal comments of Stanley Peters.

2.2   The PATR Formalism

A simple example of a formalism squarely in the constraint-based tradition will be useful as an example of the preceding considerations, as
a benchmark to indicate the research tradition from which this work
springs, and as a source for intuition in the later development. The PATR
formalism, perhaps the simplest of the constraint-based formalisms, was
developed by the author and colleagues in the Artificial Intelligence Center at SRI International as a successor to the DIALOGIC system in which
the comprehensive DIAGRAM grammar of English was written. The motivation for the particular design decisions in the PATR formalism are
discussed at length elsewhere (Shieber, 1985a).

Grammar rules written in the PATR formalism describe the relation
between strings and information about them directly. Typically, the information is thought of as being characterized by graph structures of
a certain sort. A "context-free" portion of the rule constrains the concatenation of substrings to form a whole phrase, while a set of equations
constrain the allowable information types of the constituents described.
For instance, consider the standard context-free rule postulated for a
simple English sentence (S) composed of a noun phrase (NP) followed
by a verb phrase (VP).

$$S \rightarrow NP\ VP$$

This rule would be expressed in the PATR formalism as

$$
\begin{aligned}
X_0 &\rightarrow X_1\ X_2 \\
&\langle 0\ cat \rangle \doteq S \\
&\langle 1\ cat \rangle \doteq NP \\
&\langle 2\ cat \rangle \doteq VP
\end{aligned}
\tag{R_1}
$$

The context-free portion states that the rule applies to three constituents—the string associated with the first being the concatenation of
that associated with the second and third, in that order. In addition,
it requires that the information associated with the three strings, their
graphs, simultaneously satisfy the three equations. Thus, it expresses
the possibility that an expression X_0 could be constructed as the concatenation of expressions X_1 and X_2 (in that order), under the constraint
that the *cat* (category) information associated with X_0, X_1, and X_2 be

S, *NP*, and *VP*, respectively. The rule thus corresponds directly to its context-free predecessor.

However, the PATR formalism allows more expressivity in that further independent constraints might be added. For instance, to require that the noun phrase and verb phrase agree in person and number (as they do in English), a single constraint augments the previous rule.

$$
\begin{aligned}
X_0 \;\rightarrow\; & X_1 \; X_2 \\
& \langle 0 \; cat \rangle \doteq S \\
& \langle 1 \; cat \rangle \doteq NP \\
& \langle 2 \; cat \rangle \doteq VP \\
& \langle 1 \; agr \rangle \doteq \langle 2 \; agr \rangle
\end{aligned}
\qquad (R_2)
$$

The new constraint requires that the *agr* (agreement) information associated with the noun phrase be identical to that associated with the verb phrase. This agreement information might be further decomposed into *per* (person) and *num* (number) information (as demonstrated in the lexical-item definition below), but the single equation suffices to guarantee concord of all such agreement features.

The graphs that have historically served as the carriers of information about strings in the PATR formalism are rooted, connected, directed graphs with unordered labeled arcs and labeled terminals (nodes of out-degree 0). Furthermore, the labels on arcs leaving a given node are required to be distinct. An equation $\langle f_1 \cdots f_m \rangle \doteq \langle g_1 \cdots g_k \rangle$ is satisfied by a graph if and only if the node reached from the root by traversing in order the arcs labeled f_1 through f_m is the same node as the one reached by traversing g_1 through g_k. Similarly, an equation $\langle f_1 \cdots f_m \rangle \doteq c$ is satisfied if and only if the node specified as above by the path $\langle f_1 \cdots f_m \rangle$ is a terminal node labeled with the constant c.

For the above example, then, the constraints require that the constituents belong to major categories *S* (sentence), *NP* (noun phrase), and *VP* (verb phrase), respectively, and further, that the agreement information for the noun phrase and verb phrase be identical subgraphs.

A typical graph for a string like the proper noun 'Nature'—as in the sentence 'Nature abhors vacuums',[3] which we will use throughout the

---

[3]The sentence is a mistranslation of the Latin proverb 'Natura abhorret vacuum'. The need to take liberties with the translation testifies to the difficulty of finding well-known three-word sentences of English with differing agreement in subject and object.

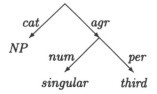

Figure 2.1
A typical graph structure

text to exemplify various points—might be as depicted in Figure 2.1. Intuitively seen, the information carried by this graph is that the string is of category *NP* and carries third person, singular number agreement. This primitive lexical item can be thought of as being defined by the rule

$$
\begin{aligned}
X_0 \quad &\rightarrow \quad \text{'Nature'} \\
&\langle 0 \; cat \rangle \doteq NP \\
&\langle 0 \; agr \; num \rangle \doteq singular \\
&\langle 0 \; agr \; per \rangle \doteq third \quad .
\end{aligned}
\qquad (R_3)
$$

2.2.1 Grammars and Their Interpretation

Using rules of the above two sorts—for combining strings and for introducing primitive strings—grammars for fragments of natural languages can be written. A PATR grammar for a tiny fragment of English will demonstrate grammar interpretation a bit more fully. The grammar, given as Figure 2.2, makes use of an abbreviatory convention that equations defining the *cat* (category) of an expression are implicit in the name chosen for the expression in the context-free portion of the rule. Thus, the first rule in the grammar—labeled (R_2)—is equivalent to the similarly labeled rule given in running text above. The sole import of the convention is to promote readability; it has no effect on expressivity.

The grammar admits the sentence 'Nature abhors vacuums', which can be verified as follows. (Since we have rigorously defined neither the formalism nor its semantics, the following description is intended merely to foster intuitions for the later, more precise, explication.)

$$S \to NP \ VP \qquad\qquad (R_2)$$
$$\langle 1 \ agr \rangle \doteq \langle 2 \ agr \rangle$$

$$VP \to V \ NP \qquad\qquad (R_4)$$
$$\langle 1 \ agr \rangle \doteq \langle 2 \ agr \rangle$$

$$NP \to \text{`Nature'} \qquad\qquad (R_3)$$
$$\langle 0 \ agr \ num \rangle \doteq singular$$
$$\langle 0 \ agr \ per \rangle \doteq third$$

$$NP \to \text{`vacuums'} \qquad\qquad (R_5)$$
$$\langle 0 \ agr \ num \rangle \doteq plural$$
$$\langle 0 \ agr \ per \rangle \doteq third$$

$$V \to \text{`abhors'} \qquad\qquad (R_6)$$
$$\langle 0 \ agr \ num \rangle \doteq singular$$
$$\langle 0 \ agr \ per \rangle \doteq third$$

$$V \to \text{`abhorred'} \qquad\qquad (R_7)$$

Figure 2.2
A tiny English fragment

The rules for the words 'abhors' and 'vacuums', respectively, incorporate constraints satisfied by the simple graphs

$$(2.2.1)$$

and

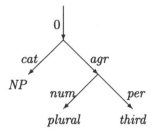

The phrases themselves are associated with the 0th subgraph of these:

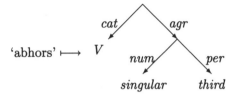

and

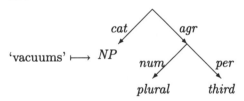

Now, the constraints in the rule for constructing verb phrases are satisfied by the graph

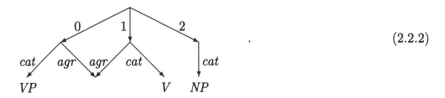

$$(2.2.2)$$

We can incorporate the phrases 'abhors' and 'vacuums' as the first and second subconstituents, respectively, in the rule, by combining their graphs with the graph for the rule as a whole, yielding the expanded graph

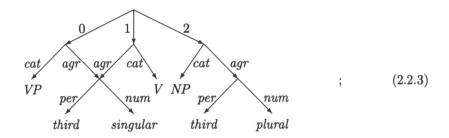

$;$ (2.2.3)

again, the 0th subgraph is associated with the full phrase:

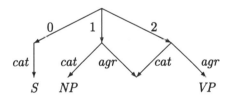

'abhors vacuums' $\longmapsto$

The sentence formation rule is associated with the satisfying graph

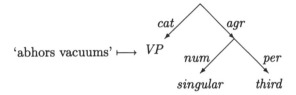

'

which can be used to combine with the graph for 'Nature' (obtained in the previously described manner)

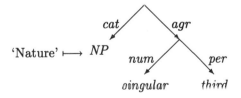

'Nature' $\longmapsto$

and the graph previously obtained for 'abhors vacuums'. The resulting graph

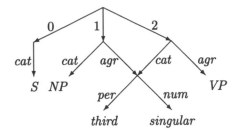

admits the entire phrase as a sentence:

$$\text{'Nature abhors vacuums'} \longmapsto \quad cat \Big|_S \quad .$$

2.2.2 Summary

The PATR formalism possesses the properties of modularity, partiality, and equationality that were described in Section 2.1. The graph structures partition information into separate modules; major-category information is separated from agreement information, for instance, and the two can be constrained separately. Only partial information about a string need be stated. The lexical entry for 'Nature', for example, gives both number and person information, but lexical entries for other words might be underspecified for one or the other feature; the word 'abhorred' is an example of a word underspecified for number and person. The equationality of the formalism follows from the ability to state equations directly.

Furthermore, grammars stated in the PATR formalism have an immediate computational interpretation. The minimal solution to all of the various equations can be found by a process of graph unification akin to the unification of terms used in resolution theorem proving. This observation allows for recognition algorithms to be built that determine the grammaticality of sentences by performing the appropriate unifications, thereby proving the satisfiability (or otherwise) of the equations.

We will not describe in any detail how the PATR formalism can be used to build actual grammars for fragments of natural language; this area has been discussed elsewhere (Shieber, 1985b; Shieber et al., 1983). Nor will we go into any further technical detail at this point to make the definition of PATR grammars more precise and to spell out their interpretation rigorously. This has also been done previously (Pereira and Shieber, 1984) and the remainder of the present work implicitly provides another method. But the example of the PATR formalism is illustrative of several important properties of constraint-based formalisms in general:

- Informational constraints are given explicitly (as equations).

- They constrain informational elements (the graphs).

- They can be interpreted computationally (by unification).

The notion of a constraint-based formalism in the abstract is defined by just such properties, parameterized by the parenthetical choices made in the design of the PATR formalism in particular. In essence, we want to define a whole class of PATR-like formalisms by broadening the class of constraints and allowing other sorts of informational structures, while still permitting computational interpretation. Consequently, we must tread a fine line, attempting to be as general as we can yet not losing sight of algorithmic considerations. As the work presented here is the first to attempt this enterprise, we must be satisfied with only a partially successful negotiating of this line. The constraint languages allowed are not as general as might be hoped, and the requisite properties of a constraint-based formalism appear more ad hoc than they might. The present results, then, should be thought of as a first step toward a more complete understanding of the mathematical and computational foundations of constraint-based grammar formalisms.

2.3 Idealizations of the Constraint-Based View

The transition from seeing linguistic information as a simple binary distinction or finite classification constitutes a movement away from an idealization of linguistic structure. But even the fuller view proposed here is a vast idealization along several dimensions concerning the structure of linguistic information. Most obviously, not all linguistic constraints are statable as equations at all; examples of such cases lie within the province of Chapter 5. Other constraints are statable as equations only with the most gymnastic effort. For this reason, we would best leave open the possibility that other types of constraints might be added to a formalism, and we will. This chapter and the next constitute an attempt to place the results concerning constraint-based formalisms in a more general setting, independent of the particular types of constraints allowed, but even this more general approach may not be sufficient for the types of informational constraints imposed by semantic and pragmatic factors not considered in the present work.

Perhaps a more basic idealization made here is that the information about phrases of a language is discrete. Properties either hold or not of phrases: number, if specified, is either singular or plural; the verb either requires its subject to be animate or it does not; and so forth. There are no preferences, no prototypes, no fuzziness. Any system based entirely on discrete information will be subject to the kind of fragility of behavior that has plagued artificial-intelligence systems in general and natural-language-processing programs in particular; constraint-based systems are no exception. However, declarative systems based on constraints at least hold open the prospect that the discrete solution of constraints can be relaxed by incorporating continuous approximations of various sorts, for instance, probabilistic or abductive interpretation of constraints. Such possibilities are much more difficult to maintain in the context of a formalism not based on the declarative statement of grammatical information. Whether the constraint-based view of linguistic information is amenable to such a relaxation is an open question with some intriguing possibilities, but one that will not be discussed further here. There is already sufficient grist for the foundational mill to make introducing this further complication presumptuous.

2.4   Constraint-Based Computer Language Description

Looking ahead to Chapter 5, we note that these same properties of structure, partiality, and primacy of equational constraints also arise in the information associated with computer-language expressions, types. For instance, the polymorphic identity function has type $\alpha \to \alpha$, where α is a type variable. Note that the type has a *modular* structure, a separate specification of domain and range type. The type information is *partial* in not fully specifying those domain and range types. Rather, an *equational* constraint is applied to them as expressed in the shared variable notation; the types of domain and range must be the same.

$R \rightarrow F \ (\ A \ )$
  $\langle 1 \ type \ constr \rangle \doteq function$
  $\langle 1 \ type \ arg \rangle \doteq \langle 2 \ type \rangle$
  $\langle 1 \ type \ result \rangle \doteq \langle 0 \ type \rangle$
  $\langle 0 \ env \rangle \doteq \langle 1 \ env \rangle$
  $\langle 1 \ env \rangle \doteq \langle 2 \ env \rangle$

$A \rightarrow \omega \qquad (\omega \in \Sigma)$
  $\langle 0 \ env \ \omega \rangle \doteq \langle 0 \ type \rangle$

$A \rightarrow \iota \qquad (\iota \in N)$
  $\langle 0 \ type \ constr \rangle \doteq int$

Figure 2.3
A tiny applicative language fragment

The analogy can be demonstrated by using the PATR formalism to define a grammar for a simple applicative language; the equations state the typing constraints. Figure 2.3 gives such a grammar.[4] Each expression is associated with a graph comprising information about its *type* and the environment (*env*) under which the typing holds. The first rule corresponds to the more traditional typing rule

$$\frac{E \vdash f : A \rightarrow R \quad E \vdash a : A}{E \vdash f(a) : R} \qquad ,$$

while the second rule (actually a rule schema) corresponds to the typing rule

$$\frac{E(w) = T}{E \vdash w : T} \qquad ,$$

where, as is typical, an environment is a function from identifiers to their types. Given such an environment encoded by the graph in Figure 2.4, the typing grammar admits the following typings:

---

[4]The implicit category convention used in the grammar of Figure 2.2 is not in force in this grammar. Furthermore, with respect to the status of the parentheses in the first rule, a more correct, but pedantic, grammar would introduce nonterminals for the parentheses and the parentheses themselves as lexical items. The intent of the grammar in this respect should, however, be clear. Such abbreviatory methods will prove useful in later examples as well.

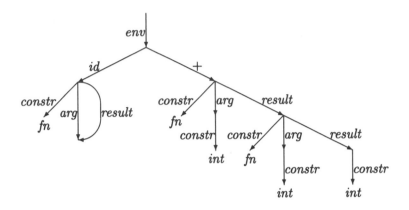

Figure 2.4
A graph that encodes an environment

- $id : \alpha \rightarrow \alpha$
- $+ : INT \rightarrow INT \rightarrow INT$
- $id(+) : INT \rightarrow INT \rightarrow INT$
- $id(+(3)(id(x))) : INT$

This last typing occurs in an environment in which x is typed as an INT. Thus, the grammar allows for type inference of subexpressions as in the ML programming language (Milner, 1978), as a consequence of the purely equational nature of the constraints.

Of course, not all expressions are typed by the grammar. For instance, the expression $+(id)(2)$ is not admitted by the grammar under any typing, as is correct. The expression $id(+)(3)(id(2))$, intuitively typable as an INT, is unfortunately not admitted by the grammar. This is because the environment defines the types of identifiers once and for all, but the expression uses the same identifier (id) with two different incompatible typings. We will return to this problem in Chapter 5, when the topic of nonequational constraints comes under consideration.

2.5 History of Constraint-Based Formalisms

Constraint-based formalisms have only recently been proposed, and their recognition as forming a single class is even more recent. Their origin may be traced to separate research efforts in computational linguistics, formal linguistics, and natural-language processing; related techniques can be found in theorem proving, knowledge-representation research, and theory of data types. Several independently initiated strains of research have converged upon the notion of constraint satisfaction, especially equational constraints, as a technique for describing languages.

Beginning with the augmented-transition-network (ATN) concept of Woods (1970) (like so much of the research in modern computational linguistics) and inspired by Bresnan's work on lexically oriented nontransformational linguistics, the lexical-functional grammar (LFG) framework of Bresnan and Kaplan was evolved (Bresnan, 1982). The formalism used within the lexical-functional theory of language allows rules with a context-free backbone and constraints of various sorts, including equational constraints, constraints requiring existence of values, set membership constraints, and others. The informational elements (in our terminology) of LFG are the so-called f-structures, a type of finite tree (as opposed to the graphs of PATR; see Section 4.1). The formalism is under constant development and new constraint types are often introduced. The LFG formalism is in general, therefore, a superset of PATR, except that, unlike PATR, LFG requires a major category to be assigned to each constituent.

Simultaneously, Kay devised the functional grammar (later unification grammar, now functional unification grammar [FUG]) formalism (Kay, 1983). FUG blurs the distinction between the language of constraints and the objects being constrained by using *functional structures* (which are similar to the graph structures of PATR) both as a language of description and as the objects of description. Besides conjunctions of equations, FUG allows disjunctions and various other descriptive extensions.

Independently, Colmerauer had produced the Q-system (Colmerauer, 1970) and metamorphosis grammar (Colmerauer, 1978) formalisms as tools for natural-language processing. The logic-programming community, specifically Pereira and Warren (Warren and Pereira, 1982; Pereira, 1983), created definite-clause grammars (DCG) on the basis of Colmerauer's earlier work on these formalisms and on the programming language Prolog. Viewed as a constraint-based formalism, DCGs describe language using first-order terms as the informational elements. Variable sharing is used to encode the equational constraints. Independent work in logic programming has employed DCG as the foundation of many constraint-based formalisms, such as extraposition, slot, and gapping grammars (Pereira, 1981; McCord, 1980; Dahl and Abramson, 1984; Dahl and McCord, 1983).

Another strain of parallel research grew out of the work on nontransformational linguistic analyses, from which Gazdar and his colleagues developed generalized phrase-structure grammar (GPSG) (Gazdar, 1982; Gazdar, Pullum, and Sag, 1982; Gazdar, 1981). In its later formalization by Gazdar and Pullum (Gazdar et al., 1985), GPSG imported a unification relation over tree-like feature structures that was used to solve implicit equations stated as language-universal principles of the theory. Later developments from GPSG, specifically, Pollard and Sag's head-driven phrase-structure grammar (HPSG) (Pollard, 1985a; Pollard, 1985b; Pollard and Sag, 1987) have moved in the direction of explicit equations as in PATR.

Most recently, influenced by early papers on GPSG, Rosenschein and Shieber (1982) devised PATR as a successor to DIALOGIC and DIAGRAM (Robinson, 1982). Although the original PATR did not use equational constraints, it developed (under the influence of FUG, later work in GPSG, and DCG) into PATR-II, the formalism we introduced above (Shieber, 1984; Shieber, Karttunen, and Pereira, 1984).

Work on the mathematical and computational background for constraint-based formalisms is an even more recent development, emerging only in the last few years. The first rigorous semantics for a constraint-based formalism was provided by Pereira and Shieber (1984); the present volume is a direct outgrowth of that line of research. Rounds and his students Kasper and Moshier have developed quite sophisticated formal analyses of feature logics and feature structures (Kasper and Rounds, 1986; Rounds and Kasper, 1986; Moshier and Rounds, 1987), concentrating on the view of feature structures as automata (as alluded to in Section 4.4). (See also the work of Dawar and Vijay-Shanker (1990) and Smolka (1988).) Their logics go well beyond those discussed here in certain aspects (allowing disjunction, negation, and set-valued features), though they make no attempt to describe classes of logics. In contrast to the present work, they do not apply their analysis to the full problem of providing a semantics for an entire formalism, or to the computational interpretation thereof. Johnson (1988) has also provided an analysis along the same lines as Kasper and Rounds, although with a more syntactic flavor. Most recently, Joseph Goguen (personal communication, 1988) has applied ideas in algebraic semantics to the problem of providing a semantics for constraint-based grammars.

The PATR formalism has been proposed previously as being especially useful as a benchmark against which various constraint-based formalisms can be compared (Shieber, 1988a). For instance, GPSG has been reconstructed by "compiling" into PATR, thereby showing that the universal principles can in fact be cashed out as equations and making clear the constraint-based methodology of GPSG that might otherwise have been hidden (Shieber, 1986). Of course, such reconstructions are only indicative in general, since no other formalism has been given the kind of rigorous semantics accorded PATR.

Work on the implementation of the formalisms has concentrated on several fronts. Nelson and Oppen (1978) describe an algorithm for computing graph closures efficiently, with an application to solving equations of the type found in constraint-based formalisms. Their algorithm forms the basis for an implementation of unification for LFG. Early implementations of PATR used a simple invisible-pointer representation for graphs that involved a large amount of copying (Shieber et al., 1983). Replacement of such representations with ones incorporating binding environments that can share structure is one method of improving efficiency (Karttunen and Kay, 1985; Pereira, 1985b), the latter based on ideas of structure-sharing for theorem proving (Boyer and Moore, 1972). Other techniques for minimizing copying have been proposed (Wroblewski, 1987).

Parsing-algorithm design is only now getting wider attention. The straightforward modeling of Earley's algorithm for PATR and the importance of using a restricted subset of information in top-down prediction (as discussed in Section 3.6.2) were first discussed by Shieber (1985c). Haas (1989) defines a variant method of restriction and uses it in extending the algorithm of Graham, Harrison, and Ruzzo (1980) to apply to a constraint based formalism. The ρ function discussed in Section 3.3 generalizes both of these methods.

Compiling of PATR grammars into Prolog programs has been investigated by Hirsh (1986). Wittenburg (1986) discusses the use of constraint-based techniques in the parsing of combinatory categorial grammars. The view of parsing as a deductive process was first espoused for DCG by Pereira and Warren (1983) and serves as the inspiration for the abstract characterization of parsing described in Chapter 3. The notion of having parsing algorithms parameterized along the control dimension appears in Kaplan's work on the General Syntactic Processor (Kaplan, 1973). The present work generalizes this to abstract the formalism as well, and to eliminate the reliance on a chart (although chart parsing is still a possible optimization, as discussed in Section 3.6.1). Kay (1985) discusses parsing FUG, although the technique provided was never contended to be fully general.

Related Formalisms and Languages from Computer Science
Besides the obvious links to logic and theorem-proving research (unification was originally discussed as a component of the resolution procedure for automatic theorem proving (Robinson, 1965), a connection that is still evident in Prolog and DCG), other research from computer science bears directly on the topic at hand.

There is a close relationship between the type theory of computer science and the algebraic structure of feature systems. Roughly speaking, the similarity is between feature structures and named product types (or numbered product types for DCG terms) with or without sum types. Building on this relationship with type theory, Aït-Kaci (1985) discusses a calculus of syntactic types that bears a remarkable resemblance to the feature structures used in constraint-based formalisms. The mathematics of subsumption, unification, and other algebraic properties of his calculus are investigated in depth. The intended application of the formalism was to knowledge representation—it was originally described as a generalization of Prolog terms—but some brief natural-language examples are given by Aït-Kaci.

Cardelli (1984), in a reconstruction of object-oriented programming, proposes a typing system based on named product types with sums for disjunction. This type system also bears a close resemblance to the feature-structure domains. He proposes this as a technique for modeling object classes with multiple inheritance in a strongly typed language.

The relationship between constraint-based formalisms and type inference for computer languages (for instance, the analogy between the use of unification for type inference (Hindley, 1969) and for natural-language parsing) has not, to our knowledge, been noted before in print. The use of subsumption to describe coordination phenomena in natural language has been in the air since the phenomenon of coordination of unlike categories was first noted (Sag et al., 1985). Our analysis seems to be the first rigorous formalization of the idea. Similarly, the idea is implicit in the description of ML type inference (Milner, 1978).

Perhaps the computer science work most closely related in spirit is the recent development of constraint logic programming (Jaffar and Lassez, 1987). The notion of defining a class of computer languages parameterized by a constraint language (and constraint satisfaction technique) seems completely analogous to the notion of defining a class of constraint-based formalisms parameterized by a constraint logic and operations on models for formulas in the logic.

Moshier (1988b), starting from a common foundation with the present work, namely, the research on unification-based grammar formalisms and their semantics (Shieber, 1985b; Pereira and Shieber, 1984; Rounds and Kasper, 1986), also investigates the mathematical aspects of these grammar formalisms, including the independently observed application of equations and inequations to problems of programming-language type inference. Although there is a sizable overlap in these independent efforts, many aspects are peculiar to one or another. Moshier covers two much more expressive logics that include disjunction, negation, and a recursion operator; the present work, on the other hand, places logics for grammar formalisms in a general framework so that their properties and alternative models can be explored. Further, the present work addresses the issue of parsing with such systems, providing parsing algorithms and proving their correctness.

2.6   The Structure of Constraint-Based Formalisms

The various constraint-based formalisms have differed historically in the details of the types of information they provide for and the types of constraints they allow. Consequently, it has been difficult to compare analyses in the various systems, to design grammar-processing algorithms of general utility, as opposed to those intended for specific formalisms, to provide uniform semantics, and so forth.

The constraint-based view of language and grammar offers a general framework in which such questions can be studied. Just as a particular language can be viewed as a relation between strings and their associated linguistic information, a grammar can be seen as expressing two types of constraints on this relation: the first, constraints on strings and

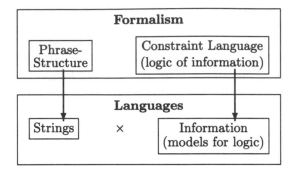

Figure 2.5
Structure of grammars and languages

their combination; the second, constraints on the associated informational elements. Figure 2.5 presents a graphical representation of this relation between grammar and language. A grammar formalism, then, merely characterizes the space of possible grammars by pinpointing a particular method of string combination and a particular language for informational constraints.

For the remainder of this work, we will assume that the method of string combination is concatenation; thus, the string-combining constraints can be seen as simple phrase-structure constraints. Although this has many ramifications for the expressiveness of formalisms, our main interest in the informational constraints and our desire for computational feasibility mandate this choice.

In order to compare various formalisms, we require a way of abstracting them with respect to the specifics of the information and constraint types that they allow for. This abstraction can be achieved by encapsulating the constraints in a *logical system* of constraints on linguistic information, comprising a logical language for stating the constraints, a class of models for the logic providing the informational elements, and a relation of satisfaction between models and formulas of the logic to relate the two.[5]

---

[5]The term 'logic' is ambiguous in common use as to whether it refers to an uninterpreted language together with some syntactic rules of inference, or to an interpreted language, that is, a set of formulas plus a class of models together with a relation of *satisfaction* between the formulas and the models. To avoid confusion, we will uniformly use the word 'logic' for the purely syntactic system, and the phrase 'log-

This view of an abstract formalism parameterized by an independent logical system of constraints supplies a framework in which different formalisms can be embedded, given uniform semantics, and compared with one another. Furthermore, under suitable conditions, general algorithms for interpreting grammars can be designed and proved correct, independently of the particulars of the constraint logic employed. Such algorithms are therefore uniformly applicable to all of the formalism instances.

2.7 Appropriate Logics for Constraint-Based Formalisms

The details of how such a logical system is used in the definition of a constraint-based formalism will be given in Chapter 3. Of course, not any logic will do for this purpose. As we have seen, the notions of structure, partiality, and equationality play a crucial role in any formalism for linguistic information; they must therefore be reflected in any logic that serves as the basis for a constraint-based formalism. This section describes the minimum criteria for expressivity of the logic.

Since information is to be thought of as modular and hierarchically structured, some notation for referring to pieces of information is necessary. Let us assume that the parts of an informational structure are labeled with elements from a set L of *labels* or *features*. Then given an information structure, a sequence of labels can be used to identify a single specified substructure by using the sequence as its "address". Such sequences will be called *paths* and will be identified with elements of $Path = L^*$. Some primitive unstructured informational elements will also be needed. These can simply be taken as a set C of constants. Because of the importance of features as the structuring method in these informational elements, we will refer to such elements generically and informally as *feature structures*, unless some more particular mathematical structure is being relied upon.

Thus, the terms of a logic will include (but are not limited to) paths and constants, each denoting a feature structure. Formulas in the logic will be finite sets of atomic formulas, each representing some constraint over feature structures. Again the choice of relations will depend on

---

ical system' for its interpreted counterpart, a triple $\langle \mathcal{L}, \mathcal{M}, \models \rangle$ consisting of a logic, a class of models, and a satisfaction relation between formulas in $\mathcal{L}$ and individual models in $\mathcal{M}$.

the logic, but because of the importance of equality, we require that, at the least, the binary relation of equality (represented by the symbol '$\doteq$' to distinguish it from the metalanguage symbol for equality, following Moshier (1988a)) be included. In particular, the atomic formulas include equations of the form

$$p_1 \doteq p_2$$

or

$$p_1 \doteq c$$

where p_1 and p_2 are members of *Path* and c is a member of C.

Formulas in the logic, finite sets of atomic formulas, are to be interpreted conjunctively and will be written using standard set notation.[6] As more atomic formulas are included, the formula describes fewer feature structures; that is, it becomes less partial, more defined. Thus, these logics allow for the structure (through labels and paths), partiality (through sets of constraints), and equationality (through the '$\doteq$' relation) of information.

A brief digression concerning notation is germane. The symbols f, g, h, etc., will conventionally represent elements of L; a, b, c, etc., elements of C; and p, q, r, etc., elements of *Path*. Concatenation of paths, and sequences in general, will be notated with a center dot ('$\cdot$'). Taken together, constants and paths comprise the set of *value descriptors* $V = C \cup Path$, elements of which are denoted by v, w, etc. The atomic formulas will conventionally be written ϕ, ψ, nonatomic formulas, Φ, Ψ, etc. Primed and subscripted symbols will also be used. The type of a symbol will often remain unstated when this is clear from its spelling or the context. For example, an equation $p \doteq c$ may stand without an explicit statement that $p \in Path$ and $c \in C$.

2.7.1   Rules of Inference

As the '$\doteq$' symbol in the logic is to be interpreted as equality, inference rules must be postulated that respect this interpretation. The notation $\Phi \vdash \phi$ will be used to state that the atomic formula ϕ can be deduced or

---

[6]The problems engendered by addition of disjunction and negation to systems of this sort have been described elsewhere (Karttunen, 1984; Kasper and Rounds, 1986; Kasper, 1987; Johnson, 1988; Dawar and Vijay-Shanker, 1990). A complete discussion is beyond the scope of the present work.

inferred from the formula Φ. The inference relation between nonatomic formulas respects their conjunctive interpretation: $\Phi \vdash \Psi$ if and only if $\Phi \vdash \psi$ for all $\psi \in \Psi$. The definition of $\vdash$ to infer atomic formulas will supervene on a formal notion of proof. Each logic $\mathcal{L}$ will provide a set of inference rules—each a relation of finite arity greater than 0 over atomic formulas of $\mathcal{L}$. The inference rules will be presented in a standard natural-deduction notation. A proof of ϕ from Φ, then, is a finite tree whose leaves are members of Φ, whose root is ϕ, and each of whose interior nodes ϕ_i and its immediate children ϕ_{i1} through ϕ_{in} are in an inference-rule relation—that is,

$$\frac{\phi_{i1} \cdots \phi_{in}}{\phi_i}$$

is an instance of a rule schema. These proof trees will again be presented in natural-deduction notation with the root at the bottom and leaves at the top, horizontal lines associating the children of a node with the node itself.

For the $\doteq$ predicate, the following inference-rule schemata suffice. They are based on those given by Pereira and Shieber (1984).

Triviality: $\dfrac{}{\langle\rangle \doteq \langle\rangle}$

Symmetry: $\dfrac{p \doteq q}{q \doteq p}$

Reflexivity: $\dfrac{R(\ldots, p \cdot q, \ldots)}{p \doteq p}$

Substitutivity: $\dfrac{q \doteq p \quad R(\vec{v})}{R(\vec{v})\langle p \rightarrow q \rangle}$

Here the notation $R(\vec{v})$ represents any atomic formula (relation applied to terms) and $\Phi\langle p \rightarrow q \rangle$, the result of textually replacing a single occurrence of a path of the form $p \cdot r$ with $q \cdot r$ in Φ. We will later use the notation $\Phi[p \rightarrow q]$ to notate the replacing of *all* paths in Φ, which must each be of the form $p \cdot r$ for some r, with the corresponding $q \cdot r$. Of course, these syntactic operations on formulas may not always be defined; the rule of inference is applicable only if its consequent is defined.

(In Section 2.7.3, we present a full proof tree using these inference rules; the reader may want to examine the proof for further intuition.)

2.7.2 Properties of ⊢

There might be other rules of inference in such a logic as well, allowing for deducing the other constraints in the language. However, it is important that any such rules of inference respect the interpretation of paths as being the terms in the logic that hierarchically structure information. In particular, if a set of paths is "about" certain information, then all deductions from constraints over those paths should be "about" the same information. We will codify this requirement in the following definition:[7]

PROPERTY 1 (LOGICAL LOCALITY) If Φ is a formula all of whose paths have some member of $\{p_i\}$ as a prefix and $\Phi \vdash \phi$, then all paths in ϕ are prefixes or extensions of some member of $\{p_i\}$.

In addition, constraints should not be sensitive to the particular syntactic forms of the paths they talk about; rather, the constraints should be sensitive only to the structural relationships among pieces of information. The inference rules must respect this insensitivity. Any uniform substitution of paths for other paths that maintains the structural relationships should therefore preserve the correctness of inference, as should uniform prefixing of paths. We will codify this requirement with a notion of prefixed homomorphism. A homomorphism over paths is defined as a function $m : Path \rightarrow Path$ such that $m(q \cdot r) = m(q) \cdot m(r)$. A homomorphism m prefixed by a path p is then a function $m_p : Path \rightarrow Path$ defined by the equation $m_p(q) = p \cdot m(q)$. We can now require that inference is invariant under prefixed homomorphisms.

PROPERTY 2 (LOGICAL TRANSPARENCY) If $\Phi \vdash \phi$ for nonempty Φ, then for any prefixed homomorphism m_p, $m_p(\Phi) \vdash m_p(\phi)$ where $m_p(\Phi)$ is the result of replacing all paths q in Φ by $m_p(q)$.

Finally, in keeping with the equational interpretation of '$\doteq$', we limit the *consistent* formulas to those not entailing a pair of atomic formulas of either of the following two forms:

Constant clash: $p \doteq a$ and $p \doteq b$ (where $a \neq b$), or

Constant/compound clash: $p \cdot \langle f \rangle \doteq v$ and $p \doteq a$.

---

[7]The notion of extension assumed here is that a path p is an extension of a path q just in case q is a prefix of p. Note that as a corollary of this property, if $\{\} \vdash \phi$, then all paths in ϕ are empty.

The former condition violates the equationality of '$\doteq$', the latter the atomicity of constants. A logic might introduce further restrictions on consistency, stemming from constraints other than equality.

2.7.3 A Simple Example Logic

A simple example of such a logic is one in which we fix the set of constraint predicates to include only the '$\doteq$' relation, and define consistency exhaustively by the clash rules above. Rather than establishing values for the set of constants and labels as well, we will refer to this logic as $\mathcal{L}_{L,C}$ to record its dependence on the set of constants C and labels L. The logic $\mathcal{L}_{L,C}$ is just the constraint logic that was used in the previous PATR grammar examples.

In the case of $\mathcal{L}_{L,C}$, the Substitutivity schema is completely characterized by the rule

Substitutivity: $\quad \dfrac{q \doteq p \quad p \cdot r \doteq v}{q \cdot r \doteq v}$

and Reflexivity by

Reflexivity: $\quad \dfrac{p \cdot q \doteq v}{p \doteq p} \quad .$

In this logic, for example, the following inference relation holds:

$$\{\langle f \rangle \doteq \langle ff \rangle, \langle fg \rangle \doteq a, \langle g \rangle \doteq b\} \vdash \langle ffg \rangle \doteq \langle ffg \rangle$$

The proof is as follows:

$$\dfrac{\dfrac{\langle f \rangle \doteq \langle ff \rangle}{\langle ff \rangle \doteq \langle f \rangle} \quad \dfrac{\overline{\langle \rangle \doteq \langle \rangle} \quad \langle fg \rangle \doteq a}{\langle fg \rangle \doteq a}}{\dfrac{\langle ffg \rangle \doteq a}{\langle ffg \rangle \doteq \langle ffg \rangle}}$$

Note that the leaf nodes of the tree ($\langle f \rangle \doteq \langle ff \rangle$ and $\langle fg \rangle \doteq a$) are elements of the antecedent in the inference relation, but do not exhaust the antecedent; the root $\langle ffg \rangle \doteq \langle ffg \rangle$ is the consequent. Each local set of nodes in the tree, corresponding to a proof step, is licensed by an inference rule; reading top to bottom and left to right, the rules used are:

Triviality, Symmetry, Substitutivity, Substitutivity again, and Reflexivity. As it turns out, this is not the minimal proof of the consequent, as the use of Triviality and the first substitution can be eliminated.

The reader can easily verify several simple properties of $\mathcal{L}_{L,C}$. For instance, in $\mathcal{L}_{L,C}$ every atomic formula is consistent. Locality holds of $\mathcal{L}_{L,C}$, as can be demonstrated by an inductive proof of the slightly stronger requirement that, if all paths in Φ have p as prefix and $\Phi \vdash \phi$, then all paths in ϕ either have p as prefix or are of the form $p' \doteq p'$ for p' a prefix of p. To give a flavor for the sort of reasoning that will predominate in the rest of this chapter, and, especially, in the Appendix, we provide the proof here.

PROPOSITION 3 (LOGICAL LOCALITY FOR $\mathcal{L}_{L,C}$) If Φ is a formula of $\mathcal{L}_{L,C}$ all of whose paths have some member of $\{p_i\}$ as a prefix and $\Phi \vdash \phi$, then all paths in ϕ are prefixes or extensions of some member of $\{p_i\}$.

Proof   We prove the stronger result that if the antecedent conditions hold, then either all paths in ϕ are extensions of some p_i or ϕ is of the form $p' \doteq p'$ for p' a prefix of some p_i.

We assume that the antecedent condition holds and prove the consequent by induction on the proof depth for $\Phi \vdash \phi$. For proofs of depth 0, either $\phi \in \Phi$ (i.e., a terminal node in the proof tree) or $\phi = \langle\rangle \doteq \langle\rangle$ (i.e., an instance of Triviality that engenders a node in the proof tree with no children). In the former case, all paths in ϕ are extensions of some p_i by assumption. In the latter case, ϕ is trivially of the form $p' \doteq p'$, where p' is a prefix of some p_i.

For proofs of depth $n + 1$, the final step in the proof is licensed by either Symmetry, Reflexivity, or Substitutivity. If Symmetry is used, the antecedent is proved using a proof of depth n; thus, it is either of the form $p_i \cdot r \doteq p_j \cdot s$ or of the form $p' \doteq p'$ for p' a prefix of some p_i. In either case, the consequent ($p_j \cdot s \doteq p_i \cdot r$ or $p' \doteq p'$, respectively) is of the required form.

Similarly, if Reflexivity is the final proof step, the antecedent must by inductive hypothesis be of the form $p_i \cdot r \doteq p_j \cdot s$ or of the form $p' \doteq p'$ for p' a prefix of some p_i. The consequent is therefore of the form $p'' \doteq p''$ for p'' a prefix or extension of either p_i or p_j, again meeting the criterion in the proposition's consequent.

Finally, for Substitutivity, the induction hypothesis guarantees that the proof antecedents are each of the required form. A case analysis reveals that only three possibilities can arise, assuming without loss of generality that no member of $\{p_i\}$ is a prefix of any other;[8] the cases are summarized below. (In the table, p_i' is a prefix of p_i and p_i'' of p_i', for p_i a member of the given path set.)

Case	Antecedent 1	Antecedent 2	Consequent
(1)	$p_i' \doteq p_i'$	$p_i \cdot r \doteq p_j \cdot s$	$p_i \cdot r \doteq p_j \cdot s$
(2)	$p_i'' \doteq p_i''$	$p_i' \doteq p_i'$	$p_i' \doteq p_i'$
(3)	$p_i \cdot t \doteq p_j \cdot u$	$p_j \cdot u \cdot r \doteq p_k \cdot s$	$p_i \cdot t \cdot r \doteq p_k \cdot s$

Note that in each case the consequent is of one of the required forms. $\square$

Furthermore, the graph models introduced informally in Section 2.2 conform to the inference rules for $\mathcal{L}_{L,C}$, that is, they possess a certain soundness property. Such desirable properties of logical systems constitute the topic of the next section.

2.8   Properties of Appropriate Constraint-Logic Models

A logic of at least this expressivity has been implicit in the constraint-based grammar formalisms used in several linguistic theories and in the natural-language-processing work of numerous computational linguists and computer scientists. Of course, we earlier begged the question of what this logic is a logic of: What precisely are the feature structures, which serve as the models for formulas? Several researchers have provided answers, starting with the information systems domain of Pereira and Shieber (1984) and including the automata-theoretic model of Kasper and Rounds (1986), the tree models of Gazdar et al. (1985) and Barwise (1988), and the normal-form models of Johnson (1988). We will reconstruct and discuss several such possibilities further in Chapter 4.

But first, we turn to the question of how to choose among such alternatives on the basis of what properties the resulting logical system possesses. In this section we will describe several such properties of logical systems; in fact, there will be sufficient properties to guarantee that

---

[8]This assumption can always be made because if p_i is a prefix of p_j, then p_j can be removed from the set without changing the set of prefixes and extensions of the paths in the set.

the logical system can be used in defining a grammar formalism and building parsing algorithms for it, as we will do in Chapter 3.

2.8.1 Soundness and Completeness Properties

The choice among these types of models depends in great part on the theoretician's proposed use of them. If we want to prove the logic consistent, we need only find a class of models for which the logical system is *denotationally sound*; that is, there are models only for consistent formulas.

Suppose we have a class of models $\mathcal{M}$ for a logic $\mathcal{L}$ and a satisfaction relation $\models$ between models and formulas of the logic.[9] Then we can define denotational soundness for the logical system consisting of $\mathcal{L}$, $\mathcal{M}$, and $\models$ as follows:

PROPERTY 4 (DENOTATIONAL SOUNDNESS) For all formulas Φ of $\mathcal{L}$, if there is a model $M \in \mathcal{M}$ such that $M \models \Phi$, then Φ is consistent.

If we want a guarantee that theorem proving in the logic is a sufficient method for revealing truths, the logical system must be *logically complete*. We can define a notion of semantic entailment in a model structure—for which we will overload the symbol '$\models$'—as follows: $\Phi \models \Phi'$ if and only if all models of Φ are models of Φ'. Then logical completeness requires that logical inferences hold for all semantically entailed formulas.

PROPERTY 5 (LOGICAL COMPLETENESS) For all formulas Φ and Φ' of $\mathcal{L}$, if $\Phi \models \Phi'$, then $\Phi \vdash \Phi'$.

Completing the set of soundness and completeness properties are the converses of the previous properties: denotational completeness[10] and logical soundness.

PROPERTY 6 (DENOTATIONAL COMPLETENESS) For all formulas Φ of $\mathcal{L}_{L,C}$, if Φ is consistent, then there is a model M in $\mathcal{M}$ such that $M \models \Phi$.

PROPERTY 7 (LOGICAL SOUNDNESS) For all formulas Φ and Φ' of $\mathcal{L}$, if $\Phi \vdash \Phi'$, then $\Phi \models \Phi'$.

---

[9]We will require as a matter of course that $\models$ reflect the conjunctive interpretation of formulas, that is, that $M \models \Phi$ if and only if $M \models \phi$ for all $\phi \in \Phi$.

[10]This property corresponds roughly to what is called *strong completeness* in the logic literature.

In summary, the denotational properties concern the faithfulness of models with respect to consistency, the logical properties faithfulness with respect to deduction. These four properties together provide a basis for viewing a model structure as an appropriate one for the purpose of imparting a semantics to a logic such as $\mathcal{L}_{L,C}$, although, for some purposes, one or another of the properties may not be necessary to appropriately deploy a logical system in certain applications. Such semantic grounding of a logic in a class of models conforming to these properties is especially useful as the basis for proving the correctness of algorithms that manipulate the formulas in various ways (as we will see in Chapter 3), so that we will uniformly require all four properties of the logical systems for constraint-based formalisms.

In addition, it is desirable that the models not display any artifactual idiosyncrasies, that is, differences among the models that are not reflected in their logical properties. Such artifacts would indicate that the models are insufficiently abstract. A logical system will be said to be *categorical* if the following property holds: [11]

PROPERTY 8 (CATEGORICITY) For any two distinct models M and M', there exists a formula Φ such that either $M \models \Phi$ and $M' \not\models \Phi$ or vice versa.

This property requires that there be a formula to distinguish any two models. Imagine a class of models just like the graph models discussed in Section 2.2, but whose nodes have, in addition to outgoing arcs, some other characteristic, say, a color. Clearly, such a class of models would not be categorical for a logic such as $\mathcal{L}_{L,C}$, which has no color constraints. For some other more expressive logic, however, colored graphs might be appropriate.

2.8.2 Subsumption Ordering and Minimality

Besides the correctness of algorithms, their efficiency is also a concern, which leads us to other properties of logical systems. In particular, we will later eschew normal theorem proving from a formula as the method for generating truths, preferring instead to operate on a representative or *canonical* model for the formula, in effect "reading off" the truths

---

[11] The notion of categoricity of models is akin to the notion of full abstraction in programming-language semantics. The term *categoricity* derives from its traditional usage in logic.

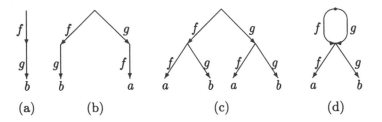

Figure 2.6
Examples of graph ordering

from it. This use of models as proxies for formulas requires, first of all, that such canonical models exist. We first define an ordering on models (called *subsumption*) such that one model subsumes another just in case it has less information—that is, fewer formulas hold of it.

DEFINITION 9 A model M *subsumes* another model M' (written $M \leq M'$) if and only if, for all formulas $\Phi \in \mathcal{L}$, $M' \models \Phi$ whenever $M \models \Phi$.

Continuing the informal example for the class of graph models, in the case of the logic $\mathcal{L}_{L,C}$, the graphs (a) through (d) in Figure 2.6 are given in increasing subsumption order.

We will require that there always be a least model (by the subsumption ordering) for any formula; this *minimal model* (which we will later prove unique) will be used as the proxy for formulas in computations.

PROPERTY 10 (EXISTENCE OF MINIMAL MODELS) If Φ is a consistent formula, then there is a model M such that $M \models \Phi$ and for all M' such that $M' \models \Phi$, it is the case that $M \leq M'$.

Since minimal-model existence is a strictly stronger property than denotational completeness (Property 6), only the former need be demonstrated for a logical system to be appropriate.

2.8.3 Compactness

Finally, a notion of compactness is required, in the sense that consequences of an infinite set of atomic formulas follow from a finite subset as well.

PROPERTY 11 (COMPACTNESS) Given a consistent (possibly infinite) set of atomic formulas S, if all models M such that $M \models \phi_i$ for all $\phi_i \in S$ are such that $M \models \Psi$, then $\Phi \vdash \Psi$ for Φ a finite subset of S.

2.8.4 Corollaries of Appropriateness Conditions

A great many consequent properties of these simple requirements will be useful in later proofs and can demonstrate the high degree of structure already imposed by the conditions. However, as the utility of these ancillary properties is motivated only in later discussion (especially Chapter 3), this section might be skimmed over at first reading, and used for reference during subsequent proofs.

It is convenient to separate the definition of the subsumption relation into two parts, corresponding to the 'if' and 'only if' components of the definition, so that they can be referred to individually.

DEFINITION 12 (UPWARD CLOSURE) If $M \leq M'$, then for all formulas Φ, whenever $M \models \Phi$, $M' \models \Phi$ as well.

DEFINITION 13 (SUBSUMPTION RESPECTS ENTAILMENT) If for all formulas Φ whenever $M \models \Phi$, $M' \models \Phi$, then $M \leq M'$.

These follow trivially from the definition of subsumption.

That definition does not in and of itself require that $\leq$ be a partial order, but this can be shown to be a consequence of categoricity.

LEMMA 14 The subsumption ordering $\leq$ is a partial order.

Proof We must show that $\leq$ is reflexive, antisymmetric, and transitive.

Reflexivity: Trivially, $M \models \Phi$ whenever $M \models \Phi$, so that $M \leq M$ by Definition 13.

Antisymmetry. Assume that $M \leq M'$ and $M' \leq M$. By the former subsumption and Definition 12, $M' \models \Phi$ whenever $M \models \Phi$, and, by the latter subsumption, conversely. Thus, $M \models \Phi$ if and only if $M' \models \Phi$. By Property 8, $M = M'$.

Transitivity: Trivial, by transitivity of implication.   □

The antisymmetry of subsumption guarantees that the minimal model is unique.

LEMMA 15 The minimal model for a formula Φ is unique.

Proof Suppose M and M' are minimal models of Φ. By Property 10, $M \models \Phi$ and $M' \models \Phi$, so since both are minimal models, $M \leq M'$ and $M' \leq M$. By Lemma 14, $M = M'$.   □

This lemma allows us to define felicitously a function mm from formulas of $\mathcal{L}$ to the unique minimal model for that formula. To demonstrate that the minimal model of a formula captures exactly those constraints that are implicit in the formula—no more, and no less—we prove the following two results:

LEMMA 16 (MINIMAL-MODEL COMPLETENESS)   If $mm(\Phi) \models \Phi'$, then $\Phi \vdash \Phi'$.

Proof Suppose $mm(\Phi) \models \Phi'$. By definition of minimal model, for all models M, if $M \models \Phi$, then $mm(\Phi) \leq M$. Now satisfaction is upward-closed (Definition 12), so if $M \models \Phi$, then $M \models \Psi$ whenever $mm(\Phi) \models \Psi$. For the particular case in which Ψ is Φ', we have that if $M \models \Phi$, then $M \models \Phi'$; that is, $\Phi \models \Phi'$. By logical completeness (Property 5), $\Phi \vdash \Phi'$.
                                                                      □

LEMMA 17 (MINIMAL-MODEL SOUNDNESS) If $\Phi \vdash \Phi'$, then $mm(\Phi) \models \Phi'$.

Proof Suppose $\Phi \vdash \Phi'$. By logical soundness (Property 7), $\Phi \models \Phi'$; that is, for all models M, if $M \models \Phi$, then $M \models \Phi'$. By definition of minimal model, $mm(\Phi) \models \Phi$, so $mm(\Phi) \models \Phi'$.   □

Finally, we show that for any formula there is a model that can be employed as its proxy, a *canonical model* that, in a sense, summarizes all and only the models of the formula. In particular, the models of the formula are exactly those that the canonical model subsumes.

LEMMA 18 (EXISTENCE OF CANONICAL MODELS) If Φ is a consistent formula, then there is a model M such that $M \models \Phi$ and for all M', $M' \models \Phi$ if and only if $M \leq M'$.

Proof Follows trivially from the existence of minimal models (Property 10) and upward closure (Definition 12).   □

The canonical model for a formula is, of course, its minimal model.

In fact, uniqueness of minimal models (Lemma 15) can be strengthened to apply to infinite sets of atomic formulas, by virtue of compactness. This will be useful in proving the functionality of various operations defined in the next section.

LEMMA 19 If a set of atomic formulas $\{\phi_i\}$ has a model, it has a unique least model.

Proof   Assume that there are two minimal models M and M' for $\{\phi_i\}$. We demonstrate that they are identical by showing mutual subsumption. Suppose that for some atomic formula ϕ we have that $M \models \phi$. Then by compactness, there must be a finite subset Φ of $\{\phi_i\}$ such that $\Phi \vdash \phi$. By logical soundness, all models for Φ are models for ϕ as well; in particular, $M' \models \phi$. By definition of subsumption, $M \leq M'$. The identical argument shows the converse subsumption. Thus, by categoricity, the two models are identical.   □

2.9   Operations on Models

If the canonical models of finite formulas of the logic are themselves finite, we can use them to compute over, replacing theorem proving over the formulas themselves. This might be advantageous if efficient algorithms exist for manipulating the minimal models in appropriate ways. With this purpose in mind, we define several operations on models. In Section 3.1 we discuss the necessary computational properties of these operations.

Informational Union   The most important operation on models is the operation that corresponds to combining the information that two models capture.

DEFINITION 20 The *informational union* of two models M and M' (written $M \sqcup M'$), if it exists, is the least model M'' such that $M \leq M''$ and $M' \leq M''$.

This is the operation that in previous work has been referred to as *unification* and that has lent its name to the class of formalisms called unification-based. The uniqueness of an informational union if it exists is proved as Lemma 32.

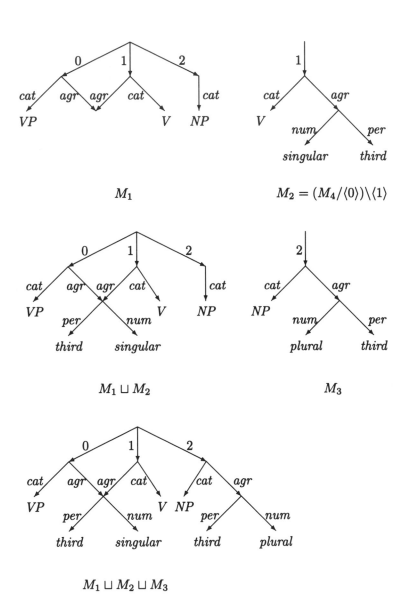

Figure 2.7
Examples of informational union, extraction, and embedding

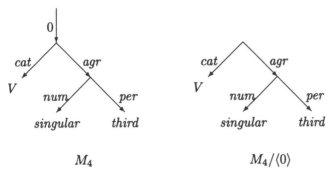

$$M_4 \qquad\qquad M_4/\langle 0 \rangle$$

Figure 2.8
Further examples of informational union, extraction, and embedding

As an example of an informational union operation, we consider the appropriate operation on graph models. The union of the graph M_1 in Figure 2.7 (given as graph (2.2.1) on page 11) with M_2 in the figure is displayed in the figure with the label $M_1 \sqcup M_2$. This, in turn, can be combined with the graph M_3 to form $M_1 \sqcup M_2 \sqcup M_3$. This latter is just the graph (2.2.3) displayed in the derivation on page 13.

Extraction   An operation that captures the intuition that the features can be used to decompose information into subparts is the extraction operation on models.

DEFINITION 21 The *extraction* of a model M at address p (written M/p) is that model M' (if there is one) such that $M' \models \Phi$ if and only if $M \models \Phi[\langle \rangle \rightarrow p]$.

Intuitively, M/p satisfies all of the constraints starting with path p, and thus serves as the "value" of the model at path p. Of course, M/p may not be defined if M models no constraints of the requisite sort, namely, all of whose paths have p as a prefix. If M satisfies no such constraints, M/p will satisfy no constraints whatever. But by Triviality, every model satisfies $\langle \rangle \doteq \langle \rangle$, so M/p must be undefined. That M/p is unique if it exists is proved as Lemma 33.

Embedding   The inverse of the extraction operation is the embedding operation.

DEFINITION 22 The *embedding* of a model M at an address p (written $M \backslash p$) is the least model M' such that $M'/p = M$.

Note that unlike the $/$ operation, the $\backslash$ operation always yields a result because proofs are invariant under prefixing (Property 2). Again, the uniqueness of M/p is proved as Lemma 34.

The examples of informational union show how that operation may play a part in defining parsers or other language processors. Extraction and embedding play a role in constructing the graphs to combine by informational union. For instance, the graph M_2 from Figure 2.7 is constructed using these operations from the minimal graph satisfying the lexical definition for the word 'abhors' displayed as (2.2.1) on page 11 and repeated as graph M_4 in Figure 2.8. The extraction of graph M_4 along the path $\langle 0 \rangle$ yields the graph $M_4/\langle 0 \rangle$ in the figure. This in turn is embedded under the path $\langle 1 \rangle$, yielding $(M_4/\langle 0 \rangle)\backslash\langle 1 \rangle = M_2$. A similar derivation forms the graph labeled M_3. Through this extended example, a natural parsing operation has been motivated, involving a single extraction, embedding, and union. Given a partially constructed graph M for a phrase that includes information about the first d of its subphrases, and a fully constructed graph M' for the $(d+1)$-st subphrase, a primitive combinatory operation is given by $M \sqcup ((M'/\langle 0 \rangle)\backslash\langle d+1 \rangle)$. In fact, this is the central component of the Scanning and Completion rules to be presented in Section 3.3.

Restriction   The final operation does not affect the "vertical" character of a model, by embedding or extracting subparts, but instead affects its "horizontal" structure, by removing features.

DEFINITION 23   The *restriction*[12] of a model M to a given domain of features F (written $M{\restriction}F$) is the least model M' such that if $M \models \Phi$ and all nonempty paths in Φ start with some element of F, then $M' \models \Phi$.

Auxiliary Notions   Useful auxiliary notions in discussing models include the domain of a model and properties of cyclicity in models.

DEFINITION 24   The *domain* of a model M (written $dom(M)$) is the set of labels $f \in L$ such that $M \models \langle f \rangle \doteq \langle f \rangle$.

DEFINITION 25   A model M is *cyclic* if and only if there are paths p and q such that q is nonempty and $M \models p \cdot q \doteq p$.

---

[12]The use of the term 'restriction' here differs from its use in previous work (Shieber, 1985c), which corresponds to the ρ function that will be introduced in Section 3.3.

DEFINITION 26 A model M is *top-cyclic* if and only if there is a path q such that q is nonempty and $M \models q \doteq \langle \rangle$.

Intuitively speaking, for the graph models top-cyclicity is the subcase of cyclicity in which the root of the graph participates in a cycle. We will refer to formulas whose minimal models are cyclic or top-cyclic as themselves having the respective properties. Equivalently (by Lemma 16), a model is cyclic or top-cyclic if it derives a formula of the kind in Definitions 25 and 26, respectively.

A useful fact about cyclicity is the following:

LEMMA 27 If Φ is a formula all of whose paths share nonempty p as a prefix, then Φ is not top-cyclic.

Proof Suppose Φ is top-cyclic; that is, $\Phi \vdash \langle \rangle \doteq p'$ for some p'. By logical locality (Property 1), p' must be a prefix or extension of p. Logical transparency (Property 2) allows us to build from the proof

$$\frac{\Phi}{\langle \rangle \doteq p'}$$

a proof, for arbitrary q, of

$$\frac{\Phi[p \to q \cdot p]}{\langle \rangle \doteq q \cdot p'}$$

(under a prefixed homomorphism $m_{\langle \rangle}$, where m takes p' or p to $q \cdot p'$ or $q \cdot p$, depending on whether p' is a prefix or an extension of p, respectively). Similarly, a prefixed homomorphism m'_q, where m' is the identity over paths, allows the proof

$$\frac{\Phi[p \to q \cdot p]}{q \doteq q \cdot p'} \quad .$$

Taken together, we can now form the following proof.

$$\frac{\dfrac{\Phi[p \to q \cdot p]}{\langle \rangle \doteq q \cdot p'} \quad \dfrac{\dfrac{\Phi[p \to q \cdot p]}{q \doteq q \cdot p'}}{q \cdot p' \doteq q}}{\dfrac{\langle \rangle \doteq q}{\dfrac{p' \doteq \langle \rangle}{\langle \rangle \doteq p'}}} \quad \frac{\Phi[p \to q \cdot p]}{\dfrac{\langle \rangle \doteq q \cdot p'}{q \cdot p' \doteq \langle \rangle}} \quad ,$$

from which it follows that $\Phi[p \to q \cdot p] \vdash \langle \rangle \doteq p'$. Since q is arbitrary, we can choose it so that p' is neither a prefix nor an extension of q (hence of $q \cdot p$); consequently, this entailment relation violates logical locality. Thus, Φ must not be top-cyclic.   □

2.9.1   Properties of Operations on Models

The final set of properties required of a logical system so that it can be used in the definition of a grammar formalism has to do with certain locality properties of inference in the logic. Although these properties could be stated directly as conditions on the inference rules, it is simpler to couch them in terms of the operations just defined, as these provide a convenient vocabulary for expressing inferential relationships.

First, the inferences drawn from an equation $p \doteq q$ should be local not only in the sense of Property 1, but also in that models should be affected only at the addresses specified.

PROPERTY 28 (MODEL LOCALITY 1) Given a model M in the range of mm, if M/p and M/q are defined, then $M \sqcup mm(\{p \doteq q\})$ is defined if and only if $M/p \sqcup M/q$ is defined.

Second, when two paths in disjoint models are combined, the ramifications should be local to the subgraphs combined.

PROPERTY 29 (MODEL LOCALITY 2) Given models M and N such that $dom(M)$ is disjoint from $dom(N)$ and M/p and N/q are defined, then

$$(M \sqcup N \sqcup mm(\{p \doteq q\})) \!\restriction\! dom(M) = M \sqcup N/q \backslash p \quad .$$

The union of two models that have disjoint domains (that is, carrying information about different aspects of a string) should be no greater than the sum of the parts.

PROPERTY 30 (MODEL LOCALITY 3) Given models M and N, if the domain $dom(M)$ is disjoint from $dom(N)$ and M and N are not top-cyclic, then $(M \sqcup N) \!\restriction\! dom(M) = M$.

Finally, the effect of informational union on a restricted model is localized to the restricted portion of the union.

PROPERTY 31 (MODEL LOCALITY 4) Given models M and N and a set of features F, if $dom(N) \subseteq F$ and M and N are not top-cyclic, then $(M \sqcup N) {\restriction} F = M {\restriction} F \sqcup N$.

Proofs for these properties for the case of $\mathcal{L}_{L,C}$ are included in the Appendix.

2.9.2   Corollaries for Operations on Models

We list some useful properties of these operations that follow from their definitions and the constraints on logical systems. Again, these are motivated by their use in later proofs.

LEMMA 32 (UNIQUENESS OF INFORMATIONAL UNION) For all models M and M' such that $M \sqcup M'$ exists, $M \sqcup M'$ is unique.

Proof   By assumption, there is a model N that is a least model such that $M \le N$ and $M' \le N$; that is, for all atomic formulas ϕ such that $M \models \phi$, $N \models \phi$ and similarly for M'. Thus, $N \models \{\phi \mid M \models \phi$ or $M' \models \phi\}$. By Lemma 19, N defined in this way is unique.   □

LEMMA 33 (UNIQUENESS OF EXTRACTION) For all models M and paths p such that M/p exists, M/p is unique.

Proof   Suppose M/p is not unique; that is, there are distinct M' and M'' obeying the definition of M/p. Since they are distinct, there must, by categoricity, exist some formula Φ such that $M' \models \Phi$ and $M'' \not\models \Phi$ (or vice versa, but without loss of generality assume the former). Then $M \models \Phi[\langle\rangle \to p]$ and $M \not\models \Phi[\langle\rangle \to p]$, a contradiction.   □

LEMMA 34 (UNIQUENESS OF EMBEDDING) For all models M and paths p such that $M \backslash p$ exists, $M \backslash p$ is unique.

Proof   Suppose $M \backslash p$ is not unique; that is, there are distinct least M' and M'' such that $M'/p = M$ and $M''/p = M$. Since $M'/p = M$, then for all Ψ, $M'/p \models \Psi$ if and only if $M \models \Psi$. By definition of $/$, this holds just in case $M' \models \Psi[\langle\rangle \to p]$. An identical argument holds for M''. In summary, $M' \models \Psi[\langle\rangle \to p]$ if and only if $M \models \Psi$, and similarly for M''. Thus, if we let $\{\psi_i\} = \{\psi \mid M \models \psi\}$, then M' is a least model such that $M' \models \{\psi_i[\langle\rangle \to p]\}$, and similarly for M''. Now since both M' and M'' are least models of a single set of atomic formulas, by Lemma 19 they are identical.   □

LEMMA 35 (UNIQUENESS OF DOMAIN RESTRICTION) For all models M and sets of features F such that $M{\upharpoonright}\backslash F$ exists, $M{\upharpoonright}\backslash F$ is unique.

Proof   As in Lemma 34.   □

LEMMA 36 For all formulas Φ and Φ' such that their union is consistent, $mm(\Phi) \sqcup mm(\Phi') = mm(\Phi \cup \Phi')$.

Proof   By Definition 20, $mm(\Phi) \leq mm(\Phi) \sqcup mm(\Phi')$. Upward closure (Definition 12) entails that if $mm(\Phi) \models \Psi$, then $mm(\Phi) \sqcup mm(\Phi') \models \Psi$; in particular, $mm(\Phi) \sqcup mm(\Phi') \models \Phi$. Similarly, $mm(\Phi) \sqcup mm(\Phi') \models \Phi'$. Thus, $mm(\Phi) \sqcup mm(\Phi') \models \Phi \cup \Phi'$, and $mm(\Phi \cup \Phi') \leq mm(\Phi) \sqcup mm(\Phi')$.

The converse is shown as follows. By Definition 13, $mm(\Phi) \leq mm(\Phi \cup \Phi')$. Similarly, $mm(\Phi') \leq mm(\Phi \cup \Phi')$. But $mm(\Phi) \sqcup mm(\Phi')$ is the *least* model obeying these subsumption relations. Thus, $mm(\Phi) \sqcup mm(\Phi') \leq mm(\Phi \cup \Phi')$. Since subsumption is antisymmetric (Lemma 14), $mm(\Phi) \sqcup mm(\Phi') = mm(\Phi \cup \Phi')$.   □

It follows from Lemma 36 and the definition of $\sqcup$ that for models M and M' in the range of mm, if there is a model N such that $M \leq N$ and $M' \leq N$, then $M \sqcup M'$ is defined and $M \sqcup M' \leq N$. In this case, we will say that M and M' are *consistent*, overloading the term as applied to formulas.

LEMMA 37 $mm(\Phi)\backslash p = mm(\Phi[\langle\rangle \to p])$.

Proof   By Lemmas 16 and 17, $mm(\Phi) \models \Psi$ if and only if $\Phi \vdash \Psi$. Since $M\backslash p$ is the least model M' such that $M'/p = M$ (by definition) and $M'/p \models \Phi$ if and only if $M' \models \Phi[\langle\rangle \to p]$ (again by definition), then by compactness (Property 11), for all formulas X, $M\backslash p \models X$ if and only if there is a Ψ such that $M \models \Psi$ and $\Psi[\langle\rangle \to p] \vdash X$. So $mm(\Phi)\backslash p \models X$ if and only if $mm(\Phi) \models \Psi$ and $\Psi[\langle\rangle \to p] \vdash X$; that is, $\Phi \vdash \Psi$ and $\Psi[\langle\rangle \to p] \vdash X$. By logical transparency (Property 2), this holds if and only if $\Phi[\langle\rangle \to p] \vdash \Psi[\langle\rangle \to p]$ and $\Psi[\langle\rangle \to p] \vdash X$, from which, by transitivity of entailment, $\Phi[\langle\rangle \to p] \vdash X$ and by Lemma 17, $mm(\Phi[\langle\rangle \to p]) \models X$. Thus, $mm(\Phi)\backslash p \models X$ if and only if $mm(\Phi[\langle\rangle \to p]) \models X$. Since models are categorical (Property 8), $mm(\Phi)\backslash p = mm(\Phi[\langle\rangle \to p])$.   □

LEMMA 38 For all formulas Φ and paths p, there exists a formula Ψ such that $mm(\Phi)/p = mm(\Psi)$.

Proof Define the class of atomic formulas $\overline{\Phi}_p$ as the set of atomic formulas ϕ such that $\Phi \vdash \phi$ and $\phi = \psi[\langle\rangle \to p]$ for some atomic formula ψ. There is a finite subset of $\overline{\Phi}_p$ that consists of those elements of $\overline{\Phi}_p$ that can be proved from Φ without using any elements of $\overline{\Phi}_p$ (except as the consequent of the proof, of course). Call this subset Φ_p; it is a well-defined formula. Any element of $\overline{\Phi}_p$ follows from Φ_p, so $mm(\Phi)/p = mm(\Phi_p[p \to \langle\rangle])$.   □

LEMMA 39 (IDEMPOTENCE OF $\sqcup$) For all models M and M', $M \leq M \sqcup M'$.

Proof Follows directly from Definition 20.   □

LEMMA 40 $dom(M\backslash\langle f\rangle \cdot q) = \{f\}$.

Proof We examine the labels g such that $M\backslash\langle f\rangle \cdot q \models \langle g\rangle \doteq \langle g\rangle$. By the argument given in the proof of Lemma 37, $M\backslash p \models X$ if and only if $M \models \Psi$ and $\Psi[\langle\rangle \to p] \vdash X$. In particular, $M\backslash\langle f\rangle \cdot q \models \langle g\rangle \doteq \langle g\rangle$ if and only if $M \models \Psi$ and $\Psi[\langle\rangle \to \langle f\rangle \cdot q] \vdash \langle g\rangle \doteq \langle g\rangle$. By Property 1, $\langle g\rangle$ must be a prefix or extension of $\langle f\rangle \cdot q$; that is, $g = f$. Thus, f is the only element in the domain of $M\backslash\langle f\rangle \cdot q$.   □

LEMMA 41 For all models M and N in the range of mm $(M \sqcup N)\backslash p = M\backslash p \sqcup N\backslash p$.

Proof Suppose $M = mm(\Phi)$ and $N = mm(\Phi')$. Then

$$
\begin{aligned}
M\backslash p \sqcup N\backslash p \ &= mm(\Phi)\backslash p \sqcup mm(\Phi')\backslash p \\
&= mm(\Phi[\langle\rangle \to p]) \sqcup mm(\Phi'[\langle\rangle \to p]) &\text{(Lemma 37)} \\
&= mm(\Phi[\langle\rangle \to p] \cup \Phi'[\langle\rangle \to p]) &\text{(Lemma 36)} \\
&= mm((\Phi \cup \Phi')[\langle\rangle \to p]) \\
&= mm(\Phi \cup \Phi')\backslash p &\text{(Lemma 37)} \\
&= (mm(\Phi) \sqcup mm(\Phi'))\backslash p &\text{(Lemma 36)} \\
&= (M \sqcup N)\backslash p \quad .
\end{aligned}
$$

□

Note that the corresponding property for / fails to hold.

LEMMA 42 $(M\backslash p)/p = M$.

Proof Follows trivially from Definition 22.   □

LEMMA 43　If $f \neq g$, then $M \backslash \langle f \rangle / \langle g \rangle$ is undefined.

Proof　The proof is by contradiction assuming $f \neq g$. Suppose that $M \backslash \langle f \rangle / \langle g \rangle$ is defined. Then it satisfies the equation $\langle \rangle \doteq \langle \rangle$ and $M \backslash \langle f \rangle$ satisfies $\langle g \rangle \doteq \langle g \rangle$, so $g \in dom(M \backslash \langle f \rangle)$. By Lemma 40, $f = g$ contra hypothesis.　　　　　　　　　　　　　　　　　　　　□

LEMMA 44　The following equality holds:

$$(M \upharpoonright F)/\langle g \rangle = \begin{cases} M/g & \text{if } g \in F \\ \text{undefined} & \text{otherwise} \end{cases}$$

Proof　Similar to those for Lemmas 42 and 43.　　　　　　　□

LEMMA 45　$M \upharpoonright F \leq M$.

Proof　Direct from the definition of $\upharpoonright$ (Definition 23) and Definition 13.　　　　　　　　　　　　　　　　　　　　　　　　　□

LEMMA 46　$M/(p \cdot q) = (M/p)/q$.

Proof　Direct from the definition of $/$ (Definition 21).　　　　□

LEMMA 47　$M/\langle f \rangle \backslash \langle f \rangle \leq M \upharpoonright \{f\}$.

Proof　By the definition of $\backslash$ and compactness (Property 11), it holds that $M/\langle f \rangle \backslash \langle f \rangle \models \Phi$ if and only if $M/\langle f \rangle \models \Psi$ and $\Psi[\langle \rangle \rightarrow \langle f \rangle] \vdash \Phi$. Expanding the definition of $/$, this holds if and only if $M \models \Psi[\langle \rangle \rightarrow \langle f \rangle]$ and $\Psi[\langle \rangle \rightarrow \langle f \rangle] \vdash \Phi$. Now $M \models \Psi[\langle \rangle \rightarrow \langle f \rangle]$ just in case $M \upharpoonright \{f\} \models \Psi[\langle \rangle \rightarrow \langle f \rangle]$, so we have that $M/\langle f \rangle \backslash \langle f \rangle \models \Phi$ if and only if $M \upharpoonright \{f\} \models \Psi[\langle \rangle \rightarrow \langle f \rangle]$ and $\Psi[\langle \rangle \rightarrow \langle f \rangle] \vdash \Phi$. Logical soundness guarantees that if $M \upharpoonright \{f\} \models \Psi[\langle \rangle \rightarrow \langle f \rangle]$ and $\Psi[\langle \rangle \rightarrow \langle f \rangle] \vdash \Phi$, then $M \upharpoonright \{f\} \models \Phi$ (though not necessarily conversely). Thus, if $M/\langle f \rangle \backslash \langle f \rangle \models \Phi$, then $M \upharpoonright \{f\} \models \Phi$. By Definition 13, $M/\langle f \rangle \backslash \langle f \rangle \leq M \upharpoonright \{f\}$.　　　　□

Actually, for $\mathcal{L}_{L,C}$, this theorem can be strengthened to equality, though this does not hold in the general case.

LEMMA 48　(IDENTITY FOR $\upharpoonright$)　For all models M, $M \upharpoonright dom(M) = M$.

Proof Suppose $M \models R(\vec{v})$. For each nonempty path p in $\vec{v}$, $M \models p \doteq p$. By the Reflexivity inference rule, $M \models \langle f \rangle \doteq \langle f \rangle$ for f the first element of p. We conclude that $f \in dom(M)$ for all such f, and $M {\upharpoonright} dom(M) \models R(\vec{v})$.

Since $M {\upharpoonright} dom(M) \leq M$ (proved as Lemma 45), by upward closure (Definition 12) $M {\upharpoonright} dom(M) \models \Phi \rightarrow M \models \Phi$. Thus, $M {\upharpoonright} dom(M)$ and M satisfy exactly the same formulas; by categoricity, they are therefore identical. □

Some extended versions of compactness (Property 11) will be employed in the sequel. These require that formulas satisfied by a union of models follow from finite formulas that hold of the models separately. Similarly, if a union is undefined, an inconsistency must follow from finite formulas that hold of the models as well.

LEMMA 49 If $M \sqcup M'$ is defined and $M \sqcup M' \models \Psi$, then there are formulas Φ and Φ' such that $M \models \Phi$ and $M' \models \Phi'$ and $\Phi \cup \Phi' \vdash \Psi$.

Proof The model $M \sqcup M'$ is the least M'' such that $M \leq M''$ and $M' \leq M''$; that is, $M'' \models \Phi$ for all Φ such that $M \models \Phi$ or $M' \models \Phi$ (by Definition 13). By compactness (Property 11), if $M \sqcup M' \models \Psi$, then $\Psi' \vdash \Psi$ for Ψ' a finite subset of $\{\phi \mid M \models \phi \text{ or } M' \models \phi\}$. Let Φ be the subset of Ψ' satisfied by M, and Φ' the subset satisfied by M'. Then $M \models \Phi$ and $M' \models \Phi'$ and $\Phi \cup \Phi' \vdash \Psi$. □

LEMMA 50 For M and M' in the range of mm, if $M \sqcup M'$ is undefined, then there are formulas Φ and Φ' such that $M \models \Phi$ and $M' \models \Phi'$ and $\Phi \cup \Phi'$ is inconsistent.

Proof We prove the contrapositive. Let $M = mm(\Psi)$ and $M' = mm(\Psi')$. Suppose there are no Φ and Φ' such that $M \models \Phi$ and $M' \models \Phi'$ and $\Phi \cup \Phi'$ is inconsistent. Since $M \models \Psi$ and $M' \models \Psi'$, the formula $\Psi \cup \Psi'$ is consistent, and $mm(\Psi \cup \Psi')$ is defined. Then by Lemma 36, $M \sqcup M' = mm(\Psi \cup \Psi')$, so $M \sqcup M'$ is defined. □

2.9.3 Monotonicity of Operations

We define a notion of monotonicity for operations on models.

DEFINITION 51 An operation *op* on models is *monotonic* if and only if whenever $M \leq M'$, $op(M) \leq op(M')$.

LEMMA 52 For all paths p and sets of features f_i, the operators $/p$, $\backslash p$, and $\upharpoonright F$ are monotonic.

Proof   Suppose $M \leq M'$. Choose an arbitrary formula Φ such that $M/p \models \Phi$. Then by definition of extraction (Definition 21), $M \models \Phi[\langle\rangle \rightarrow p]$. By upward closure (Definition 12), $M' \models \Phi[\langle\rangle \rightarrow p]$, so $M'/p \models \Phi$. Finally, Definition 13 yields $M/p \leq M'/p$.

The proofs for $\backslash p$ and $\upharpoonright F$ are only slightly more complex. $\square$

2.10   Existence of Appropriate Models for $\mathcal{L}_{L,C}$

Figure 2.9 summarizes the properties of appropriate models for constraint logics. In the illustration, an arrow connects one property with another if the property at the tail is used in the proof of the property at the head. Several incoming arrows depict the fact that several properties are needed in the proof. Properties with no incoming arrows are unproved in general, that is, postulated to hold of an appropriate logic. These properties are either definitions (shown in italics) or must be proved of an individual logic to demonstrate its appropriateness (shown in boldface). The figure reveals that, although numerous, the properties rely on just a few of these assumptions as a basis. Nevertheless, at this point, the reader might be wondering whether an appropriate class of models can be found for even the simple logic $\mathcal{L}_{L,C}$. Unfortunately, an affirmative answer must wait until Chapter 4, when we discuss at length the possibilities for classes of models for $\mathcal{L}_{L,C}$. Those especially concerned that the set of appropriate model classes might be empty can skip ahead to that chapter. More patient readers will be presented in the next chapter with a discussion regarding the uses of appropriate logical systems for grammar definition and parsing, granted the premise that such systems do in fact exist.

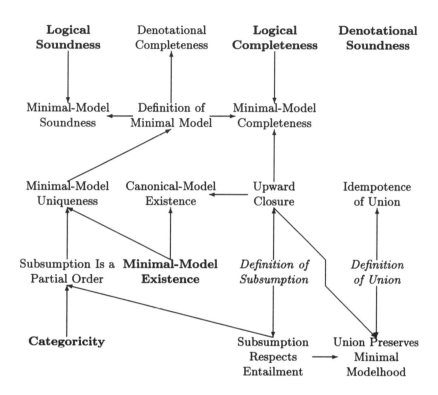

Figure 2.9
Summary of properties

3 Grammars and Parsing

Given a logical system with the requisite properties, we can define a grammar formalism based on logical constraints over information associated with phrases. The definition is quite abstract: any logical system of sufficient expressiveness satisfying the properties outlined in Chapter 2 will serve to define a formalism. It is this abstraction that justifies considering these methods as characterizing constraint-based formalisms in general, rather than an individual formalism.

Furthermore, so long as the models of the logic have some further quite strong computational properties, a general algorithm can be defined for parsing phrases with respect to a grammar in the constraint-based formalism. The construction of the algorithm and a proof of its correctness are given independently of the details of the logic upon which the formalism is based. A further abstraction in the definition of the algorithm makes the algorithm and its correctness proof independent of the control regime employed. Thus, at one stroke, a wide range of parsing algorithms are proved correct for any constraint-based formalism. Particular instances of the algorithm, including an incarnation as an extended Earley's algorithm and a simulation of LR parsing, are discussed. The latter is especially important because of its ties to psycholinguistic effects. The definition of grammar formalisms and their parsing algorithms takes up Chapter 3.

3.1 Defining Constraint-Based Formalisms

We return now to our original motivation for developing the constraint logics of the previous chapter, the definition of constraint-based grammar formalisms. As mentioned in Chapter 1, we will define constraint-based grammar formalisms—in keeping with our efforts to maintain as abstract a view of grammar as possible—by making explicit their dependence on a particular logical system of the sort described in the preceding chapter. We merely require that the logical system possess the various properties previously stipulated or proved, so that we can avail ourselves of the structure, partiality, and equationality of the logic. Beyond this requirement, almost any logic will do.

For the formalism to be computationally effective, however, stronger requirements are imposed upon the logical system, namely, that the various operations on models in the logic (i.e., $/$, $\backslash$, $|\backslash$, and $\sqcup$) be easily computable and that they preserve the finiteness of models. This is because the parsing algorithms we develop in this chapter make free use of these operations as steps in the parsing process. Thus, the operations must be computationally interpretable, and the solutions finitely representable, so that they can serve as the input to further computation.

Preservation of finiteness is given by Lemmas 36, 37, and 38, together with a requirement of the finiteness of minimal models for atomic formulas. Computability of operations, especially informational union, is a more interesting question that will receive a good deal of attention in the next chapter. For the nonce, it suffices to note that the feature-graph models developed in Chapter 4 are finite for atomic formulas, and that an algorithm for informational union will be provided.

The class of formalisms (parameterized by a constraint logic) that we will presuppose is quite simple. We assume that we are given a logical system including a logic $\mathcal{L}$ over a set of labels L and constants C, where L is required to contain the labels $0, 1, 2, \cdots, \bar{1}, \bar{2}, \cdots$.

Given such a logical system, a *grammar* G in the formalism defined by that system is a triple $\langle \Sigma, P, p_0 \rangle$, where Σ is the *vocabulary* of the grammar, P a set of *productions*, and p_0 a designated element of P, the *start production*. Each production is a pair of one of two forms: phrasal or lexical. A *phrasal production* is a pair of the form $\langle a, \Phi \rangle$. The first component is a nonnegative integer (that is, $a \in N$), and is called the *arity* of the production; it corresponds to the number of subconstituents the production allows combination of. If a is 0, then the rule allows empty constituents; if a is, say, 2, then the rule engenders binary branching. Thus, a is analogous to the length of the right-hand side of a context-free rule. The second component of the production, Φ, is a formula in L. We impose the stronger requirement that all paths in Φ have an integer from 0 to a as their first component.[1] Informally, the formula provides mutual constraints on the $a + 1$ constituents over which the rule applies: the parent constituent, numbered 0, and the a child constituents, numbered 1 to a from left to right. As an example,

---

[1] We will use the notation $[i..j]$ to denote the set of integer labels between i and j inclusive, and similarly for $[\bar{i}..\bar{j}]$. Thus, the requirement might be stated as follows: All paths in Φ have a member of $[0..a]$ as first component.

the rule given as (R_2) in Section 2.2 would be stated as

$$\left\langle 2, \left\{ \begin{array}{l} \langle 0\ cat \rangle \doteq S, \\ \langle 1\ cat \rangle \doteq NP, \\ \langle 2\ cat \rangle \doteq VP, \\ \langle 1\ agr \rangle \doteq \langle 2\ agr \rangle \end{array} \right\} \right\rangle \quad .$$

A *lexical production* is a pair of the form $\langle w, \Phi \rangle$, where w is a lexical item in Σ, and Φ is a formula, as before, all of whose paths begin with the integer 0. Rule (R_3) defining the lexical item 'Nature' would be expressed as

$$\left\langle \text{'Nature'}, \left\{ \begin{array}{l} \langle 0\ cat \rangle \doteq NP \\ \langle 0\ agr\ num \rangle \doteq singular \\ \langle 0\ agr\ per \rangle \doteq third \end{array} \right\} \right\rangle \quad .$$

Finally, the importance of the distinguished production $p_0 = \langle a_0, \Phi_0 \rangle$, the *start production*, is that only phrases admitted using it as the topmost production are considered sentences in the language of G.[2]

3.2 Grammar Interpretation

Semantics for context-free grammars have traditionally been given in one of two ways: in terms of derivations of sentential forms or fringes of admitted parse trees. The former seems to be especially prevalent both in the computer science and in the natural-language-processing literatures.[3] Aho and Ullman (1972) define the language of a grammar in terms of derivations of sentential forms, returning to the definition of parse trees as a "convenient graphical representation of an equivalence class of derivations" some 50 pages later. Similarly, Winograd's introductory text (1983) describes the interpretation of context-free grammars in terms of derivations of parse trees.

---

[2] Context-free grammars use a start symbol, as opposed to a start production. Nothing critical rests on this distinction, since if a start symbol is desired, one could just add a unary production to the grammar with that symbol as the only child and make this the start production. Thus, no generality is lost by using a start production.

[3] A third method, based on solution of systems of set equations over union and concatenation, follows from the work of Chomsky and Schutzenberger (1963). Although less prevalent these days, a similar idea underlies the original semantics of PATR-II (Pereira and Shieber, 1984).

Because of the unique character of constraint-based formalisms, a semantics for a formalism based on a naive redefinition of the notion of derivation is problematic, not only because it introduces a procedural notion where one is not needed, but also because information flow in a derivation is not easily captured by working only top-down—as in a derivation—or, for that matter, only bottom-up. Though possible, such a semantics would be geared to proving the correctness of a purely top-down or bottom-up algorithm. We would like to be more procedurally agnostic than that.

Consequently, we will define the language of a grammar directly in terms of an analogue to context-free parse trees—rather than define parse trees in terms of classes of derivations as is traditional with context-free grammars. The approach, therefore, is more reminiscent of treating grammar rules as node-admissibility conditions in the manner of Peters and Ritchie (1973) than as a product of a generative process or derivation. Informally, a parse tree can be thought of as being composed of a hierarchically structured group of local sets of nodes, each of which is admitted by a rule of the grammar. Instead of defining an entire new mathematical structure for this purpose, we will adopt the expedient of modeling parse trees with the existing feature structures. A local set of parse-tree nodes must provide information about each separate node. This will be done by placing information about each node under the labels 0 through a, where a is the arity of the rule. Such a local set of nodes must be admitted by a production $p = \langle a, \Phi \rangle$ in the grammar, so we require that the local set of nodes be a model for Φ. We must also provide for the structural relationships among the local sets of nodes. For the ith child of a node, we will place a feature $\bar{i}$ in the parse tree whose value is the parse tree of that child. Finally, we must guarantee that the child information in a local set of nodes matches the parent information in the lower set of nodes corresponding to that child; this is easily ensured by requiring that parse trees satisfy equations of the form $\langle \bar{i}\, 0 \rangle \doteq \langle i \rangle$. (Here, of course, we are relying on the minimal expressivity of $\mathcal{L}_{L,C}$ allowing such equations.)

More formally, a *parse tree* τ is a model that is a member of the infinite union of sets of bounded-depth parse trees $\Pi = \bigcup_{i \geq 0} \Pi_i$, where the Π_i are defined as follows:

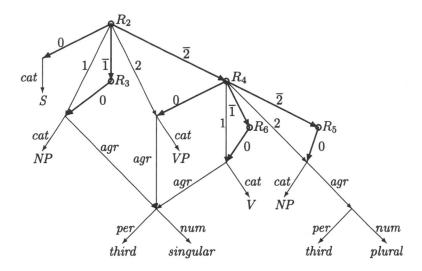

Figure 3.1
An example parse tree

1. Π_0 is the set of models τ for which there is a lexical production $p = \langle w, \Phi \rangle$ and $\tau \models \Phi$ and $dom(\tau) = \{0\}$.

2. Π_i for $i > 0$ is the set of models τ for which there is a phrasal production $p = \langle a, \Phi \rangle$ such that $\tau \models \Phi$ and $dom(\tau) \subseteq \{0, 1, \ldots, a, \bar{1}, \ldots, \bar{a}\}$ and, for $1 \leq i \leq a$, $\tau/\langle i \rangle$ is defined and $\tau/\langle i \rangle \in \bigcup_{j<i} \Pi_j$ and $\tau \models \langle \bar{i}\ 0 \rangle \doteq \langle i \rangle$.

In either case, the production p is said to *license* the parse tree.

The *yield* of a parse tree is defined in terms of the licensing production. If lexical production $\langle w, \Phi \rangle$ licenses τ, then w is a yield of τ. If phrasal production $\langle a, \Phi \rangle$ licenses τ and $\alpha_1, \ldots, \alpha_a$ are yields of $\tau/\langle \bar{1} \rangle, \ldots, \tau/\langle \bar{a} \rangle$, respectively, then $\alpha_1 \cdots \alpha_a$ is a yield of τ.

The definition of parse tree can play the role that derivation does in a context-free grammar. Existence of a parse tree whose root satisfies some formula and whose yield is the required string of terminals replaces a nonterminal deriving a string of terminals.

The *language* of a grammar can be defined in just this way. It is the set of yields of all parse trees admitted by the grammar that are licensed by the start production.

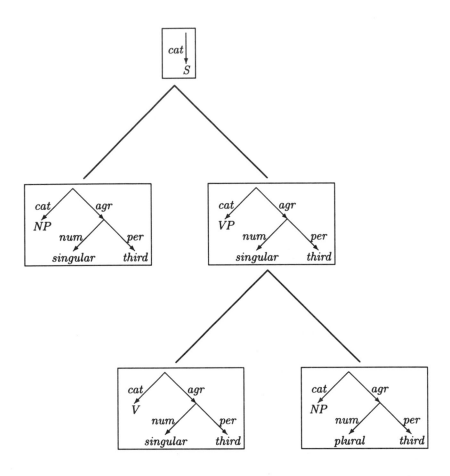

Figure 3.2
The example parse tree represented more traditionally

An Example Parse Tree   As an example of the foregoing definitions, we present the parse tree for the sample sentence and grammar described in Section 2.2. The sentence 'Nature abhors vacuums' is admitted by the grammar, as witnessed by the parse tree in Figure 3.1. The interior parse-tree nodes in the figure have been labeled with the rules that witness them. Note that the root, its immediate parse-tree children (the values of the features $\bar{1}$ and $\bar{2}$), and their parse-tree children, and so forth, are all appropriately witnessed. For each of these children, the equation $\langle \bar{i}\ 0 \rangle \doteq \langle i \rangle$ is satisfied.

Some of the information inherent in the parse tree of Figure 3.1 can be displayed in a more traditional format, as in Figure 3.2. Here, we have used the values of the 0 feature to label a traditional parse-tree node, with ordered child nodes (corresponding to the $\bar{i}$ values) similarly displayed. Of course, this representation does not capture *all* of the information of Figure 3.1—in particular, shared structure among the subconstituents is lost—which is why this more traditional representation was eschewed for the purpose of furnishing grammar semantics. However, it may be useful in conveying an intuitive notion of the role of parse trees, especially when partial parse trees and derivations are discussed later.

The parse tree given in Figure 3.1 is the minimal tree whose yield is the sample sentence. Note that the same parse tree also has a yield 'Nature abhorred vacuums', as the node labeled by the rule (R_6) is also licensed by the rule (R_7). In this case, the node corresponding to the lexical item 'abhorred' is marked as third-person singular, even though the lexical production itself states no such requirement. In a sense, the agreement features of the verb have been inferred from the surrounding context, namely, from the use of the verb with a third-person singular subject.

3.3   The Abstract Parsing Algorithm

The parsing algorithm defined here is abstract, not only by virtue of its abstraction from a particular formalism, but also by virtue of its abstraction from any particular processing regime. In effect, we define the "logic" part of the "logic + control" that Kowalski's decomposition of the notion of "algorithm" makes explicit (Kowalski, 1979). (The "control" part is discussed in Section 3.6, especially 3.6.3.) In so doing, we define a whole family of parsing algorithms by defining the logic of parsing and proving the soundness and completeness of this logic with respect to the abstract parsing problem. Then, any control method will serve to generate a particular parsing algorithm.

The parsing logic is based on *items*, structures that encode information about contextually allowed partial phrases. The item concept stems originally from the dotted rules of Knuth's LR table-building algorithms (Knuth, 1965) and is the basis of Earley's algorithm for context-free parsing (Earley, 1970). Items are found in the so-called chart-parsing algorithms (Kay, 1980; Kaplan, 1973; Thompson, 1981) under the guise of *edges* in the chart.

Here, an item will be a quintuple $\langle i, j, p, M, d \rangle$, where i and j are indices into the string being parsed; $p = \langle a, F \rangle$ is a phrasal production in the grammar; M is a model in the model structure for the logic; and d is an index into the production p, the *dot position*,[4] such that $0 \leq d \leq a$. Informally speaking, an item establishes a claim about the string, namely, that the substring between positions i and j is admitted under the grammar as the first d subconstituents of production p, that the local set of nodes in the corresponding parse tree is M, and further, that such a constituent is appropriate in the context of the string preceding position i.

Rather than make this informal characterization precise, we will give the logic for the algorithm, then return to the issue of the intended meaning for items, in preparation for proving the correctness of the algorithm relative to that intended meaning.

The Logic of the Parsing Algorithm   The parsing algorithm specifies nondeterministic rules for generating items given a grammar $G = \langle \Sigma, P, p_0 = \langle a_0, \Phi_0 \rangle \rangle$ and a string $w_1 \cdots w_n \in \Sigma^*$. These rules can be seen as inference rules in which the items are the sentences of the logic.

We start by generating an item for the start production. This corresponds to the inference rule

Initial Item: $\dfrac{}{\langle 0, 0, p_0, mm(\Phi_0), 0 \rangle}$.

---

[4]The dot position is so named for historical reasons; the index in Knuth's dotted rules was notated by insertion of an actual dot between two elements of the right-hand side of a production.

Whenever an item has been generated whose dot position has not reached the arity of the grammar rule from which the item has been instantiated (an *active* item), and when the next word in the string being parsed can match the position after the dot, we move the dot one position to the right and add the information about the word recorded in the lexicon. This corresponds to the inference rule

Scanning:
$$\frac{\langle i, j, p = \langle a, \Phi \rangle, M, d \rangle}{\langle i, j+1, p, M \sqcup ((mm(\Phi')/\langle 0 \rangle)\backslash\langle d+1 \rangle), d+1 \rangle}$$

where $d < a$ and $\langle w_{j+1}, \Phi' \rangle \in P$.

Active items also lead to the generation of items for rules that might match the position immediately after the dot. These items cover no part of the string, merely serving as predictions that such a constituent might be built through later applications of the inference rules.

Prediction:
$$\frac{\langle i, j, p = \langle a, \Phi \rangle, M, d \rangle}{\langle j, j, p', mm(\Phi') \sqcup (\rho(M/\langle d+1 \rangle)\backslash\langle 0 \rangle), 0 \rangle}$$

where $p' = \langle a', \Phi' \rangle \in P$ and $d < a$.

Here ρ is *any* monotonic operation on models obeying the restriction that for every formula Φ there is a formula $\Phi' \subseteq \Phi$ such that $\rho(mm(\Phi)) = mm(\Phi')$. As a consequence, $\rho(M) \leq M$ for M in the range of mm. For instance, the identity would suffice, as would the constant function yielding the trivial model. The utility of ρ will be explained later, in Section 3.6.2.

This inference rule, and the others presented, is applicable only if the consequent item is well defined, of course. In this case, the minimal model and the $\sqcup$ must be defined.

Finally, whenever the subconstituent after the dot position in an active item matches some inactive item that follows it contiguously, they can be combined.

Completion:
$$\frac{\langle i, j, p = \langle a, \Phi \rangle, M, d \rangle \qquad \langle j, k, p' = \langle a', \Phi' \rangle, M', a' \rangle}{\langle i, k, p, M \sqcup ((M'/\langle 0 \rangle)\backslash\langle d+1 \rangle), d+1 \rangle}$$

where $d < a$.

(Note the use of the operation $M \sqcup M'/\langle 0 \rangle\backslash\langle d+1 \rangle$ informally motivated in Section 2.9.)

Given a grammar $G = \langle \Sigma, P, p_0 = \langle a_0, \Phi_0 \rangle \rangle$, the algorithm will be said to accept a string $w_1 \cdots w_n$ if and only if it generates an item of the form $\langle 0, n, p_0, M, a_0 \rangle$. The later proof of correctness of the algorithm (Proposition 56) essentially involves proving that this notion of admitting a string and the one presented in Section 3.2 amount to the same thing.

An Example Parse   We consider the parsing of the canonical sample sentence 'Nature abhors vacuums' by the parsing algorithm just outlined. For purposes of demonstration, the function ρ used in the Prediction rule will be assumed to take any model onto a model with values for at most the paths $\langle cat \rangle$ and $\langle agr\ num \rangle$, for which the values are the same for both argument and result. In particular, the following equation holds:

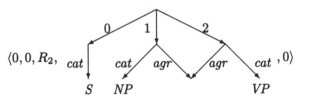

The Initial Item rule gives us the item

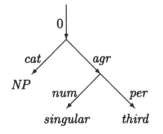

The minimal model for the formula associated with the word 'Nature' is

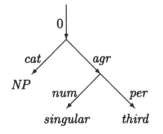

which is used in the scanning of the word to yield the item

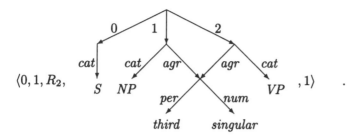

This item can feed the Prediction rule, as it requires a VP potentially defined by rule (R_4). The predicted item is

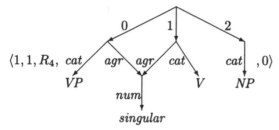

Although the required VP was marked as third-person singular, the predicted item includes only the singular agreement feature, because the person feature was eliminated by ρ.

The predicted item and the following word 'abhors' participate in the Scanning rule again, leading to the item

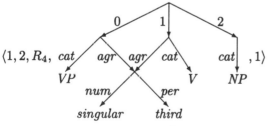

Another use of Scanning produces

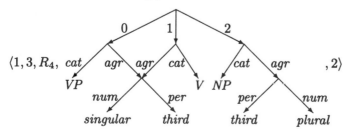

This item is not partial; its dot position is equal to the arity of the rule. It can therefore be used by the Completion rule, and is, in conjunction with the item

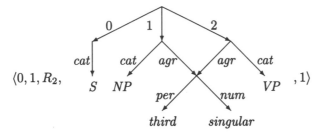

generated above. The output of Completion is the item

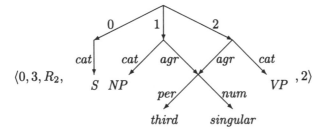

This final item is of the form $\langle 0, n, p_0, M, a_0 \rangle$ for the grammar, thus demonstrating the well-formedness of the string according to the grammar.

3.4   Auxiliary Notions for Item Semantics

We now turn to defining the meaning of an item such that the inference rules above are correct. We require certain auxiliary notions.

In discussions of context-free grammars, it makes sense to think of a string of nonterminals deriving some sentential form. For instance, the meaning of the Earley's algorithm context-free item

$$\langle i, j, A \rightarrow \alpha \bullet \beta \rangle$$

is that there exist strings of nonterminals or terminals γ and δ such that

$$\alpha \stackrel{*}{\Rightarrow} w_{i+1} \cdots w_j$$
$$S \stackrel{*}{\Rightarrow} \gamma A \delta$$
$$\gamma \stackrel{*}{\Rightarrow} w_1 \cdots w_i$$

The first condition establishes that the substring between positions i and j can be admitted as part of an A constituent, including the subconstituents listed before the dot, but excluding those after the dot. The remaining conditions establish that the left context allows such a constituent. Pictorially, we can depict the required configuration as in Figure 3.3.

Note especially the use of a string of nonterminals (α) deriving a string of terminals ($w_{i+1} \cdots w_j$). A natural way of achieving this effect with the more general class of items—without resorting to a notion of derivation—is to require the existence of a set of parse trees, one for each element of α, whose yields encompass $w_{i+1} \cdots w_j$. As it turns out, we cannot resort to modeling such derivations by this method because it ignores the fact that the production and left context from which the item was derived may place informational constraints that hold across the various subconstituents.

Instead, we will use an alternative conception of the Earley's algorithm item invariant, and generalize it to the constraint-based setting. The picture in Figure 3.3 can serve as the source of this alternative specification of the item invariant. The tree rooted at A looks much like a parse tree except that at the top level only a prefix of the subconstituents, the first d of them, have been built, where d is the dot position of the corresponding item. We can define a *partial parse tree* as such a tree. The *arity* of the partial parse tree is the number d of top-level subconstituents; the *need* of the partial parse tree is the nonterminal of the $(d + 1)$-st subconstituent (if there is one). The invariant of Earley's algorithm is, then, that a partial parse tree rooted in A with arity d and covering $w_{i+1} \cdots w_j$ must exist.

The left-context requirement can be handled by requiring that there be another partial parse tree such that its need matches the root of the first partial parse tree (that is, A), and it covers $w_{i'+1} \cdots w_i$. This second partial parse tree must fit its own left context—another partial parse tree—and so forth, until finally we have a partial parse tree rooted at S covering $w_0 \cdots w_{i''}$ where $w_{i''} + 1$ is the left edge of its need's partial parse tree.

We require, then, that there exist a cascade of partial *context-free* parse trees, the first rooted in S, the last covering the string from i to j and licensed by $A \rightarrow \alpha\beta$, such that the root of each partial parse tree is the need of its predecessor. In the case of context-free grammars, we

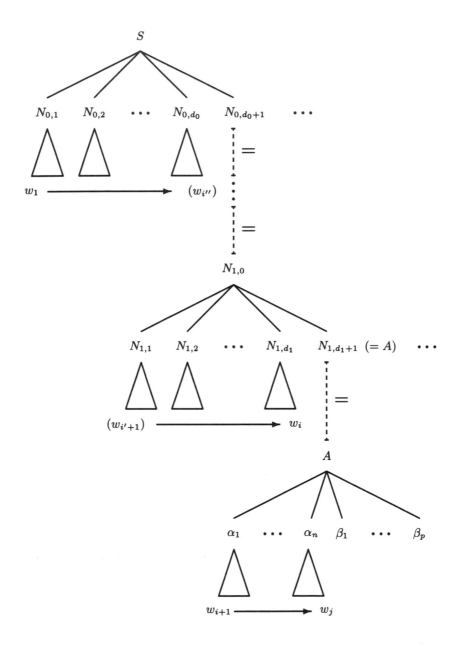

Figure 3.3
Earley's algorithm invariant as a cascade of partial context-free parse trees

could collapse these partial parse trees into a single requirement that

$$\alpha \overset{*}{\Rightarrow} w_{i+1} \cdots w_j$$
$$S \overset{*}{\Rightarrow} \gamma A \delta$$
$$\gamma \overset{*}{\Rightarrow} w_1 \cdots w_i \quad .$$

Thus, this definition is equivalent to the earlier requirement. We have merely replaced the iteration in the $S \overset{*}{\Rightarrow} \gamma A \delta$ requirement with a sequence of partial parse trees. The requirement that $\gamma \overset{*}{\Rightarrow} w_1 \cdots w_i$ is a side effect of the constraints on that sequence. The advantage of this definition is that it can be expressed completely statically, that is, non-derivationally, using only the notion of a partial parse tree.

Applying this technique to constraint-based formalisms, we will define partial parse trees and derivations thereof for the more general class of formalisms.

Formally, τ is a *partial parse tree* of arity d if and only if τ is a model that obeys one of the following two conditions:

1. $\tau \in \Pi_0$; that is, there is a lexical production p such that τ is a parse tree licensed by p as defined before. In this case, the arity of τ is 1.

2. There is a phrasal production $p = \langle a, \Phi \rangle \in G$ such that $d \leq a$ and $\tau \models \Phi$ and $dom(\tau) \subseteq \{0, 1, \ldots, a, \overline{1}, \ldots, \overline{d}\}$ and for $1 \leq i \leq d$, the value $\tau/\langle \overline{i} \rangle$ is defined and $\tau/\langle \overline{i} \rangle \in \Pi$ and $\tau \models \langle i \ 0 \rangle \doteq \langle \overline{i} \rangle$.

The yield of a partial parse tree is defined analogously to the yield of a full parse tree, except that the yields of only the first d sub-parse-trees are concatenated, where d is the arity of the partial parse tree.

When a partial parse tree of arity d is strictly partial—that is, it is licensed by a production $p = \langle a, \Phi \rangle$ and $d < a$—the information given by $\tau/\langle d + 1 \rangle$ corresponds to the next constituent that would be needed to augment the tree to make it less partial. This information will be called the *need* of the partial parse tree, again by analogy with the context-free case.

Recall that the existence of a partial parse tree covering the portion of the string that the item itself covers is only one part of an item's meaning. Existence of an item also implies that such a partial parse tree matches the left context of the string as well. That is, there must be some other partial parse tree for a section of the string to the item's left that the item's partial parse tree fits. This new partial parse tree itself must fit its own left context, and so on, until a partial parse tree licensed by the start production and covering the very beginning of the string is found.

To render this intuition concrete, we define a *derivation* as a cascade of partial parse trees, each fitting the context of the previous, just as was done for context-free grammars.

DEFINITION 53 A *derivation* is a finite sequence of partial parse trees $\tau_0, \ldots, \tau_k$ such that

1. For $0 \leq i \leq k$, τ_i is licensed by $p_i = \langle a_i, \Phi_i \rangle$ and has arity d_i, and

2. $d_k \leq a_k$ (i.e., τ_k may be a full parse tree), and

3. For $0 \leq i < k$, $d_i < a_i$ (i.e., τ_i is strictly partial), and $\rho(\tau_i/\langle d_i+1\rangle) \leq \tau_{i+1}/\langle 0 \rangle$ (i.e., τ_{i+1} fits the context of τ_i).

An informal graphical representation of a derivation is given in Figure 3.4. Each partial parse tree covers a consecutive piece of string, and each nests in the previous one in the sense that the root of each is subsumed by (some restricted portion of) the need of its predecessor.

The yield of a derivation is merely the concatenation of the yields of each of the partial parse trees. The notation $yield(\tau_0, \ldots, \tau_k)$ will be used for this concept.

One final observation is needed before we turn to the correctness proof. An important feature of the parsing rules is that all the generated models in the items are in the range of mm. This is easily shown by induction on the depth of proof of an item. For the base case, the Initial Item rule, $M_0 = mm(\Phi_0)$ is clearly in the range of mm. For the other rules, the output model is constructed using the models from the antecedent items and minimal models of rule formulas, along with the mm-preserving operations $\sqcup$, $\backslash$, $/$, and ρ. The mm preservation of the first three operations has been proved in Lemmas 36, 37, and 38, respectively. That ρ preserves minimal-modelhood follows directly from its definition. The minimal-modelhood of the output models can thus be assumed in the correctness proof in the next section.

3.5   A Correctness Proof for the Algorithm

Now that we have defined partial parse trees and derivations of them, the meaning of an item generated by this algorithm is codified by the

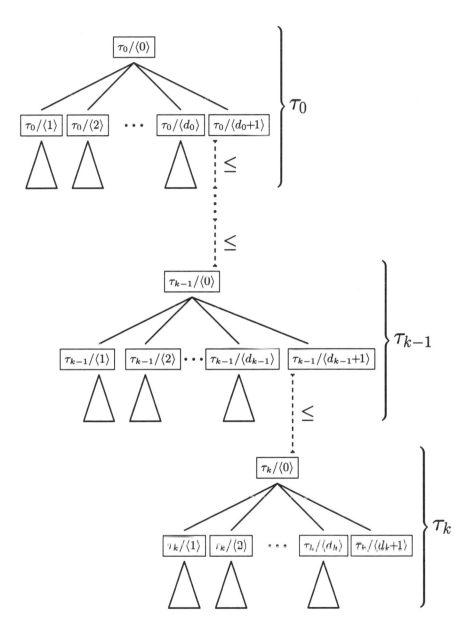

Figure 3.4
Abstract parsing algorithm invariant as a cascade of partial parse trees
$\tau_0, \tau_1 \ldots, \tau_{k-1}, \tau_k$

following algorithm invariant: Given a grammar $G = \langle \Sigma, P, p_0 \rangle$ and a
string $w_1 \cdots w_n \in \Sigma^*$, there is a derivation $\tau_0, \ldots, \tau_k$ such that[5]

1. $yield(\tau_0, \ldots, \tau_{k-1}) = w_1 \cdots w_i,$

2. $yield(\tau_k) = w_{i+1} \cdots w_j,$

3. τ_0 is licensed by p_0, the start production,

4. τ_k is licensed by $p = \langle a, \Phi \rangle$, and

5. $d = arity(\tau_k) \le a$

if and only if there is a model $M \le \tau_k \!\restriction\! [0..a]$ such that the algorithm
generates the item $\langle i, j, p, M, d \rangle$.

By proving that this invariant holds, we are essentially proving the
correctness of the algorithm, as is made explicit in Proposition 56. The
proof contains two parts. First, we must prove the 'if' direction; that is,
the algorithm generates only appropriate items, thereby yielding soundness of the algorithm. Then, completeness can be proved by showing
the 'only if' direction, that all appropriate items are generated.

PROPOSITION 54 (SOUNDNESS OF ABSTRACT ALGORITHM) Given a
grammar $G = \langle \Sigma, P, p_0 = \langle a_0, \Phi_0 \rangle \rangle$ and a string $w_1 \cdots w_n \in \Sigma^*$, if
the algorithm generates an item $\langle i, j, p, M, d \rangle$, then there is a derivation
$\tau_0, \ldots, \tau_k$ such that

1. $yield(\tau_0, \ldots, \tau_{k-1}) = w_1 \cdots w_i,$

2. $yield(\tau_k) = w_{i+1} \cdots w_j,$

3. τ_0 is licensed by p_0, the start production,

4. τ_k is licensed by $p = \langle a, \Phi \rangle$,

5. $d = arity(\tau_k) \le a$, and

6. $M = \tau_k \!\restriction\! [0..a].$

Proof   (Note that this theorem proves a stronger result than the invariant requires, as the condition on M in (6) is equality as opposed to
subsumption.)

The theorem is proved by induction on the depth of the proof tree for
the generated item.

---

[5]When $i = 0$ or $i = j$, the notations $w_1 \cdots w_i$ and $w_{i+1} \cdots w_j$, respectively, are to
be interpreted as denoting the empty string, as is standard.

Initial Item: The base case occurs with proofs of depth 0, that is, those based on the Initial Item rule. We must show that if the item $\langle 0, 0, p_0, mm(\Phi_0), 0 \rangle$ is generated, then an appropriate derivation exists. The partial parse tree $\tau_0 = mm(\Phi_0)$ obeys the various requisites. The singleton sequence containing just τ_0 is trivially a derivation. We discuss the six conditions in turn.

1. Trivial.

2. Since $arity(\tau_0) = 0$, its yield is empty as required.

3. $\tau_0 = mm(\Phi_0)$, so $\tau_0 \models \Phi_0$ by definition of mm.

4. See (3).

5. $d = arity(\tau_0) = 0 < a$.

6. By construction (and Lemma 48), $\tau_0 \upharpoonright [0..a] = \tau_0 = mm(\Phi_0)$.

To carry out the induction, we must show that each of the remaining three inference rules preserves the invariant. Since the antecedent items for application of these rules are proved by shorter proofs, we can assume that the proposition holds for them.

Prediction: We assume that the proposition holds for the antecedent item $\langle i, j, p = \langle a, \Phi \rangle, M, d \rangle$, where $d < a$, and that $p' = \langle a', \Phi' \rangle$ is the production in G to be predicted. We must show that the theorem holds for the item $\langle j, j, p', mm(\Phi') \sqcup (\rho(M/\langle d + 1 \rangle) \backslash \langle 0 \rangle), 0 \rangle$.

By the induction hypothesis, there must be a derivation $\tau_0, \ldots, \tau_{k-1}$ obeying the six constraints of the theorem. Consider the partial parse tree $\tau_k = mm(\Phi') \sqcup \rho(M/\langle d + 1 \rangle) \backslash \langle 0 \rangle$. This model was assumed to exist as a prerequisite for application of the Prediction rule. It is easily verified that τ_k is a partial parse tree of arity 0 and that its yield is the empty string, since, by Lemma 40, it is undefined for any labels $\bar{i}$. It is licensed by p' because it is subsumed by the minimal model for Φ'; by upward closure, $\tau_k \models \Phi'$. Finally, $\tau_k \upharpoonright [0..a] = \tau_k$ by construction and Lemma 48.

The sequence $\tau_0, \ldots, \tau_{k-1}, \tau_k$ is a derivation because the subsequence $\tau_0, \ldots, \tau_{k-1}$ is a derivation, and

$$\rho(\tau_{k-1}/\langle d+1 \rangle)$$
$$= \rho(\tau_{k-1} \!\upharpoonright\! [0..a]/\langle d+1 \rangle) \qquad\qquad\qquad\qquad \text{(Lemma 44)}$$
$$= \rho(M/\langle d+1 \rangle) \qquad\qquad\qquad\qquad \text{(induction hypothesis)}$$
$$= (\rho(M/\langle d+1 \rangle))\backslash\langle 0 \rangle)/\langle 0 \rangle \qquad\qquad\qquad \text{(Lemma 42)}$$
$$\leq (mm(\Phi') \sqcup (\rho(M/\langle d+1 \rangle))\backslash\langle 0 \rangle))/\langle 0 \rangle \qquad \text{(Lemmas 39 and 52)}$$
$$= \tau_k/\langle 0 \rangle \quad . \qquad\qquad\qquad\qquad \text{(Definition of } \tau_k)$$

We show that this derivation obeys the six constraints.

1. $yield(\tau_0, \ldots, \tau_{k-1}) = w_1 \cdots w_i \cdot yield(\tau_{k-1}) = w_1 \cdots w_j$.

2. Since $arity(\tau_k) = 0$, $yield(\tau_k) = \epsilon$.

3. By the induction hypothesis.

4. $mm(\Phi') \leq \tau_k$ (by Lemma 39), so $\tau_k \models \Phi'$ by upward closure (Definition 12).

5. $d = arity(\tau_k) = 0 \leq a$.

6. Follows from the fact that $\tau_k = \tau_k \!\upharpoonright\! [0..a]$.

Thus, the proposition's conditions on the item

$$\langle j, j, p', mm(\Phi') \sqcup \rho(M/\langle d+1 \rangle)\backslash\langle 0 \rangle, 0 \rangle$$

are satisfied.

Completion: We assume that the proposition holds for the two items $\langle i, j, p = \langle a, F \rangle, M, d \rangle$ (with $d < a$) and $\langle j, k, p' = \langle a', \Phi' \rangle, M', a' \rangle$, since they have shorter proof depths, and consider the case of the item inferred by Completion, $\langle i, k, p, M \sqcup ((M'/\langle 0 \rangle)\backslash\langle d+1 \rangle), d+1 \rangle$.

By the induction hypothesis applied to the first item, there exists a derivation $\tau_0, \ldots, \tau_k$ meeting the six constraints, especially that τ_k be licensed by p. Similarly, the second item gives us a derivation $\tau'_0, \ldots, \tau'_m$.

Now consider the model

$$\tau_r = \tau_k \sqcup \tau'_m\backslash\langle \overline{d+1} \rangle \sqcup mm(\langle \overline{d+1}\ 0 \rangle \doteq \langle d+1 \rangle) \quad .$$

We show that τ_r is a well-defined parse tree, and that $\tau_0, \ldots, \tau_{k-1}, \tau_r$ is an appropriate derivation for the item generated by Completion.

The model τ_r is well defined because τ_k is undefined for the feature $\overline{d+1}$, whereas $\tau'_m\backslash\langle \overline{d+1} \rangle$ is defined only for that feature (by Lemma 40). The only interaction between the two models, then, is due to the condition $\langle \overline{d+1}\ 0 \rangle \doteq \langle d+1 \rangle$. Addition of this constraint is consistent just in the case that

$(\tau'_m \backslash \langle \overline{d+1} \rangle)/\langle \overline{d+1} \ 0 \rangle \sqcup \tau_k/\langle d+1 \rangle$

is (by Property 28). But (Lemmas 46 and 42) this is just

$\tau'_m/\langle 0 \rangle \sqcup \tau_k/\langle d+1 \rangle$,

which, by construction of τ_k and τ'_m and Lemma 44, equals

$M'/\langle 0 \rangle \sqcup M/\langle d+1 \rangle$.

Since embedding is always defined, the latter is solvable just in case

$(M'/\langle 0 \rangle \sqcup M/\langle d+1 \rangle) \backslash \langle d+1 \rangle$

is, but by Lemma 41, this reduces to

$M'/\langle 0 \rangle \backslash \langle d+1 \rangle \sqcup M/\langle d+1 \rangle \backslash \langle d+1 \rangle \leq M'/\langle 0 \rangle \backslash \langle d+1 \rangle \sqcup M$

(the subsumption following from Lemmas 47 and 45). This final model was assumed to be well defined as a prerequisite of applying the Completion rule.

The derivation $\tau_0, \ldots, \tau_{k-1}, \tau_r$ is easily proved to be well formed; we must only show that $\rho(\tau_{k-1}/\langle arity(\tau_{k-1})+1 \rangle) \leq \tau_r/\langle 0 \rangle$. But this follows from the fact that $\tau_k \leq \tau_r$ (by Lemma 39) and $\rho(\tau_{k-1}/\langle arity(\tau_{k-1}) + 1 \rangle) \leq \tau_k/\langle 0 \rangle$ (since the sequence $\tau_0, \ldots, \tau_k$ is a derivation by the induction hypothesis).

Finally, we prove the six conditions on the derivation.

1. By the induction hypothesis.

2. $yield(\tau_r) = yield(\tau_k) \cdot yield(\tau_m)$
   $= w_{i+1} \cdots w_j \cdot w_{j+1} \cdots w_k$
   $= w_{i+1} \cdots w_k$.

3. By the induction hypothesis.

4. $\tau_k \leq \tau_r$, so τ_r is licensed by p.

5. $arity(\tau_r) = arity(\tau_k) + 1 = d + 1 \leq a$.

6. We must show that $\tau_r \upharpoonright [0..a] = M \sqcup M'/\langle 0 \rangle \backslash \langle d+1 \rangle$.

   Expanding the definition of τ_r, we obtain

$$\tau_r \upharpoonright [0..a] = (\tau_k \sqcup \tau'_m \backslash \langle \overline{d+1} \rangle \sqcup mm(\{\langle \overline{d+1} \ 0 \rangle \doteq \langle d+1 \rangle\})) \upharpoonright [0..a] \qquad (3.5.1)$$

Now any tree node τ, with arity d_τ, satisfies $\langle \bar{i}\, 0 \rangle \doteq \langle i \rangle$ for $0 \leq i \leq d_\tau$, so in particular, τ_k is defined at $\langle d+1 \rangle$ and τ'_m is defined at $\langle 0 \rangle$, from which it follows that $\tau'_m \backslash \langle \overline{d+1} \rangle$ is defined at $\langle \overline{d+1}\, 0 \rangle$. Furthermore, the domains of τ_k and $\tau'_m \backslash \langle \overline{d+1} \rangle$ are disjoint. Thus, Property 29 gives us that

$$
\begin{aligned}
(\tau_k \sqcup \tau'_m \backslash \langle \overline{d+1} \rangle \sqcup mm(\{\langle \overline{d+1}\, 0 \rangle &\doteq \langle d+1 \rangle\}))\!\restriction\! dom(\tau_k) \\
&= \tau_k \sqcup (\tau'_m \backslash \langle \overline{d+1} \rangle)/\langle \overline{d+1}\, 0 \rangle \backslash \langle d+1 \rangle \\
&= \tau_k \sqcup \tau'_m / \langle 0 \rangle \backslash \langle d+1 \rangle \qquad ,
\end{aligned}
$$

this last step by Lemmas 46 and 42. Restricting both sides further yields

$$
\begin{aligned}
(\tau_k \sqcup \tau'_m \backslash \langle \overline{d+1} \rangle \sqcup mm(\{\langle \overline{d+1}\, 0 \rangle \doteq \langle d+1 \rangle\}))\!\restriction\! [0..a] & \\
= (\tau_k \sqcup \tau'_m / \langle 0 \rangle \backslash \langle d+1 \rangle)\!\restriction\! [0..a] & \qquad (3.5.2) \\
= \tau_k \!\restriction\! [0..a] \sqcup \tau'_m / \langle 0 \rangle \backslash \langle d+1 \rangle & \qquad .
\end{aligned}
$$

This last step follows from Property 31, which is applicable because neither $\tau_k \!\restriction\! [0..a]$ nor $\tau'_m / \langle 0 \rangle \backslash \langle d+1 \rangle$ is top-cyclic (the latter being a consequence of Lemma 27). Substituting (3.5.2) into (3.5.1), we derive

$$
\begin{aligned}
\tau_r \!\restriction\! [0..a] & \\
= \tau_k \!\restriction\! [0..a] \sqcup \tau'_m / \langle 0 \rangle \backslash \langle d+1 \rangle & \\
= \tau_k \!\restriction\! [0..a] \sqcup (\tau'_m \!\restriction\! [0..a']) / \langle 0 \rangle \backslash \langle d+1 \rangle & \qquad \text{(Lemma 48)} \\
= M \sqcup M' / \langle 0 \rangle \backslash \langle d+1 \rangle & \qquad \text{(Definitions of } M \text{ and } M')
\end{aligned}
$$

Thus, for the generated item $\langle i, k, p, M \sqcup ((M'/\langle 0 \rangle) \backslash \langle d+1 \rangle), d+1 \rangle$, an appropriate derivation exists.

Scanning: We must show that the proposition holds for the item inferred by Scanning, $\langle i, j+1, p, M \sqcup ((mm(\Phi')/\langle 0 \rangle) \backslash \langle d+1 \rangle), d+1 \rangle$, given that $\langle i, j, p = \langle a, F \rangle, M, d \rangle$ was generated, that $d < a$, and that $\langle w_{j+1}, \Phi' \rangle \in G$. By induction applied to the antecedent item, there exists a derivation $\tau_0, \ldots, \tau_k$ such that the six constraints hold. Now, consider the model $\tau_r = \tau_k \sqcup mm(\Phi') \backslash \langle \overline{d+1} \rangle \sqcup mm(\langle \overline{d+1}\, 0 \rangle \doteq \langle d+1 \rangle)$. The proof of the well-formedness of τ_r as a partial parse tree, as well as of the well-formedness and appropriateness (with respect to the six conditions) of $\tau_0, \ldots, \tau_{k-1}, \tau_r$ as a derivation for the generated item, follows the arguments already seen in the proof for Completion. $\square$

PROPOSITION 55 (COMPLETENESS OF ABSTRACT ALGORITHM) Given a grammar $G = \langle \Sigma, P, p_0 = \langle a_0, \Phi_0 \rangle \rangle$ and a string $w_1 \cdots w_n \in \Sigma^*$, if there is a derivation $\tau_0, \ldots, \tau_k$ such that

1. $yield(\tau_0, \ldots, \tau_{k-1}) = w_1 \cdots w_i$,

2. $yield(\tau_k) = w_{i+1} \cdots w_j$,

3. τ_0 is licensed by p_0, the start production,

4. τ_k is licensed by $p = \langle a, \Phi \rangle$, and

5. $d = arity(\tau_k) \leq a$,

then there is a model $M \leq \tau_k \!\restriction\! [0..a]$ such that the algorithm generates the item $\langle i, j, p, M, d \rangle$.

Proof We define a size metric on partial parse trees as follows:

$$s(\tau) = d + \sum_{i=1}^{d} s(\tau/\langle \bar{i} \rangle) \quad ,$$

where $d = arity(\tau)$, and extend it to derivations as follows:

$$\sigma(\tau_0, \ldots, \tau_k) = k + 2 \sum_{i=0}^{k} s(\tau_i) \quad .$$

We prove the theorem by induction on the size of the derivation $\tau_0, \ldots, \tau_k$.

Base case: Suppose $\sigma(\tau_0, \ldots, \tau_k) = 0$. It follows from the definition of σ that $k = 0$, and $s(\tau_k) = s(\tau_0) = 0$, so $arity(\tau_k) = d = 0$. Since τ_0 is licensed by $p_0 = \langle a_0, \Phi_0 \rangle$, so is τ_k. Finally, since $arity(\tau_k) = 0$, we have that $yield(\tau_k) = \epsilon$, so $i = j$, and $i = 0$ because of the condition that $yield(\tau_0, \ldots, \tau_k) = w_1 \cdots w_i$.

Given, then, that $i = j = d = 0$ and $p = p_0$, we must show that the item $\langle 0, 0, p_0, M, 0 \rangle$ is generated, for some $M \leq \tau_k \!\restriction\! [0..a]$. Since τ_k is licensed by p_0, it must be the case that $\tau_k \models \Phi_0$, so $mm(\Phi_0) \leq \tau_k$. Since all paths in Φ_0 have prefixes in the path set $\{ \langle 0 \rangle, \langle 1 \rangle, \ldots, \langle a \rangle \}$, by logical locality (Property 1), if $\Phi_0 \models \langle f \rangle \doteq \langle f \rangle$, then $f \in [0..a]$, so that $dom(mm(\Phi_0)) \subseteq [0..a]$. By Lemma 48 and the monotonicity of $\restriction$ (Lemma 52), we can conclude that $mm(\Phi_0) = mm(\Phi_0) \!\restriction\! [0..a] \leq \tau_k \!\restriction\! [0..a]$. Now, let M be $mm(\Phi_0)$. By the Initial Item rule, $\langle 0, 0, p_0, M, 0 \rangle$ is generated.

Induction cases: Assume that $\sigma(\tau_0, \ldots, \tau_k) = n > 0$ and that the proposition holds for derivations of sizes smaller than n.

We prove the induction step by three mutually exclusive and exhaustive cases.

Case 1: $arity(\tau_k) = 0$.

Case 2: $arity(\tau_k) = d + 1 > 0$ and $\tau_k/\langle \overline{d+1} \rangle$ is licensed by a phrasal production.

Case 3: $arity(\tau_k) = d + 1 > 0$ and $\tau_k/\langle \overline{d+1} \rangle$ is licensed by a lexical production.

Case 1: Suppose $arity(\tau_k) = 0$. Then $s(\tau_k) = 0$. Note that since $n > 0$, k must be at least 1; that is, the derivation $\tau_0, \ldots, \tau_k$ has at least two elements. Consider the derivation $\tau_0, \ldots, \tau_{k-1}$ with size $n - 2s(\tau_k) - 1 = n - 1$. For some $i' < i$ and phrasal production p',

1. $yield(\tau_0, \ldots, \tau_{k-2}) = w_1 \cdots w_{i'}$,

2. $yield(\tau_{k-1}) = w_{i'+1} \cdots w_i$,

3. τ_0 is licensed by p_0, the start production,

4. τ_{k-1} is licensed by $p' = \langle a', \Phi' \rangle$, and

5. $d = arity(\tau_{k-1}) < a'$ (not merely $\leq$, since $\tau_k - 1$ is a strictly partial parse tree as part of the derivation $\tau_0, \ldots, \tau_k$).

By the induction hypothesis, therefore, an item $\langle i', i, p', M', d' \rangle$ is generated, where $M' \leq \tau_{k-1} \upharpoonright [0..a']$.

Consider the item $\langle i, i, p = \langle a, \Phi \rangle, M, 0 \rangle$, where

$$M = mm(\Phi) \sqcup (\rho(M'/\langle d' + 1 \rangle) \backslash \langle 0 \rangle) \quad .$$

Recall that $mm(\Phi) \leq \tau_k \upharpoonright [0..a]$ and $\rho(\tau_{k-1}/\langle d' + 1 \rangle) \leq \tau_k/\langle 0 \rangle$, from the definition of derivation. Thus,

$$
\begin{aligned}
\rho(M'/\langle d' + 1 \rangle) \backslash \langle 0 \rangle \quad &\leq \rho(\tau_{k-1}/\langle d' + 1 \rangle) \backslash \langle 0 \rangle && \text{(Lemma 52)} \\
&\leq \tau_k/\langle 0 \rangle \backslash \langle 0 \rangle && \text{(as just noted)} \\
&\leq \tau_k \upharpoonright \{0\} && \text{(Lemma 47)} \\
&\leq \tau_k \upharpoonright [0..a] \quad . && \text{(Definitions 13 and 23)}
\end{aligned}
$$

Since both $mm(\Phi)$ and $\rho(M'/\langle d'+1\rangle)\backslash\langle 0\rangle$ subsume $\tau_k\!\upharpoonright\![0..a]$, they must be consistent in the sense that their informational union must be defined; furthermore, $M = mm(\Phi)\sqcup\rho(M'/\langle d'+1\rangle)\backslash\langle 0\rangle \leq \tau_k\!\upharpoonright\![0..a]$, by Lemma 36 and the definition of informational union. (See the comment following Lemma 36.) Therefore, $\langle i,i,p,M,0\rangle$ is just the item generated from $\langle i',i,p',M',d'\rangle$ by Prediction. Thus, in this case, an appropriate item is generated.

Case 2: Suppose that $arity(\tau_k) = d+1 > 0$ and that $\tau_k/\langle\overline{d+1}\rangle$ is licensed by a phrasal production $p' = \langle a',\Phi'\rangle$. As before, τ_k is part of a derivation $\tau_0,\ldots,\tau_k$ whose size is n and that satisfies the various antecedent properties of the theorem. In particular, $yield(\tau_0,\ldots,\tau_{k-1}) = w_1\cdots w_i$ and $yield(\tau_k) = w_{i+1}\cdots w_j$. Assume that $yield(\tau_k/\langle\overline{d+1}\rangle) = w_{i'+1}\cdots w_j$, for some i' such that $i \leq i' \leq j$.

We consider two shorter derivations. The first,

$$\tau_0,\ldots,\tau_{k-1},\tau_k\!\upharpoonright\![0..a,\overline{1}..\overline{d}]\quad,$$

has size

$$n - 2s(\tau_k) + 2(s(\tau_k) - s(\tau_k/\langle\overline{d+1}\rangle) - 1)$$
$$= n - 2s(\tau_k/\langle\overline{d+1}\rangle) - 2\quad,$$

which is less than n, so that the induction hypothesis can apply. In addition, the antecedent conditions necessary for the induction hypothesis hold for this derivation, with $yield(\tau_0,\ldots,\tau_{k-1}) = w_1\cdots w_i$ and $yield(\tau_k\!\upharpoonright\![0..a,\overline{1}..\overline{d}]) = w_{i+1}\cdots w_{i'}$. By the induction hypothesis, then, there is an $M \leq \tau_k\!\upharpoonright\![0..a]$ such that the algorithm generates the item $\langle i,i',p,M,d\rangle$.

The second derivation,

$$\tau_0,\ldots,\tau_{k-1},\tau_k\!\upharpoonright\![0..a,\overline{1}..\overline{d}],\tau_k/\langle\overline{d+1}\rangle\quad,$$

has size

$$n - 2s(\tau_k/\langle\overline{d+1}\rangle) - 2 + 2s(\tau_k/\langle\overline{d+1}\rangle) + 1 = n - 1\quad,$$

which is again less than n as required for induction to apply. This is a well-formed derivation since $\tau_0,\ldots,\tau_{k-1},\tau_k\!\upharpoonright\![0..a,\overline{1}..\overline{d}]$ is, and

$$\begin{aligned}
\rho(\tau_k\!\upharpoonright\![0..a,\overline{1}..\overline{d}]/\langle d+1\rangle) &\leq \rho(\tau_k/\langle d+1\rangle)\\
&= \rho(\tau_k/\langle\overline{d+1}\,0\rangle)\\
&= \rho((\tau_k/\langle\overline{d+1}\rangle)/\langle 0\rangle)\\
&\leq (\tau_k/\langle\overline{d+1}\rangle)/\langle 0\rangle\quad,
\end{aligned}$$

as required. Again, this derivation meets the antecedent conditions of the proposition, with $yield(\tau_0, \ldots, \tau_{k-1}, \tau_k \upharpoonright [0..a, \overline{1}..\overline{d}]) = w_1 \cdots w_{i'}$ and $yield(\tau_k / \langle \overline{d+1} \rangle) = w_{i'+1} \cdots w_j$. By the induction hypothesis, there is an $M' \leq (\tau_k / \langle \overline{d+1} \rangle) \upharpoonright [0..a']$ such that the algorithm generates the item $\langle i', j, p', M', a' \rangle$.

We must show, then, that the model $M \sqcup ((M'/\langle 0 \rangle) \backslash \langle d+1 \rangle)$ is well defined as the final precondition for applying Completion. Now, from the induction hypothesis, $M \leq \tau_k \upharpoonright [0..a]$ and $M' \leq (\tau_k / \langle \overline{d+1} \rangle) \upharpoonright [0..a']$, so

$$
\begin{aligned}
(M'/\langle 0 \rangle) \backslash \langle d+1 \rangle &\leq (((\tau_k / \langle \overline{d+1} \rangle) \upharpoonright [0..a']) / \langle 0 \rangle) \backslash \langle d+1 \rangle \\
&\leq (\tau_k / \langle \overline{d+1} \; 0 \rangle) \backslash \langle d+1 \rangle \\
&= (\tau_k / \langle d+1 \rangle) \backslash \langle d+1 \rangle \\
&= \tau_k \upharpoonright \{d+1\} \\
&\leq \tau_k \upharpoonright [0..a] \qquad .
\end{aligned}
$$

Consequently, the two models are consistent, and, furthermore,

$$
M \sqcup ((M'/\langle 0 \rangle) \backslash \langle d+1 \rangle) \leq \tau_k \upharpoonright [0..a] \qquad ,
$$

as required. Thus, the item

$$
\langle i, j, p, M \sqcup ((M'/\langle 0 \rangle) \backslash \langle d+1 \rangle), d+1 \rangle
$$

is generated by Completion.

Case 3: Suppose that $arity(\tau_k) = d+1 > 0$, as in Case 2, but that $\tau_k / \langle \overline{d+1} \rangle$ is licensed by a lexical production $p' = \langle w_{j+1}, \Phi' \rangle$. Once again τ_k is part of a derivation $\tau_0, \ldots, \tau_k$ whose size is n and that satisfies the various antecedent properties of the theorem. In particular, $yield(\tau_0, \ldots, \tau_{k-1}) = w_1 \cdots w_i$, and $yield(\tau_k) = w_{i+1} \cdots w_{j+1}$.

Construct the smaller derivation $\tau_0, \ldots, \tau_{k-1}, \tau_k \upharpoonright [0..a, \overline{1}..\overline{d}]$. Note that $yield(\tau_k \upharpoonright [0..a, \overline{1}..\overline{d}]) = w_{i+1} \cdots w_j$. The size of this derivation is

$$
\begin{aligned}
n - 2s(\tau_k) &+ 2s(\tau_k \upharpoonright [0..a, \overline{1}..\overline{d}]) \\
&= n - 2(s(\tau_k \upharpoonright [0..a, \overline{1}..\overline{d}]) \\
&\qquad + s(\tau_k / \langle \overline{d+1} \rangle) + 1) + 2s(\tau_k \upharpoonright [0..a, \overline{1}..\overline{d}]) \\
&= n - 2s(\tau_k / \langle \overline{d+1} \rangle) - 2 \qquad ,
\end{aligned}
$$

which is less than n, so that the induction hypothesis applies. By the same argument as in Case 2, this derivation is well formed, leading us to conclude that an item $\langle i, j, p, M, d \rangle$ was generated for some $M \leq \tau_k \!\restriction\! [0..a]$.

We must show, then, that the model $M \sqcup ((mm(\Phi')/\langle 0 \rangle)\backslash\langle d + 1 \rangle)$ is well defined as the final precondition for application of the Scanning rule. From the induction hypothesis, we conclude that $M \leq \tau_k \!\restriction\! [0..a]$. Since $\tau_k / \langle \overline{d + 1} \rangle$ is licensed by p', we can conclude that $\tau_k / \langle \overline{d + 1} \rangle \models \Phi'$, so $mm(\Phi') \leq \tau_k / \langle \overline{d + 1} \rangle$. From this, we have that

$$(mm(\Phi')/\langle 0 \rangle)\backslash\langle d + 1 \rangle \leq (mm(\tau_k / \langle \overline{d + 1} \rangle)/\langle 0 \rangle)\backslash\langle d + 1 \rangle \quad ,$$

whence, by the analogous argument in Case 2,

$$(mm(\Phi')/\langle 0 \rangle)\backslash\langle d + 1 \rangle \leq \tau_k \!\restriction\! [0..a] \quad .$$

Thus, the two models are demonstrated consistent, and, furthermore,

$$M \sqcup ((mm(\Phi')/\langle 0 \rangle)\backslash\langle d + 1 \rangle) \leq \tau_k \!\restriction\! [0..a] \quad ,$$

as required. Therefore, the item

$$\langle i, j + 1, p, M \sqcup ((mm(\Phi')/\langle 0 \rangle)\backslash\langle d + 1 \rangle), d + 1 \rangle$$

is generated by the Scanning rule.

Since the three cases are exhaustive, the induction step has in general been proved, and thereby, the proposition itself. □

The preceding theorem allows us to prove the following corollary, a simple statement of the correctness of the algorithm for recognizing the language of a grammar.

PROPOSITION 56 (PARTIAL CORRECTNESS OF ABSTRACT ALGORITHM) Given a grammar $G = \langle \Sigma, P, p_0 = \langle a_0, \Phi_0 \rangle \rangle$ and a string in Σ^*, $w_1 \cdots w_n$, the algorithm generates the item $\langle 0, n, p_0, M, a_0 \rangle$ for some M if and only if $w_1 \cdots w_n$ is grammatical according to G.

Proof We prove the two implication directions separately, the 'if' direction first. Assume that $w_1 \cdots w_n$ is grammatical. Then there is a parse tree τ such that τ is licensed by p_0 and $yield(\tau) = w_1 \cdots w_n$. By Proposition 55, the trivial derivation consisting of the single parse tree τ guarantees the generation of an item $\langle 0, n, p_0, M, a_0 \rangle$ for some M.

For the 'only if' direction, we assume that the algorithm generates $\langle 0, n, p_0, M, a_0 \rangle$ for some M. Proposition 54 guarantees the existence of a derivation $\tau_0, \ldots, \tau_k$ such that $yield(\tau_k) = w_1 \cdots w_n$, and τ_k is licensed by p_0 and $arity(\tau_k) = a_0$. Thus, the parse tree τ_k provides a witness for admitting $w_1 \cdots w_n$ as a sentence of the language of G. □

3.6   Instances of the Abstract Algorithm

The process of parsing (more properly, recognition) as described by the abstract algorithm just presented involves searching a (potentially infinite) space of items for one of the form $\langle 0, n, p_0, M, a_0 \rangle$. The partial correctness of the algorithm, proved as Proposition 56, guarantees that any method for complete search of this space yields a partially correct parsing algorithm. However, the problems of termination and efficiency of the search method have not been addressed.

Two basic problems in this vein are considered in this section. First, the search space can be massively redundant; exhaustive search will therefore entail superfluous work in general. Second, in certain cases, the Completion and Prediction rules can feed themselves recursively and indefinitely, thus leading to nontermination in an exhaustive search.

3.6.1   Eliminating Redundancy

To eliminate the redundant generation of items, we can import the idea of a *chart* or *tableau* from tabular context-free parsing schemes, or a *cache* of lemmas as used in automatic theorem-proving algorithms. The analogous modification for parsing with the more general constraint-based formalisms is more akin to the subsumption check in theorem proving than to the tableau of Earley's algorithm.

The central observation is the following: We augment the algorithm with a tableau or cache of generated items. Then an item $\langle i, j, p, M, d \rangle$ need be added to the tableau only if no previously generated item $\langle i, j, p, M', d \rangle$ exists therein for which $M' \leq M$. Traversal of the search space below the omitted item can be pruned as well.

This modification of the abstract algorithm is clearly sound because although a subset of the items in the full search space is generated, no item outside of the full space is. Recall that completeness (Proposition 55) requires that if there is a derivation $\tau_0, \ldots, \tau_k$ satisfying the antecedent criteria, then an item $\langle i, j, p, M, d \rangle$ be generated such that $M \leq \tau_k \upharpoonright [0..a]$. Now, if the item $\langle i, j, p, M, d \rangle$ is omitted in the tabular modification of the algorithm, there must have been an item $\langle i, j, p, M', d \rangle$ generated for which $M' \leq M \leq \tau_k \upharpoonright [0..a]$, so that completeness is still guaranteed. In sum, the modified algorithm is complete because an omitted item makes a stronger "claim" about the string than the subsuming item.

3.6.2   Nontermination

Addition of a tableau and the subsumption check can dramatically improve the efficiency of parsing while retaining the soundness and completeness results. Even with such improvements, nontermination is a possibility, stemming from two sources: the Prediction and Completion rules.

Prediction Nontermination   Since items inferred by Prediction are of the form of the antecedent, the Prediction rule can (potentially at least) feed itself recursively. For example, imagine a rule $p' = \langle a', \Phi' \rangle$ such that $mm(\Phi')/\langle 1 \rangle$ is consistent with $mm(\Phi')/\langle 0 \rangle$; suppose also that ρ is the identity function. Then an item

$$\langle i, i, p', mm(\Phi'), 0 \rangle$$

would predict the item

$$\langle i, i, p', mm(\Phi') \sqcup mm(\Phi')/\langle 1 \rangle \backslash \langle 0 \rangle, 0 \rangle$$

(which is consistent by assumption), in turn predicting

$$\langle i, i, p', mm(\Phi') \sqcup (mm(\Phi') \sqcup mm(\Phi')/\langle 1 \rangle \backslash \langle 0 \rangle)/\langle 1 \rangle \backslash \langle 0 \rangle, 0 \rangle \qquad,$$

and so forth, indefinitely. In general, none of the various models in these items need subsume any of the others, so that subsumption checking does not break this chain of prediction. The example given involves an immediate left recursion of sorts in the rule p', but nonimmediate recursions (even involving some interspersed Completion steps if both antecedent items cover the empty string) can also manifest this kind of nontermination.

A simple condition guarantees, however, that this potential nontermination will not be realized. It is at this point that the importance of introducing the function ρ into the parsing algorithm is revealed. If the range of ρ is finite in size—say r—then there is only a finite number of items that could ever be generated by the Prediction rule, namely, $rn|G|$ where n is the string length and $|G|$ is the number of phrasal productions in G. Consequently, after a finite number of applications of Prediction, a previously generated item would be built and the subsumption check would prune further applications. Since the correctness proof for the algorithm holds for any ρ, we can choose a ρ of finite range without sacrificing soundness or completeness, but regaining termination in these cases.

In a sense, ρ serves to specify how much information is to be used in the top-down phase of parsing. If ρ is the constant function yielding the trivial model, no top-down information is used; all productions are predicted at each point in the string and parsing proceeds strictly bottom-up without taking into account any aspects of the preceding context. If, on the other hand, ρ is the identity function, all available information from the left context is used top-down in predicting production instances. As long as we are satisfied by a finite amount of top-down information employed in guiding the parse, we can guarantee termination of the prediction process.

Furthermore, by tuning the ρ function—thereby adjusting which finite subset of the available information is used in processing—the behavior of the algorithm can be fine-tuned to the grammar. Indeed, this possibility was the original motivation for adding ρ to previous implementations of parsers for the constraint-based PATR formalism. As previously described by Shieber (1985c), appropriate choice of ρ can be used not only to regain termination when parsing left-recursive grammars, but also to reduce greatly the number of generated items in parsing by using information top-down that restricts parsing possibilities, but not using top-down that information that merely makes distinctions that are unimportant for later parsing.

In that paper, a particular class of monotonic ρ functions is used, which restrict the information to a particular set of paths. Haas (1989) uses a different function in generalizing the parsing algorithm of Graham, Harrison, and Ruzzo (1980) to a constraint-based formalism. His function eliminates recursive structure in the graph, thereby generating a finite range; Sato and Tamaki (1984) use a similar function in their work on analysis of logic programs. In keeping with the overall aim for generality, our ρ subsumes these and other methods of "weakening" information by requiring only very general properties of ρ: namely, that it be a monotonic, finite-ranged, weakening function.

Completion Nontermination   The most insidious form of nontermination is associated with the unconstrained application of Completion. We will have little to say about this problem here. Fortunately, it has not appeared historically as a factor in the natural-language-processing work that has been based on constraint-based formalisms, unlike prediction nontermination; the latter is responsible, for instance, for the well-known difficulty of parsing with left-recursive definite-clause grammars.

It is important to realize that no complete solution to completion nontermination is possible, even in principle. As has been previously observed, recognition of constraint-based formalisms such as PATR or DCG is in general undecidable. A complete solution to nontermination would contradict this undecidability.

However, partial solutions are possible. For instance, we can allow only grammars with a decidable property sufficient (though not in general necessary) to guarantee the termination of Completion. The lexical-functional grammar constraint of *off-line parsability* described by Kaplan and Bresnan (1982, page 266) and Pereira and Warren (1983) is one such sufficient condition. Generalized for the more abstract setting of constraint-based grammar formalisms, an off-line-parsable grammar can be defined as follows:

DEFINITION 57 A grammar G is *off-line parsable* if and only if there exists a finite-ranged function ρ on models such that $\rho(M) \leq M$ for all M and there are no parse trees τ admitted by G such that $\rho(\tau/\langle 0 \rangle) = \rho(\tau'/\langle 0 \rangle)$ for some τ' a sub-parse-tree of τ with identical yield.

This is a sufficient condition for guaranteeing completion termination (by a pigeonhole argument analogous to that given above for prediction termination). However, there are non-off-line-parsable grammars for which termination holds. Nonetheless, if off-line parsability can be proven of a grammar, we at least know that it can safely be employed.[6]

This definition of off-line parsability is more general than the definition implicit in LFG; there a particular ρ is given a priori, namely, the function taking (the LFG correlate of) a model to one of a finite set of atomic syntactic categories. The special case, then, merely requires that the "context-free backbone" of the grammar disallow derivations of the form $A \Rightarrow^* A$. The importance of off-line parsability for LFG is that off-line-parsable grammars are finitely ambiguous, which implies the decidability of the parsing problem.

---

[6]Haas (1989) defines a slightly stronger criterion for termination of his parsing algorithm, depth-boundedness, and gives a semi-decision procedure for it.

The restrictiveness of the LFG special case of off-line parsability is discussed by Johnson (1988), who presents an argument contending that a particular LFG analysis of the Dutch cross-serial verb construction violates the LFG off-line-parsability constraint. However, it should be possible to prove that the analysis is off-line parsable in the more general sense just presented, although the details are not pursued here. Furthermore, if a grammar is off-line parsable in the more general sense, then it still follows that it is finitely ambiguous. Again, this allows for the decidability of parsing.

3.6.3 Specifying a Control Regime

Even with subsumption checking and the various techniques for guaranteeing termination, considerable latitude remains in how to search the space of items. In this section we describe how this flexibility can be used to develop constraint-based analogues of standard context-free parsing algorithms by specifying particular control regimes for searching. Given that all such regimes that completely search the space generate identical items, the ability to mimic various complete parsing algorithms may be of only academic interest. However, certain *incomplete* context-free parsing algorithms—which, as we have argued in previous work, provide a good model for human sentence-processing behavior as illuminated by psycholinguistic research—can also be modeled. Their psycholinguistic quality makes these variants of more immediate interest.

Finally, the ability to specify a control regime permits the basic parsing architecture explored here to be used for generation as well. This possibility has been described in separate work (Shieber, 1988b).

Modeling Earley's Algorithm   As a simple example of the use of the abstract architecture to model a standard context-free parsing algorithm in the more general setting of constraint-based grammar formalisms, we describe a search strategy for mimicking Earley's algorithm. Simply put, Earley's algorithm corresponds to the tabular variant of the abstract architecture under a strictly left-to-right control strategy. That is, items are generated in such a way that if an item $\langle i, j, p, M, d \rangle$ is generated before $\langle i', j', p', M', d' \rangle$, then $j \leq j'$. This constraint on ordering does not fully determine the order of searching the item space. It should be noted, however, that the standard nondeterministic statement of Earley's algorithm allows exactly the same ordering freedom.

This algorithm, as applied in particular to the PATR formalism, has been previously proposed by Shieber (1985c). This chapter constitutes the first proof of the correctness of that proposal—in a more general setting, of course.

Modeling Shift-Reduce Parsing   As another example of the use of the control abstraction, we turn to the mimicking of shift-reduce parsing. Pereira and the present author independently observed that certain psycholinguistic phenomena could be modeled by postulating that the parsing algorithm used to interpret a standard formulation of a competence grammar was an incomplete shift-reduce algorithm utilizing certain quite simple disambiguation strategies. Pereira (1985a) used the technique to model the phenomena of right association and minimal attachment described by Frazier and Fodor (1978) and first observed by Kimball (1973). In previous work (Shieber, 1983), we extended the method to the lexical-preference phenomena of Ford, Bresnan, and Kaplan (1982), as well as to the garden-path phenomena whose computational analysis was pioneered by Marcus (1980).

Simply put, the technique rests on the following observation. A standard context-free grammar for a natural language—say English—will exhibit certain local and global ambiguities. These ambiguities make it impossible to build a correct and complete shift-reduce table in accordance with any of the standard methods (SLR, LALR, and so forth) since these algorithms will generate multiple actions for a single table entry. These are the so-called shift/reduce and reduce/reduce conflicts.

A strategy for resolving these conflicts—to determine whether to shift or reduce, or which possible reduction to choose—defines a disambiguation of the language. A particular strategy was shown to model right association and minimal attachment phenomena, namely:

- In case of a shift/reduce conflict, choose the shift operation.

- In case of a reduce/reduce conflict, choose the longer reduction.

A slight variation models the lexical-preference data as well. Furthermore, the resolution of local ambiguities in a globally unambiguous string in conformance with this strategy can lead to the incorrect local choice, thus causing the parser to fail to parse a grammatical string. This garden-path phenomenon has been shown to accord well with the corresponding psycholinguistic phenomenon of garden-path sentences.

There are problems with the shift-reduce technique for modeling human sentence disambiguation. First, the technique assumes that the competence grammar is stated in the form of a context-free grammar. As current theories of competence grammar eschew such simple formalisms, it is unclear how the results can be carried over to current theories of linguistic competence. Second, all information used to guide the parse must be encoded in the finite set of atomic nonterminal symbols of the grammar. Thus, semantic or contextual information is not available to the disambiguation strategy, eliminating any simple solution to the modeling of the contextual priming effects of Crain and Steedman (1985) by means of more complex disambiguation strategies. Finally, since all the (finite amount of) information associated with a phrase is used to guide the parse (that is, to build the shift-reduce tables), the parser cannot be fine-tuned to differentially use only certain information in the top-down guidance phase of processing. For any given kind of information, it must be either used in guiding the parse or eliminated from the grammar entirely.

These problems can be solved by developing an instance of the abstract parsing algorithm to mimic a shift-reduce parser operating under a disambiguation strategy such as the one above. In a context-free grammar, all possible distinctions that could be pertinent to guiding a parse are explicit in the grammar itself as the set of nonterminal symbols. In a constraint-based grammar, this is not so. The number of distinctions among phrases is potentially infinite (since the set of informational elements is); thus, precompilation of an exhaustive set of tables is impossible. Instead, we must mimic the shift-reduce parsing regime on the fly, building the pertinent portions of a potentially infinite shift-reduce table at run time.

The states of an LR parser correspond to sets of items quite similar to the items that the abstract algorithm generates. All state sets are closed under the Prediction inference rule. States are associated with positions on a stack, but we will take them to be associated with positions in the string, distinguishing at any point a current string position to mark the top of the stack (and hence a current state). Rather than move elements to and fro between a stack and an input buffer, we will merely move the current string position to mark the boundary between the stack and the input buffer. A shift operation corresponds to the completion of a set of items in the current state by a lexical item. The new state is the prediction closure of the completed items, and is associated with the position following the lexical item shifted. A reduce operation corresponds to the changing of the current state to the one at the current left edge of an inactive item (one in which the dot position d equals the arity of the rule a) in the current state set, followed by a shifting of the item thus traversed. In sum, the inactive item is incorporated into a previous state set by Completion. The output state is again achieved by closing the resultant item under Prediction.

Disambiguation is simply modeled. If the current state set both can incorporate the following lexical item (allowing a shift) and includes an inactive item (allowing reduction), the shift operation is chosen and parsing proceeds from that generated state. Since the new state has no record of the old, the ability to perform the reduction is thus lost forever; that Completion operation will never be performed. If the current state has no shift possibility, but several inactive items, the one based on the longer rule will be chosen. Again, parsing possibilities may be lost by this choice.

In this way, the abstract algorithm can be employed to mimic a generalized shift-reduce parser operating over constraint-based grammars in a provably sound (though clearly not complete) manner. The psycholinguistic results demonstrated for context-free grammars thus apply more broadly, and in a more linguistically attractive formal setting. Since the informational elements are much richer, more complex disambiguation schemes involving arbitrarily large amounts of information built up by the grammar (for instance, semantic or contextual information) can be envisaged. Finally, the ability to use the ρ parameter allows certain information to be excluded in the top-down guidance of the parse, even though the grammar maintains that information correctly.

4 A Compendium of Model Classes

In this chapter we return to the topic of appropriate classes of models for the constraint logics, and develop a series of possible classes of models for the logic $\mathcal{L}_{L,C}$, with an eye toward their utility for logical and computational purposes. We begin with the class of finite-tree models, but a desire for completeness requires that we allow infinite trees as well. Both types of tree models, however, are too extensional, compelling us to augment them with a stronger notion of intensional identity, which we make precise in the eqtree models. Although the eqtree models serve as a perfectly acceptable semantics for $\mathcal{L}_{L,C}$, they do not possess the computational properties required for use in the parsing algorithm of the preceding chapter. To serve this purpose, we develop the graph models as finite encodings of the rational eqtrees. This exercise of developing models for $\mathcal{L}_{L,C}$ explicates the trade-offs that have only been implicit in previous research in this area.

Having defined the appropriate desiderata with which to evaluate the logical systems in Chapter 2 and having seen the use of the models for definition of grammars, languages, and parsing algorithms in Chapter 3, we can now return to the task of describing some of the possibilities for models of $\mathcal{L}_{L,C}$ and examine how the logical systems based on them fare.

In general, to define an appropriate logical system incorporating $\mathcal{L}_{L,C}$, we must specify a class of models $\mathcal{M}$ along with a satisfaction relation. These, in turn, will determine a subsumption ordering, and operations of informational union, extraction, embedding, and restriction in accordance with the definitions in Chapter 2. The set of independent properties that must be proved of the logical system are

- Denotational soundness,
- Logical soundness,
- Logical completeness,
- Minimal-model existence, and
- Categoricity.

For computational reasons, we also require the following properties (as stated in Section 3.1)

- Finiteness of minimal models of atomic formulas,
- Finiteness preservation for model operations, and
- Computability of operations.

Figure 2.9 codifies the dependence of other properties on these.

The development of an appropriate class of models for $\mathcal{L}_{L,C}$ will progress in stages, each triggered by a frailty in the previous. The finite-tree models fail to provide models for all formulas; in particular, the existence of cyclic formulas underlies the need for infinite trees. The infinite-tree models, in turn, are too extensional. The eqtree class of models makes the necessary intensional distinctions lacking in the tree models. Computational considerations will impel us toward the graph models introduced informally and used extensively in previous chapters. The progression provides grounds for the use of graph models over other alternatives in the present work and elsewhere, as well as serving as an exemplar for the development of similar models for the extended logics of Chapter 5.

4.1   Finite-Tree Models

The *finite feature trees* constitute by far the simplest of the proposed model classes. The class of finite feature trees is defined as the infinite union of a hierarchy of larger and larger bounded trees. The smallest trees comprise the class $\mathcal{T}_0$ and include just the constants C plus an element for the undefined tree, $\perp$. Classes of larger trees, $\mathcal{T}_i$ for $i > 0$, are given as all partial functions with finite domain from L to $\bigcup_{j<i} \mathcal{T}_j$. Then $\mathcal{T}_{L,C}$, the set of finite feature trees over L and C, is the infinite union of the $\mathcal{T}_i$, that is,

$$\mathcal{T}_{L,C} = \bigcup_{i \geq 0} \mathcal{T}_i$$

The finite feature trees look at first glance like excellent models for $\mathcal{L}_{L,C}$ as they possess a natural hierarchical structure, modularity, and partiality. Hierarchical structure is given by the recursive definition. Modularity, the ability to extract subparts, is achieved simply by function application. Partiality of the trees supervenes on the partiality of functions that define them.

A logical system based on finite feature trees can be fixed by defining a notion of *satisfaction*. First, we extend the function application notation to apply to paths as well as labels: $t(\langle f_1 \cdots f_n \rangle)$ will be used to express the iterated application $t(f_1) \cdots (f_n)$. A finite feature tree t *satisfies* or *models* a formula $\Phi = \{\phi_1, \ldots, \phi_n\}$ (written $t \models \Phi$) just in case it models all the ϕ_i individually. For atomic formulas, $t \models p \doteq q$ if and only if the subtrees at p and q are identical (i.e., $t(p) = t(q)$); $t \models p \doteq c$ if and only if the subtree at p is the constant c (i.e., $t(p) = c$).

As it turns out, the extraction operation t/p corresponds exactly to the iterated application $t(p)$. We can show that this definition actually satisfies the definition of the extraction operation, namely, that $t/p \models \Phi$ if and only if $t \models \Phi[\langle\rangle \to p]$. We need only consider cases where Φ is atomic. For the 'if' direction, suppose that $t \models \Phi[\langle\rangle \to p]$. If Φ is of the form $q \doteq r$, then $\Phi[\langle\rangle \to p]$ is of the form $p \cdot q \doteq p \cdot r$. Since t satisfies this equation, $t(p \cdot q) = t(p \cdot r)$; that is, $t(p)(q) = t(p)(r)$. The extraction definition entails that $(t/p)(q) = (t/p)(r)$, so $t/p \models q \doteq r$. A similar argument holds for atomic formulas of the variety $q \doteq c$.

Proof of the 'only if' direction presupposes that $t/p \models \Phi$. Again, we consider only the case of $\Phi = q \doteq r$; the other atomic case is similar and the nonatomic case trivial. By definition of extraction for finite trees, $t(p) \models q \doteq r$, so $t(p)(q) = t(p)(r)$, and $t(p \cdot q) = t(p \cdot r)$, from which $t \models p \cdot q \doteq p \cdot r$ follows immediately.

We thus conclude that, for the finite-tree models, extraction is iterated application. Similarly, we can discover definitions for restriction (corresponding to restricting the domain of the partial function), subsumption, and embedding.

As a side note, observe that feature trees fall under a natural partial ordering, determined by the hereditary partiality of functions. Under this ordering, $t \leq t'$ if and only if t is $\perp$ or both are identical atomic trees or both are compound trees such that for all $f \in dom(t)$, $t'(f)$ is defined and $t(f) \leq t'(f)$. That subsumption on trees is a partial ordering is obvious from the definition. However, this naive ordering is not the notion of subsumption required by Definition 9. In particular, this ordering respects entailment (Definition 13) but is not closed upward (Definition 12). For instance, consider the trees in Figure 4.1. The tree in Figure 4.1(a) is less than the one in Figure 4.1(b) in the naive ordering, yet the former satisfies $\langle f \rangle \doteq \langle g \rangle$ and the latter does not. The true finite-tree subsumption ordering must leave these two trees unordered with

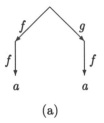
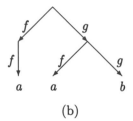

(a)   (b)

Figure 4.1
Failure of upward closure

respect to each other. We will return to this problem in Section 4.2.2.

4.1.1 Properties of Finite-Tree Models

This simple model of feature structures generates a logical system possessing certain of the potential properties of logical systems defined above. In particular, the soundness properties, both logical and denotational, hold.

PROPOSITION 58 (LOGICAL SOUNDNESS OF FINITE-TREE MODELS) For all $t \in \mathcal{T}_{L,C}$ and $\Phi \in \mathcal{L}_{L,C}$, if $t \models \Phi$ and $\Phi \vdash \phi$, then $t \models \phi$.

Proof The proof is by induction on the depth of the proof tree for $\Phi \vdash \phi$. The base case occurs where $\Phi \vdash \phi$, either by Triviality or because $\phi \in \Phi$. For these, we must show that $t \models \langle \rangle \doteq \langle \rangle$ and $t \models \phi$ if $\phi \in \Phi$ and $t \models \Phi$. The former follows from the fact that $t/\langle \rangle$ is always defined and is t. The latter follows from the definition of modeling a set of equations.

For the induction step, assume that the theorem holds for proofs of depth n or less. We must show that if $t \models \phi_i$ for ϕ_i the antecedents of the final proof step, then $t \models \phi$. Since $\Phi \vdash^n \phi_i$, the induction hypothesis guarantees that $t \models \phi_i$, which is why the antecedents can be assumed to be modeled. The proof is by cases depending on the rule invoked in the final step. If Symmetry is used, we assume that $t \models p \doteq q$. Then t/p and t/q are defined, $t/p = t/q$; consequently, $t/q = t/p$ and $t \models q \doteq p$. For Reflexivity, assume that $t \models p \cdot q \doteq v$. Then $t/(p \cdot q) = (t/p)/q$ is defined, and therefore so is t/p. Thus, $t/p = t/p$ and $t \models p \doteq p$. If the final step is Substitutivity, we assume that $t \models q \doteq p$ and $t \models p \cdot r \doteq v$. Then $t/q = t/p$ and $t/(p \cdot r) = t/v$ (or v depending on whether v is a constant or a path). So $t/(q \cdot r) = (t/q)/r = (t/p)/r = t/(p \cdot r) = t/v$ (respectively v). Thus, $t \models q \cdot r \doteq v$.   □

PROPOSITION 59 (DENOTATIONAL SOUNDNESS OF TREE MODELS) For all sets of equations $\Phi \in \mathcal{L}_{L,C}$, if there exists a feature tree $t \in \mathcal{T}_{L,C}$ such that $t \models \Phi$, then Φ is consistent.

Proof   Suppose that $t \models \Phi$ but Φ is inconsistent, that is, that Φ derives a clash. We consider the two cases of clash type. If the clash is a constant clash, then $\Phi \vdash p \doteq a$ and $\Phi \vdash p \doteq b$ for some p, a, and b such that $a \neq b$. Now, since $t \models \Phi$, $t/p = a$ and $t/p = b$ by Proposition 58, so $a = b$, contradicting the assumption. Similarly, if the clash is a constant/compound clash, then $\Phi \vdash p \doteq a$ and $\Phi \vdash p \cdot \langle f \rangle \doteq v$. Then $t/p = a$ and $t/(p \cdot \langle f \rangle)$ is defined. So $t/(p \cdot \langle f \rangle) = (t/p)(f) = a(f)$ is defined. But a is not a partial function, so $a(f)$ cannot be defined. Thus, no clashes can exist, so Φ must be consistent.   □

4.1.2   Problems with Finite-Tree Models

However, finite feature trees do not provide a complete model structure for the logic. For example, consider the cyclic formula $\{\langle f \rangle \doteq a, \langle g \rangle \doteq \langle \rangle\}$. This formula derives all equations of the form $\langle g^i f \rangle \doteq a$ for $i \geq 0$. Now, since every finite feature tree t is a member of some $\mathcal{T}_i$ and since all elements of $\mathcal{T}_i$ have a maximum defined path length $i - 1$ (by a simple induction), any finite feature tree has a finite maximum path length. Thus, no finite feature tree satisfies all of the equations of the required form; the logical system is thus not denotationally complete.

Logical completeness also fails. Given a finite label domain L, all models of the formula $\Phi = \{\langle f\ x \rangle \doteq a \mid f \in \{f_1, f_2\}, x \in L\}$ also model $\phi = \langle f_1 \rangle \doteq \langle f_2 \rangle$. But $\Phi \not\vdash \phi$.

From these last examples, certain trade-offs are revealed that we will mention but not demonstrate rigorously. First, the counterexample to logical completeness relied on the finiteness of the label domain L. If L is taken to be infinite, no such finite formula Φ can exist, and logical completeness will hold (as long as infinite formulas are excluded from the logic). Similarly, if both cyclic formulas and infinite formulas are proscribed, denotational completeness can be recovered. Finally, it might be the case that completeness properties are incidental to the proposed use for the logical system, in which case tree models such as these would be effective.

Looking ahead to Section 4.2.2, however, we note in passing that even if appropriate restrictions are placed so that the models are sound and complete both logically and denotationally, the simple finite-feature-tree model cannot satisfy the property of minimal-model existence, which we desire for computational reasons.

4.2   Infinite-Tree Models

To regain denotational completeness, we can augment the class of models with infinite trees. Infinite-tree models have been proposed under various guises by Pereira and Shieber (1984, the domain F) and Barwise (1988). Rather than define the set of models using recursive domain equations (Pereira and Shieber, 1984), we will use a technique reminiscent of the method of Courcelle (1983). We define $T_{L,C}^{\infty}$, the set of (possibly) infinite trees over labels L and constants C, as the set of all partial functions from $Path$ to $C \cup \{\bot\}$, where $\bot$ is a distinguished constant not an element of C. Informally speaking, an element of t defines a tree by supplying, for every path from the root to a node in the tree, the label of that node. We require an additional provision of *prefix closure*, that all interior tree nodes are labeled with $\bot$. That is, for all paths p, if $t(p \cdot \langle f \rangle)$ is defined for some $f \in L$, then $t(p) = \bot$, so that only the terminal tree nodes will be labeled with constants (as was the case for the finite trees). Finally, we require that $t(\langle \rangle)$ be defined for all $t \in T_{L,C}^{\infty}$.

We must provide a definition of satisfaction so that infinite trees may serve as models for $\mathcal{L}_{L,C}$ in a logical system. As was the case for the finite-tree models, we will use extraction as an aid in defining satisfaction. The extraction of t at p (written t/p) is defined by the following condition: $(t/p)(q) = v$ if and only if $t(p \cdot q) = v$. Under this definition of extraction, an infinite tree t satisfies atomic formulas as follows: $t \models p \doteq q$ if and only if $t/p = t/q$ and $t \models p \doteq c$ if and only if $t(p) = c$. Modeling of nonatomic formulas is conjunctive, as for the finite trees.

We can now prove the correctness of the definition of extraction by showing that $t/p \models \Phi$ if and only if $t \models \Phi[\langle \rangle \rightarrow p]$. As before, we will restrict attention to the formulas of the form $q \doteq r$. Suppose that $t \models p \cdot q \doteq p \cdot r$. Then by definition of satisfaction, $t/(p \cdot q) = t/(p \cdot r)$, that is, $t(p \cdot q \cdot s) = t(p \cdot r \cdot s)$ for all s for which the applications are defined. Associativity of concatenation allows the conclusion that $(t/p)(q \cdot s) = (t/p)(r \cdot s)$, so $(t/p)(q) = (t/p)(r)$. But this is the requirement for

$t/p \models q \doteq r$. The proof for $\Phi = p \doteq c$ is similar, and for nonatomic formulas, trivial.

4.2.1   Properties of Infinite-Tree Models

We demonstrate that certain soundness and completeness properties hold for infinite-tree models.

PROPOSITION 60 (LOGICAL SOUNDNESS OF INFINITE-TREE MODELS) For all $t \in T_{L,C}^{\infty}$ and $\Phi \in \mathcal{L}_{L,C}$, if $t \models \Phi$ and $\Phi \vdash \phi$, then $t \models \phi$.

Proof   The proof is similar to that for Proposition 58. We must verify that if $t \in T_{L,C}^{\infty}$ is a model for Φ, then it is a model for ϕ as well. The proof is by induction on the depth of the proof tree for $\Phi \vdash \phi$. The base case occurs when $\Phi \vdash \phi$, either by Triviality or because $\phi \in \Phi$. In the former case, if $\phi = \langle\rangle \doteq \langle\rangle$, then $t \models \phi$, since $t/\langle\rangle = t = t/\langle\rangle$ for all t. In the latter, if $\phi \in \Phi$ and $t \models \Phi$, then $t \models \phi$ by definition of satisfaction.

The induction step requires a demonstration that the other rules of inference preserve modeling. For the Reflexivity rule, assume $\Phi \vdash p \cdot q \doteq v$. By the induction hypothesis, $t \models p \cdot q \doteq v$, that is, $t/(p \cdot q) = t/v$ (or v, depending on whether $v \in Path$ or $v \in C$, respectively). Thus, $(t/p)/q = t/v$ (respectively v) and t/p is defined. Since $t/p = t/p$ if defined, $t \models p \doteq p$. Preservation of modeling by the Symmetry rule follows in the same manner. For Substitutivity, we assume that $\Phi \vdash q \doteq p$ and $\Phi \vdash p \cdot r \doteq v$, giving us $t \models q \doteq p$ and $t \models p \cdot r \doteq v$ by the induction hypothesis. So $t/q = t/p$ and $t/(p \cdot r) = t/v$ (respectively v) $= (t/p)/r$. Substituting for t/p, we obtain $(t/q)/r = t/v$ (respectively v) $= t/q \cdot r$. We can conclude that $t \models q \cdot r \doteq v$.   □

PROPOSITION 61 (DENOTATIONAL SOUNDNESS OF INFINITE-TREE MODELS) For all $\Phi \in \mathcal{L}_{L,C}$, if there is a $t \in T_{L,C}^{\infty}$ such that $t \models \Phi$, then Φ is consistent.

Proof   Suppose $t \models \Phi$ and Φ is inconsistent. Then there are atomic formulas ϕ and ϕ' that follow from Φ and that clash. By Proposition 60, t is a model for both ϕ and ϕ'. Now, the clash can be either a constant clash or a constant/compound clash. In the former case, $\phi = p \doteq a$ and $\phi' = p \doteq b$ for $a \neq b$. Thus, $t(p) = a$ and $t(p) = b$, contradicting the functionality of t. In the latter case, $\phi = p \doteq a$ and $\phi' = p \cdot \langle f \rangle \doteq v$. Then $t(p) = a$ and $t(p) = \bot$ (by the restriction on labeling interior nodes), again contradicting the functionality of t.   □

PROPOSITION 62 (DENOTATIONAL COMPLETENESS OF INFINITE-TREE MODELS) For all $\Phi \in \mathcal{L}_{L,C}$, if Φ is consistent, then there is a $t \in T_{L,C}^{\infty}$ such that $t \models \Phi$.

Proof   Define $t = itm(\Phi)$, an infinite-tree model of Φ, as follows: $t(p) = v$ if and only if either

1. $v \in C$ and $\Phi \vdash p \doteq v$, or

2. $v = \bot$ and $\Phi \vdash p \doteq p$, but $\Phi \nvdash p \doteq c$ for any $c \in C$.

We must show that t is one of the models for Φ, that is, that it is well defined (a true function), prefix-closed, and satisfies Φ.

t is a function: Suppose t were not a function, that is, the definition of $itm(\Phi)$ assigned two distinct values v and v' to a single path p. If $v, v' \in C$, then $\Phi \vdash p \doteq v$ and $\Phi \vdash p \doteq v'$, so Φ is inconsistent by a constant clash, contra assumption of consistency. If $v \in C$ and $v' = \bot$, then $\Phi \vdash p \doteq v$ and $\Phi \nvdash p \doteq v$ for any $v \in C$, here too a contradiction. Thus, t must be a function.

t is prefix-closed: Suppose $t(p \cdot \langle f \rangle)$ is defined. We must show that $t(p) = \bot$ to conclude that t is prefix-closed. Now, by definition of itm, either $\Phi \vdash p \cdot \langle f \rangle \doteq v$ or $\Phi \vdash p \cdot \langle f \rangle \doteq p \cdot \langle f \rangle$. By Reflexivity, $\Phi \vdash p \doteq p$. Since Φ is consistent, $\Phi \nvdash p \doteq c$ for any $c \in C$. Thus, $t(p) = \bot$ by definition, and t is prefix-closed. Since $\Phi \vdash \langle \rangle \doteq \langle \rangle$, the function t must be defined at $\langle \rangle$, as required.

t satisfies Φ: Finally, we show that t is a model for Φ by proving the stronger result that t is a model for all consequences ϕ of Φ. Any ϕ such that $\Phi \vdash \phi$ is of one of the two forms of atomic formulas. If $\phi = p \doteq c$, then $t(p) = c$ by definition and $t \models \phi$.

If $\phi = p \doteq q$, we must show that t/p and t/q are defined and that $t/p = t/q$, that is, $t(p \cdot r) = t(q \cdot r)$ for all r such that $t(p \cdot r)$ is defined. First, t/p is defined because if $\Phi \vdash p \doteq q$, then $\Phi \vdash p \doteq p$, so $t(p)$ is defined (by definition of itm); similarly for t/q. Now, suppose $t(p \cdot r)$ is defined. Then either $\Phi \vdash p \cdot r \doteq c$ or $\Phi \vdash p \cdot r \doteq p \cdot r$ and $\Phi \nvdash p \cdot r \doteq c$ for any $c \in C$. In the former case, we have $\Phi \vdash q \cdot r \doteq c$ by Substitutivity, so $t(q \cdot r) = c = t(p \cdot r)$. In the latter case, we can conclude that $\Phi \vdash q \cdot r \doteq q \cdot r$

by Symmetry and Substitutivity. Also, $\Phi \not\vdash q \cdot r \doteq c$ for any $c \in C$. (If Φ did derive such a formula, then $\Phi \vdash p \cdot r \doteq c$ by Substitutivity and $t(p \cdot r) \neq \bot$, contrary to assumption.) Thus, $t(q \cdot r) = \bot = t(p \cdot r)$. As a consequence, $t/p = t/q$ and $t \models p \doteq q$. The tree t is therefore a model for ϕ.

Since t is a model for any equation that follows from Φ, it must be a model for Φ itself. We have shown that if Φ is consistent, there exists a model for Φ, namely, that given by $itm(\Phi)$. □

4.2.2 Problems with Infinite-Tree Models

Infinite-tree models are an advance over the finite-tree models because they provide denotational completeness. Unfortunately, logical completeness does not inhere in the new class of models. As a counterexample, consider the formula

$$\Phi_c = \{\langle x\ y\rangle \doteq a \mid x, y \in L\} \qquad ,$$

which requires that the values for each label be the same, namely, a tree taking all labels to the constant a. Because this specification defines values for every label on every interior node, only one infinite-tree model can exist for Φ_c. The unique model—thus every model—obeys the equation $\langle x\rangle \doteq \langle y\rangle$ for all $x, y \in L$. But $\Phi_c \not\vdash \langle x\rangle \doteq \langle y\rangle$. The logical system based on infinite trees is thus not logically complete.

The counterexemplifying formula Φ_c is finite only if L is finite. Thus, if L is not restricted to be finite, then the argument fails. We conjecture that in this case, the models are in fact logically complete.

A second problem with tree models, both finite and infinite, involves definition of the subsumption ordering on trees. As noted in Section 4.1, the natural ordering on finite trees does not satisfy upward closure. The same holds for the natural ordering on infinite trees, given by: $t \leq t'$ if and only if, whenever $t(p)$ is defined, $t(p) \leq t'(p)$, where, for elements v and v' of $C \cup \{\bot\}$, we take $v \leq v'$ to hold if and only if $v = v'$ or $v = \bot$. It is possible to show that the function itm defined in the proof of Proposition 62 actually defines the minimal infinite-tree model with respect to the natural ordering; it might therefore seem a desirable candidate for the subsumption ordering. However, under this ordering, the trees in Figure 4.1 (now viewed as elements of $T_{L,C}^\infty$) are ordered; Figure 4.1(a) subsumes Figure 4.1(b). Yet the former satisfies $\langle f\rangle \doteq \langle g\rangle$, whereas the latter does not. Thus, upward closure is violated, and the ordering is not appropriate for subsumption.

On the other hand, the subsumption ordering prescribed by Definition 9 leaves the two trees unordered, for each satisfies a formula unsatisfied by the other. In particular, Figure 4.1(a) satisfies $\langle f \rangle \doteq \langle g \rangle$ and Figure 4.1(b) satisfies $\langle g\ g \rangle \doteq b$. By enumerating all smaller models in the subsumption ordering—of which there are only finitely many—we can show that no model smaller than these two satisfies the formula $\Phi = \{\langle f\ f \rangle \doteq a, \langle g\ f \rangle \doteq a\}$. Therefore, no minimal tree model exists for Φ.

These various problems with tree models arise because the models (both finite and infinite) are *extensional*; that is, two nodes in the tree are identical if they take the same labels onto identical values. But the formulas in the logic are *intensional*, in that all the individual equations for two paths can be the same without entailing that the paths themselves participate in an equality relationship.

In summary, the tree models of both the finite and infinite variety lose information, since the only available notion of identity in the models is extensional identity. Because of this problem, canonical tree models for formulas do not in general exist, thereby removing the possibility of computing over them as an alternative to performing deduction in the logic. A preferable alternative model would restore the distinction between intensional and extensional identity that the tree models blur.

4.3   Eqtree Models

The most direct method for constructing a class of models that can distinguish intensional from extensional identity is to augment the infinite-tree models directly with an intensional identity relation. Eqtree models do just that.

An *eqtree* is a pair $\langle t, R \rangle$, where $t \in T_{L,C}^{\infty}$ is a possibly infinite tree, and R is a relation over $dom(t)$ (the paths of the tree) such that

1. R is an equivalence relation,

2. If pRp' then $t(p) = t(p')$, and

3. If pRp' and $p \cdot \langle f \rangle \in dom(t)$, then $p \cdot \langle f \rangle R p' \cdot \langle f \rangle$.

These conditions make R a *congruence relation* over *dom(t)*. We will use the notation $T_{L,C}^=$ for the class of eqtrees.

As a consequence of the constraints on R, if pRp', then $t/p = t/p'$; the equivalence relation R is a stronger relation than extensional identity. In fact, R will correspond to intensional identity.

PROPOSITION 63 For all eqtrees $\langle t, R \rangle$ and paths p and p', if pRp', then $t/p = t/p'$.

Proof We must show that $(t/p)(q) = (t/p')(q)$ for all q such that $(t/p)(q)$ is defined as well. Suppose that $(t/p)(q)$ is defined. Then $t(p \cdot q)$ is defined. Now pRp', so by a simple induction, $p \cdot qRp' \cdot q$ and $t(p \cdot q) = t(p' \cdot q)$. But the latter is just $(t/p')(q)$. □

Satisfaction will be defined much as it was in the tree models. An eqtree $\langle t, R \rangle$ satisfies or models an equation $p \doteq c$ just in case t itself models the equation, that is, if and only if $t(p) = c$. The eqtree models an equation $p \doteq q$ just in case pRq, that is, the subtrees of t at p and q are *intensionally* identical. This implies that $t/p = t/q$, which was the definition of satisfaction in the tree models. Thus, satisfaction in an eqtree model is strictly stronger than the notion for tree models, again because of the distinction between extensional and intensional identity.

Subsumption is defined pointwise. That is, $\langle t, R \rangle \leq \langle t', R' \rangle$ if and only if $t \leq t'$ and $R \subseteq R'$. Here we are using the natural subsumption ordering on trees. Recall that for this ordering, minimal infinite-tree models exist. Although, as we have shown, the ordering on infinite-tree models does not satisfy upward closure by itself, it does in conjunction with the ordering on R. We show that subsumption as here defined respects entailment and is upward-closed.

PROPOSITION 64 (SUBSUMPTION ON EQTREES RESPECTS ENTAILMENT) If whenever $\eta \models \Phi$, $\eta' \models \Phi$ for all $\Phi \in \mathcal{L}_{L,C}$, then $\eta \leq \eta'$.

Proof Suppose we have two eqtrees $\eta = \langle t, R \rangle$ and $\eta' = \langle t', R' \rangle$ such that whenever $\eta \models \Phi$, $\eta' \models \Phi$ for all $\Phi \in \mathcal{L}_{L,C}$. We examine the relationship between the two components of the eqtrees separately.

First, if $t(p) = c$, then $\eta \models p \doteq c$, so $\eta' \models p \doteq c$ as well and $t'(p) = c$. Similarly, if $t(p) = \bot$, then $\eta \models p \doteq p$, so $\eta' \models p \doteq p$ as well. Now, it either holds or not that $\eta' \models p \doteq c$ for some $c \in C$. If so, by definition of satisfaction for infinite trees, $t(p) = c$; if not, $t(p) = \bot$. In either of these two cases $t(p) \leq t'(p)$ whenever $t(p)$ is defined, so that $t \leq t'$ in general.

Second, if pRq, then $\eta \models p \doteq q$, so $\eta' \models p \doteq q$ as well and $pR'q$. Hence, $R \subseteq R'$. By definition of subsumption on eqtrees, $\eta \leq \eta'$.   □

PROPOSITION 65 (UPWARD CLOSURE OF SUBSUMPTION ON EQTREES)
If $\eta \leq \eta'$, then whenever $\eta \models \Phi$, $\eta' \models \Phi$ for all $\Phi \in \mathcal{L}_{L,C}$.

Proof   Assume that we have two eqtrees $\eta = \langle t, R \rangle$ and $\eta' = \langle t', R' \rangle$ such that $\eta \leq \eta'$. Furthermore, suppose $\eta \models \Phi$. We must show that $\eta' \models \Phi$, proved by cases depending on the form of the equations in Φ. Without loss of generality, we can assume that Φ is atomic, since the case for nonatomic formulas reduces trivially to that for atomic ones.

If Φ is of the form $p \doteq q$, then pRq. By definition of subsumption, $pR'q$ as well, so $\eta' \models p \doteq q$. If Φ is of the form $p \doteq c$, then $t(p) = c$. Again, by definition of subsumption, $t'(p) = c$ so $\eta' \models p \doteq c$.   □

4.3.1   Properties of Eqtree Models

The appropriateness properties satisfied by the tree models also inhere in eqtrees. We prove them here.

PROPOSITION 66 (LOGICAL SOUNDNESS OF EQTREE MODELS)   For all $\eta = \langle t, R \rangle \in \mathcal{T}_{L,C}^{\doteq}$ and $\Phi \in \mathcal{L}_{L,C}$, if $\eta \models \Phi$ and $\Phi \vdash \phi$, then $\eta \models \phi$.

Proof   The proof is by induction on the size of the proof tree for $\Phi \vdash \phi$. The base case occurs where $\Phi \vdash \phi$ is proved either by Triviality or because $\phi \in \Phi$. Clearly, if $\phi \in \Phi$ and $\eta \models \Phi$, then $\eta \models \phi$ by definition of satisfaction for eqtrees. For Triviality, if $\phi = \langle \rangle \doteq \langle \rangle$, then $\eta \models \phi$, since for all trees, $t(\langle \rangle)$ is defined; hence, $\langle \rangle R \langle \rangle$.

The induction step requires that we demonstrate that the other rules of inference preserve modeling. For the Reflexivity rule, assume $\Phi \vdash p \cdot q \doteq v$. By the induction hypothesis, $\eta \models p \cdot q \doteq v$, so either $p \cdot qRv$ or $t(p \cdot q) = v$ (depending on whether $v \in Path$ or $v \in C$, respectively). In either case, $t/(p \cdot q) = (t/p)/q$ is defined, guaranteeing the definition of t/p. Since R is an equivalence on $dom(t)$, we have that pRp; thus, $\eta \models p \doteq p$. Preservation of modeling by Symmetry follows similarly. Finally, for Substitutivity, we assume that $\Phi \vdash q \doteq p$ and $\Phi \vdash p \cdot r \doteq v$, giving $\eta \models q \doteq p$ and $\eta \models p \cdot r \doteq v$ by the induction hypothesis. So qRp and either $p \cdot rRv$ or $t(p \cdot r) = v$ (again depending on whether

$v \in Path$ or $v \in C$, respectively). If the former, a simple induction on the length of r yields $(q \cdot r)Rv$; hence, $\eta \models q \cdot r \doteq v$. If the latter, then $t/(p \cdot r) = (t/p)/r = (t/q)/r = t/(q \cdot r) = v$, so that once again, $\eta \models q \cdot r \doteq v$. □

PROPOSITION 67 (DENOTATIONAL SOUNDNESS OF EQTREE MODELS)
For all formulas $\Phi \in \mathcal{L}_{L,C}$, if there exists an eqtree $\eta = \langle t, R \rangle \in \mathcal{T}^{=}_{L,C}$ such that $\eta \models \Phi$, then Φ is consistent.

Proof By definition of satisfaction for eqtrees, if $\eta \models \Phi$, then $t \models \Phi$. But by Proposition 61, Φ must be consistent. □

PROPOSITION 68 (MINIMAL-MODEL EXISTENCE FOR EQTREE MODELS)
If $\Phi \in \mathcal{L}_{L,C}$ is consistent, then there is a least $\eta = \langle t, R \rangle \in \mathcal{T}^{=}_{L,C}$ such that $\eta \models \Phi$.

Proof Define $\eta = metm(\Phi)$, the *minimal eqtree model* of Φ, as follows: $\eta = \langle t, R \rangle$ where $t = itm(\Phi)$ and pRq if and only if $\Phi \vdash p \doteq q$.

We show that η is a well-formed eqtree, that $\eta \models \Phi$, and that η is the least such eqtree.

η is a well-formed eqtree: As proved in Proposition 62, t is a well-formed infinite tree. We must only prove that R is a relation over $dom(t)$ satisfying the properties of a congruence. Now, if pRq, then $\Phi \vdash p \doteq q$ and $\Phi \vdash p \doteq p$ by Reflexivity. Furthermore, it either holds or not that $\Phi \vdash p \doteq c$ for some $c \in C$. If so, $t(p) = c$; if not, $t(p) = \bot$, according to the *itm* construction. In either case, $p \in dom(t)$ so R is a relation over $dom(t)$.

We turn to the three conditions on the well-formedness of R. First, R is an equivalence relation, since it is reflexive (trivially), symmetric (if pRq, then $\Phi \vdash p \doteq q$; hence, $\Phi \vdash q \doteq p$ by Reflexivity, and qRp), and transitive (if pRq and qRs, then $\Phi \vdash p \doteq q$ and $\Phi \vdash q \doteq s$, so by Substitutivity, $\Phi \vdash p \doteq s$, and pRs).

Second, if pRp', then $\Phi \vdash p \doteq p'$. Again we consider two cases as to whether it holds that $\Phi \vdash p \doteq c$ for some $c \in C$. If so, $t(p) = c$, and by Substitutivity, $\Phi \vdash p' \doteq c$, so $t(p') = c$. If not, $t(p) = \bot$ and $\Phi \not\vdash p' \doteq c$ for any $c \in C$, for otherwise we would have $\Phi \vdash p \doteq c$ by Substitutivity; hence, $t(p') = \bot$ as well. In either case, $t(p) = t(p')$, as required.

Third, assume that pRp' and $p' \cdot \langle f \rangle \in dom(t)$. Then $\Phi \vdash p \doteq p'$ and $\Phi \vdash p' \cdot \langle f \rangle \doteq v$ for some v. By Reflexivity, $\Phi \vdash p' \cdot \langle f \rangle \doteq p' \cdot \langle f \rangle$, whence, by Substitutivity, $\Phi \vdash p \cdot \langle f \rangle \doteq p' \cdot \langle f \rangle$, so $p \cdot \langle f \rangle R p' \cdot \langle f \rangle$. This concludes the proof of the well-formedness of R and therefore η.

η is a model for Φ: Suppose $\Phi \vdash p \doteq q$. Then by construction, pRq and $\eta \models p \doteq q$. If $\Phi \vdash p \doteq c$, then $t(p) = c$ by the itm construction (see Proposition 61); hence, $\eta \models p \doteq c$. Since η is a model for any equation that follows from Φ, it is a model for Φ itself.

η is the least model for Φ: Consider any model $\eta' = \langle t', R' \rangle$ such that $\eta' \models \Phi$. By logical soundness (Proposition 66), $\eta' \models \Phi'$ for all $\Phi \vdash \Phi'$. In particular, if pRq, then $\Phi \vdash p \doteq q$, so $\eta' \models p \doteq q$ and $pR'q$. Thus, $R \subseteq R'$. If $t(p) = c$, then $\Phi \vdash p \doteq c$, so $\eta' \models p \doteq c$ and $t'(p) = c$. Similarly, if $t(p) = \bot$, then $\Phi \vdash p \doteq p$, so $\eta' \models p \doteq p$ and, by definition of satisfaction, either $t'(p) = \bot$ or $t'(p) = c$ for some $c \in C$. In either case, $t(p) \leq t(p')$, so $t \leq t'$ in general. By definition of subsumption on eqtrees, $\eta \leq \eta'$.   □

PROPOSITION 69 (CATEGORICITY FOR EQTREE MODELS) If $\eta = \langle t, R \rangle$ and $\eta' = \langle t', R' \rangle$ are distinct eqtrees in $\mathcal{T}_{L,C}^{=}$, then there exists a formula $\Phi \in \mathcal{L}_{L,C}$ such that $\eta \models \Phi$ and $\eta' \not\models \Phi$, or vice versa.

Proof   If η and η' are distinct, they must differ either in t or in R. The possibilities can be divided exhaustively into six cases. The first three cases are as follows:

Case 1: $t(p)$ defined and $t'(p)$ undefined.

   Then $\eta \models p \doteq p$ but $\eta \not\models p \doteq p$.

Case 2: $t(p) = c$ and $t'(p) = \bot$.

   Then $\eta \models p \doteq c$ but $\eta' \not\models p \doteq c$.

Case 3: pRq but not $pR'q$.

   Then $\eta \models p \doteq q$ but $\eta' \not\models p \doteq q$.

The remaining three cases, the symmetric versions of the first three, where t' or R' is more defined, are proved similarly.   □

PROPOSITION 70 (LOGICAL COMPLETENESS OF EQTREE MODELS)   If for all $\eta \in \mathcal{T}_{L,C}^{=}$ such that $\eta \models \Phi$, $\eta \models \Phi'$, then $\Phi \vdash \Phi'$.

Proof Without loss of generality, we can restrict ourselves to the case where Φ' is atomic. (For nonatomic wffs, satisfaction holds just in case it holds for the atomic elements, so the problem reduces to the atomic case.) Suppose that for all $\eta \in \mathcal{T}_{L,C}^{=}$ such that $\eta \models \Phi$, it is the case that $\eta \models \Phi'$. Then, in particular, $metm(\Phi) = \langle t, R \rangle \models \Phi'$. We prove that $\Phi \vdash \Phi'$ by cases, depending on the form of Φ'. If Φ' is of the form $p \doteq q$, then $\langle t, R \rangle \models p \doteq q$ and pRq. By the *metm* construction, $\Phi \vdash p \doteq q$. If Φ' is of the form $p \doteq c$, then $\langle t, R \rangle \models p \doteq c$ and $t(p) = c$. Now, by the *itm* construction employed in the *metm* construction, $\Phi \vdash p \doteq c$. Thus, in general, $\Phi \vdash \Phi'$. □

We have proved all five of the crucial properties for demonstrating the appropriateness of eqtree models as a semantic system for the logic $\mathcal{L}_{L,C}$. As described in Section 3.1, the resulting logical system can be used to define a constraint-based grammar formalism.

4.3.2 Problems with Eqtree Models

The eqtree models comprise the first class of models for $\mathcal{L}_{L,C}$ for which the engendered logical system satisfies the appropriateness conditions defined in Chapter 2. As such, eqtrees can provide a semantics for the grammar formalism based on $\mathcal{L}_{L,C}$.

The stronger requirements placed on a logical system to allow for the computational efficacy of the parsing algorithm described in Chapter 3 do not, however, inhere in the eqtree class of models. There are two related problems. First, the models are too large. Section 3.1 requires that the minimal model of an atomic formula be finite, but the minimal model for, say, $\langle f \rangle \doteq \langle \rangle$ is an eqtree whose first component is an infinitely large infinite tree and whose second component is an infinite relation over paths. On the other hand, the model is highly regular in its structure, a fact that we might take advantage of in representing it finitely. This leads us to the second problem with eqtrees: there are too many of them. Besides the nicely behaved eqtrees like the minimal model of $\langle f \rangle \doteq \langle \rangle$, there are also eqtrees that are both infinite and unstructured. For instance, consider the eqtree satisfying all equations of the form $\langle f^n \ g \rangle \doteq \pi_n$, where π_n is the nth digit in the decimal expansion of π.

These problems are not unique to eqtrees; they apply to the infinite-tree models as well. We delayed their introduction only because other problems with infinite trees rendered moot any thought of using them computationally, whereas the success of eqtrees as a model class for $\mathcal{L}_{L,C}$

raises hopes that they might serve as the basis of a computationally appropriate class of models.

Both problems with eqtrees (and infinite trees as well), their size and numerousness, can be solved with one method: elimination of all but the *rational* eqtrees. An eqtree $\langle t, R \rangle$ is rational if and only if it contains just a finite number of distinct sub-eqtrees. As usual, we opt for the strong reading of the term 'distinct', that is, the intensional one. Two subtrees are identical if the paths that address them are R-equivalent, distinct if they are not. This leads to the following formal definition of a rational eqtree:

DEFINITION 71 An eqtree $\langle t, R \rangle$ is *rational* if and only if R partitions $dom(t)$ into a finite set of equivalence classes.

For example, the minimal model of $\langle f \rangle \doteq \langle \rangle$ has only one distinct subtree—itself—and one equivalence class of paths—all paths of the form $\langle f^n \rangle$—and is therefore rational. The minimal model for the formula $\{\langle f \rangle \doteq \langle \rangle, \langle g \rangle \doteq a\}$ has as subtrees the vestigial tree $\langle a, \{\langle \rangle \doteq \langle \rangle\}\rangle$ and itself, hence is also rational. The two equivalence classes of paths are $\langle f^n \rangle$ and $\langle f^n g \rangle$. The eqtree based on the decimal expansion of π, on the other hand, contains distinct eqtrees corresponding to the infinite set of distinct postfixes of the π expansion; it is clearly irrational.

As we will shortly prove, the minimal models for formulas are all rational eqtrees, and, since the basic operations $\sqcup$, $/$, $\backslash$, and so forth, all preserve minimal-modelhood (Lemmas 36, 37, and 38), we can safely retreat to using the rational subset as the model class. Furthermore, since the rational eqtrees by definition contain only a finite number of distinct subtrees, we can hope to represent them finitely.

In fact, this observation is the basis of our next and final model class, the graph models. By reifying the distinct subtrees of an eqtree and representing multiple instances of the same subtree only once, we can represent any rational eqtree finitely as a graph. For instance, the rational eqtree corresponding to $\{\langle f \rangle \doteq \langle \rangle, \langle g \rangle \doteq a\}$ (represented in Figure 4.2(a)) has two distinct subtrees; the corresponding graph (Figure 4.2(b)) thus has two nodes. In Section 4.4 we describe the graph models directly and then show their relationship to the eqtrees.

4.3.3   Properties of Rational Eqtrees

PROPOSITION 72 For all $\Phi \in \mathcal{L}_{L,C}$, $metm(\Phi)$ is rational.

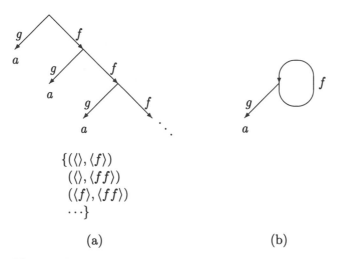

$$\{(\langle\rangle, \langle f\rangle)$$
$$(\langle\rangle, \langle f f\rangle)$$
$$(\langle f\rangle, \langle f f\rangle)$$
$$\cdots\}$$

(a)   (b)

Figure 4.2
Eqtree and corresponding graph

Proof   Without loss of generality, we can assume that Φ is nonempty. Let $metm(\Phi) = \langle t, R\rangle$. We must show that there is only a finite number of R-equivalence classes. We do so by demonstrating that for any path $p \in dom(t)$, p must be in an equivalence class with some prefix of a path in Φ, of which there are only finitely many. If $p \in dom(t)$, then pRp, and by definition of the *metm* construction, $\Phi \vdash p \doteq p$. So it suffices to show, for each p such that $\Phi \vdash p \doteq p$, that $\Phi \vdash p \doteq q$ for some q a prefix of a path in Φ. We can prove this by induction on the depth of the proof tree for $\Phi \vdash p \doteq p$.

The base case occurs when $\Phi \vdash p \doteq p$ is proved either by the Triviality rule or because $p \doteq p \in \Phi$. In the former case, $p = \langle\rangle$, which is the prefix of all paths, therefore of some path in Φ. In the latter case, $p \doteq p \in \Phi$, so p is itself a path in Φ.

For the induction step, we assume that the hypothesis holds for proofs of depth smaller than n and show it for proofs of depth n by cases depending on the final proof step. If the final proof step is Reflexivity or Symmetry, the paths in the consequent are exactly those in the antecedent. Since the induction hypothesis holds for the paths in the antecedent, it holds for those in the consequent. For the Substitutivity rule, we assume that the hypothesis holds for p, q, $p \cdot r$, and v (if $v \in Path$), and, moreover, that $\Phi \vdash p \doteq q$ and $\Phi \vdash p \cdot r \doteq v$. We must show that $\Phi \vdash q \cdot r \doteq s$ for s a prefix of a path in Φ. By Reflexivity and Substitutivity, we can conclude that $\Phi \vdash p \cdot r \doteq q \cdot r$. The induction hypothesis gives us $\Phi \vdash p \cdot r \doteq s$ for some s a prefix of a path in Φ. Using Substitutivity again, we can prove that $\Phi \vdash q \cdot r \doteq s$. (The length of this latter proof—though perhaps longer than n—is irrelevant to the argument; the induction hypothesis is never applied to its antecedents.)

Thus, there are at most as many equivalence classes as there are prefixes of paths in Φ. Since this is finite, $metm(\Phi)$ is rational.   □

4.4   Graph Models

We arrive at our final class of models for $\mathcal{L}_{L,C}$, the graph models. Similar models have been used implicitly since the earliest implementations of constraint-based formalisms, and have been proposed as a theoretical basis for feature structures by Kasper and Rounds (1986), and Pereira and Shieber (1984).

Feature Frames   We use the notion of feature frame (a kind of rooted directed graph with labeled arcs) as a precursor to feature graphs with which we can model the formulas in $\mathcal{L}_{L,C}$.

A *feature frame* is a triple $s = \langle N, n_0, \delta \rangle$ where

- N is a set of *nodes*;

- n_0 is a distinguished node, the *root node*;

- δ is a partial function from $N \times L$ to N, the *next node* function.

The set of *terminals* of a feature frame s, notated as $terminals(s)$, is the set of nodes $n \in N$ such that $\delta(n, f)$ is undefined for all $f \in L$.

Furthermore, we introduce notation for traversing feature frames (and, later, feature graphs). For $p = \langle f_1 \cdots f_k \rangle$ a path, and $s = \langle N, n_0, \delta \rangle$ a frame, and $n \in N$, define n/p to be the node in g given as follows: If $k = 0$, then $n/p = n$. Otherwise $n/p = \delta(n, f_1)/\langle f_2 \cdots f_k \rangle$ if this is defined. We will use the notation s/p to mean n_0/p for n_0 the root node of s. (Although we use the extraction notation here, we have still to prove that the operation corresponds to the definition of extraction. See Section 4.4.1.)

Feature Graphs   A *feature graph* g is a quadruple $\langle N, n_0, \delta, \pi \rangle$, where

- $s = \langle N, n_0, \delta \rangle$ is a feature frame, and

- π is a partial function from $terminals(s)$ to C, the *labeling* function.

Thus, feature graphs are feature frames with certain labeled terminal nodes.

Feature graphs can be regarded—as in the work of Kasper and Rounds (1986)—as deterministic finite-state automata with final states defined intensionally (i.e., states with no outgoing transitions) rather than extensionally, and with a labeling function on final states.

Given a frame $s = \langle N, n_0, \delta \rangle$ and a partial function $\pi : terminals(s) \rightarrow C$, we will write $\langle s, \pi \rangle$ for the graph $\langle N, n_0, \delta, \pi \rangle$.

4.4.1 Feature Graphs as Models for the Feature Logic

Graphs can be used as models for formulas in $\mathcal{L}_{L,C}$. A graph $g = \langle N, n_0, \delta, \pi \rangle$ *satisfies* (is a *model* for) an equation $p \doteq v$ (written $g \models p \doteq v$) if and only if

- If v is a path $p' \in Path$, then g/p and g/p' are defined and $g/p = g/p'$, and

- If v is a constant $c \in C$, then g/p is defined and terminal, and $\pi(g/p) = c$.

As usual, satisfaction for nonatomic formulas is defined conjunctively; a graph $g \models \Phi$ if and only if $g \models \phi$ for all $\phi \in \Phi$.

In the following discussion, we omit explicit statements that terms in an equation are well defined under the convention that writing an equation $x = y$ implies that x and y are both defined.

Extraction We can now prove that the $/$ operator conforms to the definition for the extraction operator.

PROPOSITION 73 $M/p \models \Phi$ if and only if $M \vdash \Phi[\langle\rangle \rightarrow p]$.

Proof Suppose $M/p \models \Phi$. Without loss of generality, we consider only the cases where Φ is atomic. If Φ is of the form $q \doteq r$, then $(M/p)/q = (M/p)/r$, so $M/(p \cdot q) = M/(p \cdot r)$ and $M \models p \cdot q \doteq p \cdot r$. The argument when Φ is of the form $q \doteq c$ is similar.

Conversely, if $M \models p \cdot q \doteq p \cdot r$, then $M/(p \cdot q) = M/(p \cdot r)$ and $(M/p)/q = (M/p)/r$, so $M/p \models q \doteq r$. Again, the argument when Φ is of the form $q \doteq c$ is similar. $\square$

Subsumption Ordering on Graphs   We first define a graph homomorphism $m : g \to g'$ from $g = \langle N, n_0, \delta, \pi \rangle$ to $g' = \langle N', n_0', \delta', \pi' \rangle$ as a function $m : N \to N'$ such that

1. $m(n_0) = n_0'$,

and, for every $f \in F$ and $n \in N$,

2. If $\delta(n, f)$ is defined, then $\delta'(m(n), f)$ is defined and $m(\delta(n, f)) = \delta'(m(n), f)$, and

3. If $\pi(n)$ is defined, then $\pi'(m(n))$ is defined and $\pi(n) = \pi'(m(n))$.

By a simple induction, if n/p is defined, then so is $m(n)/p$ and $m(n/p) = m(n)/p$.

A graph $g = \langle N, n_0, \delta, \pi \rangle$ *subsumes* a graph $g' = \langle N', n_0', \delta', \pi' \rangle$ (written $g \le g'$) if and only if there is a graph homomorphism m from g to g'. The homomorphism m is called the *witness* to the subsumption relationship.

Graph subsumption as defined here is a preorder, since distinct graphs can subsume one another. Intuitively, this is because the set of nodes might be different, whereas the interrelationships among the nodes given by δ and π are the same. An equivalence relation on graphs to remove such artifactual distinctions will allow us to treat graphs (actually equivalence classes of graphs) as a partial order; this equivalence relation is the one given by collapsing all graphs that subsume each other. Furthermore, if we assume that all graphs $g = \langle N, n_0, \delta, \pi \rangle$ are *connected*, in the sense that for all $n \in N$ there is a path p such that $n = n_0/p$, then the equivalence classes constitute the isomorphism classes of graphs. We will notate that two graphs g and g' are isomorphic with $g \approx g'$. (The reason that connectedness is required is exemplified in Figure 4.3, which exhibits two nonisomorphic graphs that subsume each other. The witness homomorphism from the (b) to the (a) graph can map the single disconnected node to any node in the (a) graph.)

PROPOSITION 74   If g and g' are connected and $g \le g'$ and $g' \le g$, then $g \approx g'$.

Proof   It suffices to show that the witnesses of the two subsumption relations are inverses. If the witnesses to the two subsumption relationships are m and m', respectively, then we must show that $m'(m(n)) = n$

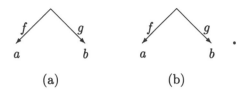

Figure 4.3
Two mutually subsuming but nonisomorphic graphs

for all nodes n in g. Now, for the root node of g, n_0, $m'(m(n_0)) = m'(n_0') = n_0$ (where n_0' is the root node of g'). By connectedness, any other node n in g is n_0/p for some p. Therefore, $m'(m(n)) = m'(m(n_0/p)) = m'(m(n_0)/p) = m'(n_0'/p) = m'(n_0')/p = n_0/p = n$. Similarly, $m(m'(n')) = n'$ for all nodes n' in g'. $\square$

In the sequel, we will assume that graphs (but, crucially, not frames) are connected,so that the isomorphism classes on graphs form a partial order.

To demonstrate that the ordering defined here is truly a subsumption ordering, we prove that it matches the definition of subsumption given in Chapter 2, that is, that it respects entailment and is upward-closed.

PROPOSITION 75 (SUBSUMPTION ON GRAPHS RESPECTS ENTAILMENT)
If whenever $g \models \Phi$, $g' \models \Phi$ for all $\Phi \in \mathcal{L}_{L,C}$, then $g \leq g'$.

Proof Suppose we have two graphs g and g' where $g = \langle N, n_0, \delta, \pi \rangle$ and $g' = \langle N', n_0', \delta', \pi' \rangle$ such that whenever $g \models \Phi$, $g' \models \Phi$ for all $\Phi \in \mathcal{L}_{L,C}$. Construct the witness m such that $m(g/p) = g'/p$. Since g is connected, this function is total on N. Furthermore, g'/p is defined whenever g/p is, since if g/p is defined, then $g' \models p \doteq p$; therefore, $y' \models p \doteq p$ and g'/p is defined.

To prove m is a well-defined function, we observe that if $g/p = g/p'$, then $g \models p \doteq p'$, so $g' \models p \doteq p'$ as well, and $g'/p = y'/p'$. We must demonstrate that m is a graph homomorphism. First, $m(n_0) = m(g/\langle\rangle) = g'/\langle\rangle = n_0'$. Second, let $n = g/p$. If $\delta(n, f)$ is defined, then $\delta(n, f) = g/(p \cdot \langle f \rangle)$, so $m(\delta(n, f)) = m(g/(p \cdot \langle f \rangle)) = g'/(p \cdot \langle f \rangle) = \delta'(g'/p, f) = \delta'(m(n), f)$. Finally, if $\pi(n) = c$, then $\pi(n) = \pi(g/p) = c$, so $g \models p \doteq c$. By assumption, then, $g' \models p \doteq c$ and $\pi'(g'/p) = \pi'(m(g/p)) = \pi'(m(n)) = c$. Thus, m provides a witness for the subsumption $g \leq g'$. $\square$

PROPOSITION 76 (UPWARD CLOSURE OF SUBSUMPTION ON GRAPHS)
If $g \leq g'$, then whenever $g \models \Phi$, $g' \models \Phi$ for all $\Phi \in \mathcal{L}_{L,C}$.

Proof   Assume that we have two graphs $g = \langle N, n_0, \delta, \pi \rangle$ and $g' = \langle N', n'_0, \delta', \pi' \rangle$ such that $g \leq g'$ by some witness homomorphism m. Further, suppose $g \models \Phi$. We must show that $g' \models \Phi$, which we do by cases depending on the form of the equations in Φ. Without loss of generality, we can assume that Φ is atomic, since the case for nonatomic formulas reduces trivially to that for atomic ones.

If Φ is of the form $p \doteq q$, then $g/p = g/q$, so $m(g/p) = m(g/q)$. By definition of subsumption, $m(n_0)/p = m(n_0)/q$ as well, so $g'/p \doteq g'/q$ and $g' \models p \doteq q$. If Φ is of the form $p \doteq c$, then $\pi(g/p) = c$. Again by definition of subsumption, $\pi'(g'/p) = \pi'(m(n_0)/p) = \pi'(m(n_0/p)) = \pi(n_0/p) = c$, so $g' \models p \doteq c$. $\square$

4.4.2   Eqtrees and Feature Graphs

The close relationship between eqtrees and feature graphs is given by the following proposition:

PROPOSITION 77 The eqtrees are isomorphic to the isomorphism classes of feature graphs.

Proof   The proof is structured as follows. We define two mappings: τ from graphs to eqtrees, and γ from eqtrees to graphs. Each mapping is total, one-to-one, and satisfaction-preserving. (The mapping γ is one-to-one in the sense that it takes each distinct eqtree onto a graph in a distinct equivalence class of graphs.) Since the mappings are satisfaction-preserving, $\tau(\gamma(\eta))$ satisfies the same formulas as η. By categoricity of eqtrees, $\tau(\gamma(\eta)) = \eta$; that is, τ is the inverse of γ. Since τ is total, γ must be onto, as well as total and one-to-one; γ is therefore an isomorphism (with inverse τ).

It merely remains to display the claimed mappings τ and γ.

Given a feature graph $g = \langle N, n_0, \delta, \pi \rangle$, let $\tau(g) = \langle t, R \rangle$, where

$t(p) = c$ if and only if $\pi(g/p) = c$
$t(p) = \perp$ if and only if g/p is defined but $\pi(g/p)$ is undefined

pRp' if and only if $g/p = g/p'$

We must show that τ is a total, one-to-one function with respect to isomorphism classes of feature graphs and that τ preserves satisfaction, that is, that $\tau(g) \models \Phi$ if and only if $g \models \Phi$.

$\tau(g)$ **is a well-formed eqtree:** Clearly, t is a well-defined function, for if it were not, g would be an ill-defined graph. For all paths p, if $t(p \cdot \langle f \rangle)$ is defined for some feature f, then $g/(p \cdot \langle f \rangle)$ is defined as well and so is g/p. Furthermore, by the conditions of well-formedness of feature graphs, $\pi(g/p) \neq c$ for any $c \in C$. Thus, $t(p) = \bot$; t is prefix-closed. In sum, t is a well-formed tree in $T_{L,C}^{\infty}$.

We must also show that R obeys the congruence constraints on eqtree relations.

1. The relation R is an equivalence relation because $=$ is.

2. If pRp', then $g/p = g/p'$. Therefore, if $\pi(g/p)$ is undefined, then $t(p) = t(p') = \bot$ and if $\pi(g/p) = c$, then $t(p) = t(p') = c$. In either case, $t(p) = t(p')$.

3. If pRp' and $p \cdot \langle f \rangle \in dom(t)$, then $g/p = g/p'$ and $g/(p \cdot \langle f \rangle)$ is defined. By definition, $g/(p \cdot \langle f \rangle) = (g/p)(f) = (g/p')(f) = g/(p' \cdot \langle f \rangle)$. So $(p \cdot \langle f \rangle)R(p' \cdot \langle f \rangle)$.

Since t is a well-formed tree and R an appropriate relation, $\tau(g)$ is a well-formed eqtree.

τ **is total and one-to-one:** The function τ is total by construction. We show that τ is one-to-one; that is, if $\tau(g) = \tau(g')$ for some $g' = \langle N', n_0', \delta', \pi' \rangle$, then $g \approx g'$.

Suppose that $\tau(g) = \tau(g') = \langle t, R \rangle$. It suffices to show that $g \leq g'$. By symmetry, $g' \leq g$, whence $g \approx g'$ by Proposition 74. Consider the graph homomorphism $m : g \to g'$, defined by $m(g/p) = g'/p$. (By connectedness, all nodes n are of the form g/p for some p, so m is total. Also, if g/p is defined, then pRp, so g'/p is defined as well.)

- m *is a well-defined function:* We must show that if $g/p = g/p'$, then $g'/p = g'/p'$. If $g/p = g/p'$, then pRp' and $g'/p = g'/p'$.
- $m(n_0) = n_0'$: $m(n_0) = m(g/\langle \rangle) = g'/\langle \rangle = n_0'$.
- *For all* $f \in L$, $n \in N$, *if* $\delta(n, f)$ *is defined, then* $m(\delta(n, f)) = \delta'(m(n), f)$: Suppose $n = g/p$. Existence of such a p is guaranteed by connectedness. Then $m(\delta(n, f)) = m(\delta(g/p, f)) = m(g/p \cdot \langle f \rangle) = g'/p \cdot \langle f \rangle = \delta'(g'/p, f) = \delta'(m(n), f)$.

- *For all $n \in N$, if $\pi(n)$ is defined, then $\pi'(m(n)) = \pi(n)$:* Suppose $n = g/p$. Then $\pi'(m(n)) = \pi'(m(g/p)) = \pi'(g'/p) = t(p) = \pi(g/p) = \pi(n)$.

Thus, $g \leq g'$ by witness m. As mentioned above, this suffices to show that $g \approx g'$ and concludes the proof that τ is one-to-one.

τ **is satisfaction-preserving:** By its definition, $\tau(g) \models \Phi$ if and only if $g \models \Phi$. For instance, for equations of the form $p \doteq q$, $g \models p \doteq q$ if and only if $g/p = g/q$ if and only if pRq if and only if $\tau(g) \models p \doteq q$. Similar arguments hold for other formulas.

We now turn to γ, the inverse of τ. Given an eqtree $\eta = \langle t, R \rangle$, let $\gamma(\eta) = \langle N, n_0, \delta, \pi \rangle$, where

- N is the set of R-equivalence classes of paths in $dom(t)$ (the notation $[p]$ being used for the equivalence class containing p),
- n_0 is the equivalence class $[\langle \rangle]$,
- δ is exhaustively defined by $\delta([p], f) = [p \cdot \langle f \rangle]$ for all $p \cdot \langle f \rangle \in dom(t)$, and
- $\pi([p]) = c$ if and only if $t(p) = c$.

We must show that γ is a well-defined function, that the range of γ contains only well-formed graphs, and that it is total, one-to-one, and satisfaction-preserving.

$\gamma(\eta)$ **is a well-formed graph:** We must show that δ and π are well-defined functions, that the domain of π includes only terminals in the graph, and that the graph is connected.

To show that δ is a well-defined function, it suffices to demonstrate that if $[p] = [q]$ (i.e., pRq), then $p \cdot \langle f \rangle R q \cdot \langle f \rangle$ wherever defined. Assume pRq and $p \cdot \langle f \rangle \in dom(t)$. Then, by definition of eqtree, $p \cdot \langle f \rangle R q \cdot \langle f \rangle$.

Similarly, if pRq, then $t(p) = t(q)$, so that if $t(p) = c$, then $t(q) = c$. Thus, π is a well-defined function as well. Furthermore, if $t(p) = c$, then t is undefined at $p \cdot \langle f \rangle$ for any $f \in L$. Consequently, $\delta([p], f)$ is undefined as well, so the domain of π includes only terminals in the graph.

Finally, for all nodes $[p]$ in the graph, $[p] = [\langle \rangle]/p$, so the graph is connected.

γ **is total and one-to-one:**   The function γ is trivially total by construction. We show that it is one-to-one; that is, if $\gamma(\eta) \approx \gamma(\eta')$, then $\eta = \eta'$. For ease of reference, let $\eta = \langle t, R \rangle$, and $\eta' = \langle t', R' \rangle$.

Suppose $\gamma(\eta) \approx \gamma(\eta')$. Because of categoricity (Property 8), it suffices to show that $\eta \leq \eta'$, or equivalently by Definition 13, if $\eta \models \Phi$, then $\eta' \models \Phi$ for all Φ. We need only consider atomic formulas, since the definition of satisfaction reduces satisfaction of nonatomic formulas to satisfaction of atomic formulas.

If $\eta \models p \doteq q$, then pRq and $[p] = [q]$. Since nodes in $\gamma(\eta)$ are the equivalence classes of paths in $dom(\eta)$, it holds that $\gamma(\eta)/p = \gamma(\eta)/q$; the same must hold for any isomorphic graph, so $\gamma(\eta')/p = \gamma(\eta')/q$. Thus, $pR'q$ and $\eta' \models p \doteq q$.

If $\eta \models p \doteq c$, then $t(p) = c$, so $\pi(p) = c$ for π the labeling function of $\gamma(\eta)$. The labeling function π' for the isomorphic graph must also obey $\pi'(p) = c$; therefore, $t'(p) = c$ and $\eta' \models p \doteq c$.

γ **is satisfaction-preserving:**   We must show that $\eta \models \Phi$ if and only if $\gamma(\eta) \models \Phi$. Since satisfaction for nonatomic formulas is defined identically for the two model classes, we need consider only the atomic cases. By definition of satisfaction for eqtrees, $\eta \models p \doteq q$ if and only if pRq if and only if $[p] = [q]$ by definition of γ. Since in general $[r] = [\langle \rangle]/r = n_0/r = \gamma(\eta)/r$, it holds that $\gamma(\eta)/p = \gamma(\eta)/q$, so, by definition of satisfaction for graphs, $\gamma(\eta) \models p \doteq q$.

For equations of the form $p \doteq c$, $\eta \models p \doteq c$ if and only if $t(p) = c$ if and only if $\pi([p]) = c$ by definition of γ. Replacing $[p]$ with the equivalent $\gamma(\eta)/p$ as before, we conclude that $\pi(\gamma(\eta)/p) = c$, so $\gamma(\eta) \models p \doteq c$. $\square$

This theorem allows us to conclude immediately that the equivalence classes of graphs are at least as good a model class for $\mathcal{L}_{L,C}$ as the eqtrees. In particular, we are guaranteed that graph models are logically and denotationally sound and complete, as well as categorical, and that minimal graph models exist. The minimal graph model for Φ is merely $\gamma(metm(\Phi))$.

Furthermore, nodes in the graph corresponding to an eqtree correspond to equivalence classes of paths in the eqtree. Thus, if the eqtree is rational, the graph will be finite. Since τ and γ are inverses, we can conclude that the rational eqtrees are isomorphic to equivalence classes of finite graphs. The finite graphs then have all the semantic advantages of the eqtrees, yet all the computational advantages of being finite.

4.4.3   Computational Properties of Graph Models

To complete the demonstration of the utility of finite graph models, we must demonstrate that the computational properties stated in Section 3.1 hold. In particular, we show the following properties:

- Finiteness of minimal models of atomic formulas

- Finiteness preservation for model operations

- Computability of operations

Since all minimal eqtree models are rational (Proposition 72), all minimal graph models are finite.

Finiteness is preserved for the model operations because minimal-modelhood is preserved (Lemmas 36, 37, and 38).

Computing the extraction and embedding operations is quite straightforward. To extract the subgraph of g at address p, we merely take the subgraph of g rooted at g/p. More formally stated, given a graph $g = \langle N, n_0, \delta, \pi \rangle$, the extraction g/p is the graph $\langle N', n_0/p, \delta', \pi' \rangle$ where N' is the subset of N reachable by δ from n_0/p, δ' is the subset of δ' whose first argument domain is N', and π' is the corresponding subset of π with domain N'.

To embed g under the path p, we add a chain of nodes above the previous root node of g, and make the topmost one the new root. The embedding $g\backslash\langle f_1 \cdots f_k \rangle$ is the graph $\langle N \cup \{n'_0, \ldots, n'_{k-1}\}, n'_0, \delta', \pi' \rangle$, where the n'_i are k new nodes, δ' is an extension of δ that takes $\delta'(n'_{i-1}, f_i)$ onto n'_i for $1 \leq i < k - 1$ and $\delta'(n'_{k-1}, f_k)$ onto n_0.

Graphical representations of these two procedures appear in Figure 4.4. The input graph g is so labeled; the output graph of the operation is printed with darker lines.

Finally, we resolve the question of computing the informational union of two models, which lies at the heart of the computational use of any model class.

4.4.4   Relation of Graph Models to Congruence Closure

Unfortunately, the definition of minimal graphs as $\gamma(metm(\Phi))$ is not computationally effective, relying in part on the computation of all consequences of Φ (in the $metm$ construction). In this section we show how a computationally effective construction can be defined that is consistent

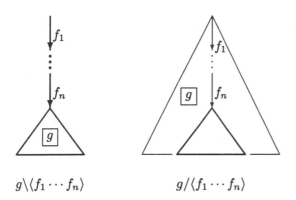

$$g \backslash \langle f_1 \cdots f_n \rangle \qquad\qquad g / \langle f_1 \cdots f_n \rangle$$

Figure 4.4
Extraction and embedding on feature graphs

with the earlier definition of informational union (Definition 20). The construction is based on a congruence closure computation, for which efficient algorithms are known. Thus, this section can be viewed as a general proof of the correctness of a graph-construction algorithm that computes congruence closure. It is interesting to note that virtually every implementation of an interpreter for a constraint-based grammar formalism we know of uses such an algorithm.

Given a frame $s = \langle N, n_0, \delta \rangle$ and a relation R on N, the *congruence closure* of R is the least equivalence relation $\equiv$ on N containing R such that if $u \equiv v$, $\delta(u, f) = u'$, and $\delta(v, f) = v'$, then $u' \equiv v'$.

Congruence closure can be used to define a notion of informational union of graphs that, we show, is consistent with Definition 20—which in turn depends on the foregoing definition of subsumption.

Given graphs $g_1 = \langle N_1, n_1, \delta_1, \pi_1 \rangle$ and $g_2 = \langle N_2, n_2, \delta_2, \pi_2 \rangle$, we construct the frame $s = \langle N_1 \oplus N_2, n_1, \delta_1 \cup \delta_2 \rangle$.[1] Here $\oplus$ is disjoint union and the union of the δs is over that disjoint-union domain. This union is a function, since the two domains are kept disjoint.

Now form the congruence closure $\equiv$ of R over s, where R is given exhaustively by $n_1 R n_2$. Construct the contracted frame

$$s_= = \langle (N_1 \oplus N_2)/\equiv, [n_1], (\delta_1 \cup \delta_2)/\equiv \rangle$$

---

[1] The reader may have noticed that s is not connected, thus necessitating our weakening the connectedness requirement on frames.

Again, $\delta_\equiv = (\delta_1 \cup \delta_2)/\equiv$ is a function, since if $\delta_\equiv([m], f) = u$, $\delta_\equiv([n], f) = v$, and $[m] = [n]$, then $u = v$ by definition of congruence closure. In addition, the contracted frame is connected, since the roots of the two unconnected parts of s have been identified.

Under certain conditions stated in the next proposition, it is possible to define a partial labeling function $\pi_\equiv : terminals(s) \rightarrow C$, defined as follows:

$$\pi_\equiv([n]) = \begin{cases} \pi_i(n) & \text{if } n \in N_i \text{ and } \pi_i(n) \text{ is defined} \\ \text{undefined} & \text{otherwise} \end{cases} \qquad (4.4.1)$$

In general, $\pi_\equiv$ may not be well defined—for instance, if $[n] = [m]$ and $\pi_1(n) \neq \pi_2(m)$. Furthermore, even if well defined, $\pi_\equiv$ may not be an appropriate labeling function for $s_\equiv$, as its domain may not be limited to just the terminals.

Finally, define the informational union of g_1 and g_2 (written $g_1 \sqcup g_2$) as follows:

$$g_1 \sqcup g_2 = \begin{cases} \langle s_\equiv, \pi_\equiv \rangle & \text{if } \pi_\equiv \text{ exists and } dom(\pi_\equiv) \subseteq terminals(s_\equiv) \\ \text{undefined} & \text{otherwise} \end{cases}$$

That the operation just defined is in fact an informational union is proved in the next proposition.

PROPOSITION 78 Given graphs g_1, g_2, and g, if $g_1 \leq g$ and $g_2 \leq g$, then $g_1 \sqcup g_2$ is defined and $g_1 \sqcup g_2 \leq g$.

We must show first that $g_1 \sqcup g_2$ is defined.

Let $g = \langle N, n_0, \delta, \pi \rangle$ and $g_i = \langle N_i, n_i, \delta_i, \pi_i \rangle$ for $i = 1, 2$. Since the g_i individually subsume g, there must exist witness graph homomorphisms $m_i : g_i \rightarrow g$ given by

$$\begin{aligned} m_i(n_i) &= n_0 \\ m_i(\delta_i(n, f)) &= \delta(m_i(n), f) & \text{for all } n \in N_i, f \in F \\ \pi_i(n) &= \pi(m_i(n)) & \text{for all } n \in N_i \end{aligned} \quad .$$

Consider the frame $s = \langle N_1 \oplus N_2, n_1, \delta_1 \cup \delta_2 \rangle$. Construct the mapping $m : s \rightarrow g$ such that

$$m(n) = m_i(n) \quad \text{if} \quad n \in N_i \quad .$$

The construction above defines the congruence relation $\equiv$ and the contracted frame

$$s_\equiv = \langle (N_1 \oplus N_2)/\!\equiv, [n_1], (\delta_1 \cup \delta_2)/\!\equiv \rangle \quad .$$

We use the same congruence to define the contracted mapping

$$m_\equiv([n]) = m(n) \quad .$$

To show that $m_\equiv$ is a well-defined function, we must prove that if $n \equiv n'$, then $m_\equiv([n]) = m_\equiv([n'])$—that is, $m(n) = m(n')$—or alternatively, that the kernel of m (written $ker(m)$) contains $\equiv$. Since $\equiv$ is the least equivalence relation closed under δ such that $n_1 \equiv n_2$, it is sufficient to show that $ker(m)$ is a congruence relation such that $n_1 \, ker(m) \, n_2$. Clearly, $ker(m)$ is an equivalence relation, since it is the kernel of a function, and $n_1 \, ker(m) \, n_2$ because $m(n_1) = m_1(n_1) = n_0 = m_2(n_2) = m(n_2)$. Assume now that $n \, ker(m) \, n'$ with $n \in N_i$ and $n' \in N_j$. Then, if $m((\delta_1 \cup \delta_2)(n, f))$ is defined, we can conclude that

$$
\begin{aligned}
m((\delta_1 \cup \delta_2)(n, f)) &= m_i(\delta_i(n, f)) \\
&= \delta(m_i(n), f) \\
&= \delta(m(n), f) \\
&= \delta(m_j(n'), f) \\
&= m_j(\delta_j(n', f)) \\
&= m((\delta_1 \cup \delta_2)(n', f)) \quad ;
\end{aligned}
$$

that is, $(\delta_1 \cup \delta_2)(n, f) \, ker(m) \, (\delta_1 \cup \delta_2)(n', f)$, and $ker(m)$ is a congruence containing $\equiv$. Thus, $m_\equiv$ is a well-defined function.

Continuing the $\sqcup$ construction, we must now show that the graph $\langle s_\equiv, \pi_\equiv \rangle$, where $\pi_\equiv$ is given by

$$
\pi_\equiv([n]) = \begin{cases} \pi_i(n) & \text{if } n \in N_i \text{ and } \pi_i(n) \text{ is defined} \\ \text{undefined} & \text{otherwise} \end{cases} \quad ,
$$

is well defined; that is, $\pi_\equiv$ is a function from the terminals of $s_\equiv$.

We have shown above that if $n \equiv n'$, then $m(n) = m(n')$. Assume that $n \in dom(\pi_i)$ and $n' \in dom(\pi_j)$. Then,

$$
\begin{aligned}
\pi_\equiv([n]) &= \pi_i(n) \\
&= \pi(m_i(n)) \\
&= \pi(m(n)) \\
&= \pi(m(n')) \\
&= \pi(m_j(n')) \\
&= \pi_j(n') \\
&= \pi_\equiv([n']) \quad ,
\end{aligned}
$$

so $\pi_\equiv$ is a well-defined function. Now, assume that $\pi_\equiv([n])$ is defined for some $n \in N_i$, and also that $\delta_\equiv([n'], f)$ is defined for some $n \in N_j$ such that $n \equiv n'$. Then, $\pi_i(n) = \pi(m_i(n)) = \pi(m(n))$ is defined, as is $\delta_j(n', f)$, and $m_j(\delta_j(n', f)) = \delta(m_j(n'), f) = \delta(m(n'), f)$. Since $m(n) = m(n')$, both $\pi(m(n))$ and $\delta(m(n), f)$ are defined, contradicting the well-formedness of the graph g. By contradiction, $\pi_\equiv$ must take its domain in $terminals(s)$. In sum, $g_1 \sqcup g_2$ is a well-defined graph.

We demonstrate further that $g_1 \sqcup g_2 \leq g$, by using $m_\equiv$ as a witness to the subsumption relationship.

The mapping $m_\equiv : g_1 \sqcup g_2 \to g$ obeys the following conditions:

$$m_\equiv([n_1]) = m_1(n_1) = n_0$$

$$
\begin{aligned}
m_\equiv(\delta_\equiv([n], f)) &= m_\equiv([[(\delta_1 \cup \delta_2)(n, f)]]) \\
&= m((\delta_1 \cup \delta_2)(n, f)) \\
&= m(\delta_i(n, f)) && \text{if } n \in N_i \\
&= m_i(\delta_i(n, f)) && \text{if } n \in N_i \\
&= \delta(m_i(n), f) && \text{if } n \in N_i \\
&= \delta(m(n), f) \\
&= \delta(m_\equiv([n]), f)
\end{aligned}
$$

$$
\begin{aligned}
\pi(m_\equiv([n])) &= \pi(m(n)) \\
&= \pi(m_i(n)) && \text{if } n \in N_i \\
&= \pi_i(n) && \text{if } n \in N_i \\
&= \pi_\equiv([n])
\end{aligned}
$$

Thus, $m_\equiv$ is a witness of the subsumption $g \sqcup g' \leq g''$.   □

We can conclude from this proposition that the presented $\sqcup$ construction based on congruence closure actually computes the informational union of two feature graphs.

5 Parsing as Type Inference

Finally, we turn to a more speculative topic: the relation between these techniques and those devised for characterizing computer languages. In so doing, we attempt to bring out more clearly the similarities and differences between the two classes of languages.

As a concrete example of the techniques described in Chapters 2 and 3, and as an application of those techniques to both natural and computer languages, we define a more expressive logic than $\mathcal{L}_{L,C}$, extending the equational constraints of $\mathcal{L}_{L,C}$ to encompass inequations; we provide a class of models for the logic and algorithms for computing with the models on the basis of the foundations built up in Chapter 4. The existence of the logic and its model structure with appropriate properties immediately gives rise to algorithms for interpreting grammars in the formalism constructed around the logic. This chapter discusses the connections to computer languages and the inequality logic.

Constraint-based grammar formalisms have been proposed separately in linguistics, computational linguistics, and artificial-intelligence research as alternatives to previous formalisms in use in the respective areas, but independently of work in the active field of computer-language specification. Yet natural languages and computer languages share a reliance on well-formedness conditions that, one might hope, would facilitate a concomitant sharing of tools and technology.

In this chapter, we discuss a view alluded to previously in Section 2.4 under which the methods for describing well-formedness conditions for natural languages and computer languages can be unified, so that the study of natural-language grammar formalisms might benefit from existing results for computer languages, and vice versa, and so that the similarities and differences between the two classes of languages can be more accurately pinpointed. In particular, the informational constraints of the constraint-based grammar formalisms can be viewed as filling the role of typing rules for a programming language. Consequently, we refer to this unifying analogy under the rubric *parsing as type inference*, using the term 'type inference' in its sense from computer science type theory—the inference of a type or types for an expression according to explicit rules in a deductive calculus of types. According to this view, the notions of *category* from linguistic theory and *type* from computer science are identified.

Such a rapprochement of the fields of computer- and natural-language description would have several benefits:

- It would provide another mathematical foundation to current practice in linguistics and computational linguistics.

- It would allow the use of insights from type theory in extending linguistic formalisms.

- It would make possible the application of current techniques in computational linguistics to increase the flexibility of computer languages.

- It would permit a fairer and more accurate comparison of well-formedness issues that arise in the two classes of languages.

Each of these benefits will be seen, to a greater or lesser extent, in the following sections. We start (in Section 5.1) by examining traditional wisdom as to the differences between natural-language and computer-language structure, and argue that the analogy of parsing as type inference provides the basis for a fairer analysis. Section 5.2 describes some less often noted distinctions between the two classes of languages that the analogy highlights and, as a digression, proposes an application to computer-language design. Section 5.3 describes in more detail the topic introduced in Section 2.4—the use of constraint-based techniques for describing computer-language well-formedness conditions, including typing constraints. This application will reveal insufficiencies in the purely equational system based on $\mathcal{L}_{L,C}$ for the purposes of describing computer languages, and, surprisingly, natural languages as well; two extensions to $\mathcal{L}_{L,C}$ will be motivated thereby. One of these, the addition of inequalities, will serve as the topic of Section 5.4, which develops an extended logic $\mathcal{L}_{L,C}^{\leq}$ following the techniques of previous chapters. A discussion of models for $\mathcal{L}_{L,C}^{\leq}$ occupies Section 5.5.

5.1   Natural and Computer Languages

A proposal to unify the techniques for specifying the structures of computer and natural languages may seem surprising. The inclination at first blush is to believe that the structural similarity of the two kinds of language is minimal. In support of this view, note that the fields of natural-language parsing and programming-language parsing have been viewed as exhibiting different properties and requirements. For instance, it is commonly held that

- Programming languages require only coarse-grained distinctions among types of expressions (e.g., *nonterminals* in a BNF grammar) whereas linguistic theories postulate vast numbers of such expression *categories*, and

- Natural languages are fraught with ambiguity, whereas programming languages can be designed to be completely unambiguous.

Such comparisons can be misleading, however. Because the fields of programming-language and natural-language processing have diverged, there is a danger that putative comparisons between the two may not actually cover comparable areas. In particular, much of the difference at this level of detail (and, as we will see, at a much finer grain) may be epiphenomena stemming from a difference in terminology, especially a distinction between what is referred to as "syntax" in the two fields versus the actual techniques for describing *well-formedness*.

Traditionally, computer-language designers have described the "syntax" of their languages by means of simple context-free grammars or their equivalents. Such a description does not, however, exhaust what might be regarded as well-formedness conditions on computer-language expressions. In recent years programming languages have increasingly incorporated the idea of *types* and type constraints into their well-formedness conditions. That is, certain expressions are well typed, and thus well formed; other "syntactically allowed" expressions are ill typed, hence ill formed. Computer-language well-formedness is thus typically described in two tiers of description: syntax proper and typing constraints.[1]

As seen in previous chapters, natural languages are typically described by grammatical formalisms from linguistic theory that are much richer and more expressive in their descriptive apparatus than context-free grammars; indeed, they perform the same work as the context-free and

---

[1] The fact that typing constraints are often referred to as "static semantics" does not deny their role in defining well-formedness. It does, however, provide evidence of the divergence in terminology in the two fields.

LT terminology	Concept	CS terminology
Syntax {	Coarse-grained distributional properties	Syntax
	Fine-grained typing constraints }	Semantics }
Semantics	Denotation	

Figure 5.1
Well-formedness terminology in computer science (CS) and linguistic theory (LT)

typing constraints on computer languages combined. Thus, a comparison of the two fields of language processing on the basis of what they respectively consider "syntax" or "parsing" is inherently prone to confusion. Figure 5.1 highlights the terminological situation.

Looking again at the two distinctions cited above from this new perspective, the mismatch between the fields seems less prominent. First, type theory in computer science enables quite fine-grained distinctions to be made among the expressions in a language. It admits means of associating structured information—types—with expressions, in a way remarkably reminiscent of that used in linguistic grammatical formalisms. Thus, the mismatch in the granularity of expression types all but vanishes if we view the task of typing in computer science as paralleling the notion of grammaticality in linguistics. Indeed, our claim extends further; the actual type-structuring mechanisms postulated in computer science are of direct relevance to linguistic theory.

Second, the difference in ambiguity between the language classes may in some cases be more superficial than actual. The nonambiguity of programming languages is to a great extent a consequence of the two-tier method of defining well-formedness. Ambiguity at the first level is minimized by fiat. When ambiguity does arise (as with dangling *elses*), ad hoc rules are typically introduced to choose a structuring before types are inferred, so that the ambiguity does not extend into the second tier. Finally, local ambiguity at the type level (overloading, multiple typings, polymorphic type schemas, and the like) is generally not considered in informal statements of the "nonambiguity of programming-language syntax." Again the difference is terminological.

Thus, these apparent structural differences between computer and natural languages lessen when perceived from this vantage on what constitutes well-formedness in the fields. In computer languages, well-typing is not considered as being a part of "syntax in the small", whereas in natural languages, current linguistic theories make the fine-grained "well-typing" the critical factor. If we normalize for this distinction, that is, if we view the two tiers of computer-language description as parallel to the single tier of well-formedness constraints postulated in formal syntactic theories, the superficial differences in the two problems become less prominent. Instead, we are left with a metaphor for parsing in general that allows useful insights into both linguistic theory and computer-language design.

Indeed, not only do certain of the differences between the well-formedness properties of the two classes of language appear diminished, but under this view, a rich set of commonalities can be mapped. As alluded to in Section 2.4, the properties of structure, partiality, and primacy of equational constraints arise in the information associated with computer-language expressions, the types, as well as the grammatical information presupposed in linguistic work. For instance, consider the type $\alpha \rightarrow \alpha$ of the polymorphic identity function. This type exhibits structure in that it includes specifications for the component types of the function's argument and result. Polymorphism introduces a partiality into the description: the type is less constrained than the integer identity function $INT \rightarrow INT$; expressions of the polymorphic type therefore participate in more grammatical constructions than do expressions of the more specific type. Finally, constraints on types are expressed as identities of subtypes; in the example, a shared-variable notation is used to constrain the types of the argument and result to be identical. Similarly, type-inference rules use logical variables (implicit equations) in stating typing constraints.

Just as unification of graphs is used to solve sets of equational constraints that arise in the course of parsing, yielding a minimal model for the equations, unification can serve as the basic technique for type inference by using it to build the most general typing for an expression, as first proposed by Hindley (1969).

There are, of course, fundamental differences between computer and natural languages, stemming from their disparate functions and their quite distinct genetic processes. These differences include important issues of determinacy and precision of meaning, degree of context dependence, and other semantic and pragmatic factors. The previous discussion notwithstanding, the differences even impinge on the well-formedness conditions for the two language classes; much of linguistics is predicated on a somewhat artificial distinction between grammatical and ungrammatical strings, a distinction that is perfectly felicitous for programming languages, as anyone knows who has waded through long lists of compiler-generated syntax errors, ephemera of the rigidness of programming-language syntax. It should be clear that we are not claiming that natural and computer languages are uniformly similar in all areas. Rather, we argue that the differences that do exist—specifically with respect to well-formedness conditions—may not reside in the places traditionally thought of, and that a view of natural-language syntax as analogous to typing constraints for computer languages elucidates both the similarities and the differences. One important difference identified in this way is the topic of the next section.

5.2   A Difference in Semantics

Traditionally, the semantics for type theories have assigned types a denotation that is the set of all values of that type. Under this conception, value expressions denote values and type expressions denote sets of values. In a correct type-inference system for the language, a typing (composed of a value expression and a type expression) can be inferred just in case the denotation of the value expression is a member of the denotation of the type expression.

Type information in a type system with this sort of correctness property necessarily conflates information about two independent properties of an expression: its *denotation*—the value specified by the expression of that type—and its *distribution*—the grammatical context in which it can occur. Because computer languages can be carefully constructed so as to exhibit maximal orthogonality of constructs, it is typically unnecessary to limit the contexts in which an expression can occur as long as it is semantically meaningful to allow it. Therefore, in computer languages, the type information governing distribution is completely characterized by that governing denotation, and a semantics for types in terms of semantic domains (i.e., in terms of *denotational* properties) is felicitous.[2]

Such an approach seems inappropriate for natural languages, however, because, in contrast to programming languages, the permissible combinatorial arrangements of expressions are only partially governed by properties of what is most naturally considered the appropriate semantic domain of the expressions, that is, something corresponding to semantic content. This statement is merely a weak and nondogmatic version of the thesis of autonomy of syntax; it states that syntax is not completely supervenient upon semantics.[3] Thus, in natural language there is far more information in a type expression than could reasonably be expected to impinge on a semantic value.

Instead, a more natural view of semantics for natural-language type expressions is a (partial) description of the *distributional* properties of a particular value. Such a set of properties, of course, has an extension. Thus, one can say of certain values that they belong to a given type or not. But, in the case of natural languages, the values will be associated to value expressions only indirectly through the typing mechanism, so that this phase can be seen to contribute nothing of real interest at this conceptual level. (We have seen how it can contribute at the implementation stage, however.) Thus, although the parsing as type inference analogy is quite robust in both natural and computer languages, important differences between the two remain. One ramification of this observation is that the notion of correctness of a typing, which is implicit in the conflation of distributional and denotational information in a type system, lacks the independent justification in natural languages that it enjoys in computer languages.

---

[2]Of course, this is a gross simplification. Until recently, explicit examination of programming-language semantics was a post hoc phenomenon, and so such considerations were not taken into account in language design. Furthermore, implementation issues can cause designers to override the elegance of orthogonality of constructs. Since these gratuitous distributional distinctions are small in number, they can typically be hidden in the first tier of well-formedness description.

[3]Even linguistic methodologies that do try to draw a strong relationship between denotation and distribution—categorial grammars being the foremost example—are forced to use diacritics (multiple slashes, subscripts, side conditions on application, and so forth) to limit the overgeneration of the system. The prevalence of such diacritics provides a good yardstick of the "distance" between denotational and distributional properties of natural-language expressions, at least at our current level of linguistic knowledge.

A Digression   We have argued above that natural-language descriptions can be seen as conflating the computer-language notions of parsing and type inference in a single specification. Such a conflation might in certain cases have benefits for computer-language specification as well. For instance, expressions that are ambiguous according to a simple context-free grammar but disambiguated by typing are, under current methods, disambiguated without recourse to their typing information, thereby leading to anomalous behavior. For instance, in a language with an infix syntax for conditionals (like C), one of the two expressions

$$x \le y \to x; y$$

and

$$x \le positive(y) \to y; -y$$

would be deemed ungrammatical, although typing completely disambiguates both. Under the intuitive (well-typed) disambiguation, the first expression computes the minimum of x and y, while the second determines whether x is less than or equal to $|y|$.

Another example is notorious among cognoscenti of the ML programming language.[4] Suppose we define a datatype of binary trees with

```
datatype tree = Leaf | Node of tree * tree;
```

and attempt to use it in a function to compute the size of a tree as the number of leaves, that is,

```
fun size Leaf = 1
  | size Node(left, right) = size left + size right;
```

Although this definition by cases is quite natural, it fails to type-check, because the parse takes the expression `size Node(left, right)` to be a function applied consecutively to a constructor function `Node` and a pair `(left, right)`, rather than the intended application of `size` to the application `Node(left, right)`. It is therefore necessary to introduce parentheses to force the alternate parse:

```
fun size Leaf = 1
  | size (Node(left, right)) = size left + size right;
```

---

[4]I am indebted to Carl Gunter for pointing out the pertinence of this example.

This annoyance is familiar to anyone who has programmed in ML; the elegance of ML's quite natural pattern-matching notation for defining functions by cases based on the type constructors used to construct the data is degraded by the requirement to fully parenthesize the data. Here again, types could disambiguate the otherwise ambiguous syntax in the intuitive way.

Thus, the use of the two-tiered model of well-formedness, a reflection of the separation of parsing and type inference in computer languages, results in anomalous behavior that can be easily prevented by adopting the view of parsing as type inference for computer languages as well. Such a move, which seems in keeping with the philosophy behind the use of strong typing, has at least anecdotal evidence supporting its utility.

An objection to the conflation of parsing and type inference in computer languages, however, is that the efficiency of context-free—especially unambiguous context-free—parsing would be lost. This problem has been addressed to a certain extent in the computational linguistic work in this area, and methods have been devised for the efficient parsing of constraint-based formalisms. Of special interest is the use of LR-like techniques in linguistics to model psycholinguistic phenomena (Shieber, 1983). It was shown that in cases in which other linguistic constraints fail to disambiguate, a simple LR disambiguation strategy mimics exactly the types of parsing preferences humans have been shown to exhibit. It is presumably no coincidence that these disambiguation techniques are similar to those found in parsing solutions to the dangling-*else* and other computer-language parsing problems. The ability to view parsing as type inference opens up the possibility of efficient algorithms for parsing computer languages that resort to such ad hoc disambiguation techniques only if typing constraints fail to disambiguate, as seems to be appropriate for natural languages.[5]

5.3   Constraint-Based Computer-Language Formalisms

At present, type-inference algorithms for computer languages are described on a language-by-language basis by explicit procedural description or specialized inference rules. The availability of simple mecha-

---

[5]Recall that Section 3.6.3 describes how shift-reduce parsing—including the LR disambiguation method (Shieber, 1983)—can be modeled with the abstract algorithm of Chapter 3.

nisms for grammar formalisms that can describe types directly—a by-product of research in computational linguistics—opens the possibility that these mechanisms could serve as tools for declaratively describing type-inference algorithms for a variety of computer languages in a uniform manner, and with immediate implementations available.[6] In this section, we pursue the possibility of using constraint-based techniques for computer languages, but first turn to the modeling of categorial grammars as an initial step toward applicative languages.

Constraint-Based Categorial Grammars Recently, a style of analysis based on categorial grammar has become influential in the constraint-based grammar formalism community. By adding the structuring and partiality of constraint formalisms to simple categorial rules, many of the difficulties of using categorial grammars for natural languages can be overcome (Uszkoreit, 1986; Karttunen, 1986; Zeevat, 1988). We will demonstrate how a classical categorial grammar can be embedded in a constraint formalism as an intermediate step toward using the formalism for computer-language type inference. The formalism will be based on $\mathcal{L}_{L,C}$.

The categorial grammar will have two rules corresponding to forward and backward application.[7]

$R \rightarrow F\ A$
   $\langle F\ type\ constr \rangle \doteq rightfunctor$
   $\langle F\ type\ result \rangle \doteq \langle R \rangle$
   $\langle F\ type\ arg \rangle \doteq \langle A \rangle$

$R \rightarrow A\ F$
   $\langle F\ type\ constr \rangle \doteq leftfunctor$
   $\langle F\ type\ result \rangle \doteq \langle R \rangle$
   $\langle F\ type\ arg \rangle \doteq \langle A \rangle$

The first rule allows combination of a functor and its argument to the right just in case the functor is one that takes its argument to the right.

---

[6] A similar goal is pursued quite successfully by Kahn (1987).

[7] In the grammar rules in the remainder of this text, we will use a rule notation in which the small integers in constraints are replaced by the "names" of the corresponding constituents; thus, $\langle F\ type\ arg \rangle \doteq \langle A \rangle$ will be written, rather than $\langle 1\ type\ arg \rangle \doteq \langle 2 \rangle$. The modification can be viewed purely as syntactic sugar for readability.

The rule is a direct encoding of the standard categorial rule of forward application,[8]

$$R \to R/A \; A \quad ,$$

where the forward slash (/) corresponds to a rightward functor. Similarly, the second rule encodes

$$R \to A \; R\backslash A \quad .$$

Here the backward slash (\) corresponds to a leftward functor.

Lexical entries for proper nouns or plural common nouns (type NP) and transitive verbs (type $(S\backslash NP)/NP$) can also be encoded.

$A \; \to \;$ 'Nature'
     $\langle A \; type \; constr \rangle \doteq np$
     $\langle A \; type \; agr \; num \rangle \doteq singular$
     $\langle A \; type \; agr \; per \rangle \doteq third$

$A \; \to \;$ 'vacuums'
     $\langle A \; type \; constr \rangle \doteq np$
     $\langle A \; type \; agr \; num \rangle \doteq plural$
     $\langle A \; type \; agr \; per \rangle \doteq third$

$F \; \to \;$ 'abhors'
     $\langle F \; type \; constr \rangle \doteq rightfunctor$
     $\langle F \; type \; result \; constr \rangle \doteq leftfunctor$
     $\langle F \; type \; result \; constr \; result \; constr \rangle \doteq s$
     $\langle F \; type \; result \; constr \; arg \; constr \rangle \doteq np$
     $\langle F \; type \; result \; constr \; arg \; agr \; num \rangle \doteq singular$
     $\langle F \; type \; result \; constr \; arg \; agr \; per \rangle \doteq third$
     $\langle F \; type \; arg \; constr \rangle \doteq np$

$F \; \to \;$ 'abhorred'
     $\langle F \; type \; constr \rangle \doteq rightfunctor$
     $\langle F \; type \; result \; constr \rangle \doteq leftfunctor$
     $\langle F \; type \; result \; constr \; result \; constr \rangle \doteq s$
     $\langle F \; type \; result \; constr \; arg \; constr \rangle \doteq np$
     $\langle F \; type \; arg \; constr \rangle \doteq np$

---

[8]We will use the Steedman rather than the Lambek conventions for slash notation.

The reader can verify that parsing according to this grammar involves confirming that the types of the functors match (in the appropriate sense of model existence) their arguments to the left or right as specified lexically. For instance, the string 'Nature abhors vacuums' is admitted, but 'vacuums abhors Nature' is not, as the phrase 'abhors Nature' is a functor taking a singular *NP* to the left. The inferred type for the phrase 'Nature abhors vacuums' is S, as expected.

A Simple Applicative Language   Modifying the grammar above to perform type inference for a simple applicative programming language is straightforward. Let us assume that all operators in the language are unary and prefix. In this case, only a forward application rule is needed. We will assume that arguments are always parenthesized, so as to eliminate a source of local ambiguity.

$R \rightarrow F (A)$

   $\langle F\ type\ constr \rangle \doteq fn$
   $\langle F\ type\ arg \rangle \doteq \langle A\ type \rangle$
   $\langle F\ type\ result \rangle \doteq \langle R\ type \rangle$
   $\langle F\ env \rangle \doteq \langle A\ env \rangle$
   $\langle A\ env \rangle \doteq \langle R\ env \rangle$

This rule is just the forward application rule above, but with no need to distinguish leftward versus rightward functors, and with an extra feature *env* for keeping track of the environment—the mapping from symbols to their types. The final two equations in this rule state that the environments within which the functor and the argument are interpreted are the same, and are identical to the environment for the whole expression. Another way to view this rule is as the direct encoding of the more traditional type inference rule

$$\frac{E \vdash f : A \rightarrow R \quad E \vdash a : A}{E \vdash f(a) : R}$$

Environments will be encoded as follows: if a symbol s is mapped to a given type encoded as t, the environment e will obey $e/\langle s \rangle = t$. For instance, the environment given in Figure 2.4 encodes the typings $id : \alpha \rightarrow \alpha$ and $+ : INT \rightarrow INT \rightarrow INT$. This environment could well serve as the start structure of the grammar.

For any identifier, its type is just that given by the environment. We can have a single schematic lexical entry for all identifiers ω.

$A \rightarrow \omega$

$\quad \langle A \ env \ \omega \rangle \doteq \langle A \ type \rangle$

Similarly, for all integers ι a schematic entry will suffice.

$A \rightarrow \iota$

$\quad \langle A \ type \ constr \rangle \doteq int$

What we have done is merely to state the constraints on types and environments for a simple applicative language. (The whole grammar can be seen in Figure 2.3.) The general definition of a grammar's language, as defined in Section 3.2, determines a relation between strings and their associated types and binding environments. For instance, the string '$id(+(3)(id(2)))$' is typed as an INT. As a side effect, this grammar/type system can be utilized directly for type inference by the algorithm of Chapter 3, since $\mathcal{L}_{L,C}$, the constraint logic on which it is based, has been shown (in Chapter 4) to satisfy the requisite properties.

5.3.1 Problematic Cases

There are two computer-language phenomena that serve as problematic cases for describing computer-language type inference with the constraint-based techniques introduced so far: binding of variables and generic usage of functions. We will describe both problems here, as well as their relation to problems in natural-language specification, but will develop a full solution only to the second of the problems.

Variable Binding The first problematic case involves the source of the environment. The environment itself should be specified through object-language expressions. In extending the object language with such a construct, say, a '$let \ldots in \ldots$' construct, an extension of the equational constraints of $\mathcal{L}_{L,C}$ will be needed. We might consider adding the following rule·

$E \rightarrow$ 'let' ω '$=$' D 'in' B

$\quad \langle E \ env \rangle \doteq \langle D \ env \rangle$

$\quad \langle E \ type \rangle \doteq \langle B \ type \rangle$

$\quad \langle E \ env \rangle \doteq \langle B \ env \rangle$

$\quad \langle B \ env \ \omega \rangle \doteq \langle D \ type \rangle$

This would admit the string '$let \ x = 3 \ in \ id(x)$' to be typed as an INT, as expected. As a side effect, however, the environment of the entire expression, not only that of the body, has the identifier x bound as type INT. Thus, the expression '$let\ x = id\ in\ let\ x = 3\ in\ id(x)$' would be deemed ill typed, as the environment would require x to be typed both as an INT and as $\alpha \rightarrow \alpha$. What is needed is a way of expressing the fact that the environment of the body is identical to the environment of the entire expression *except* that the identifier is bound to the type of the definiens. We introduce a new type of constraint to the constraint logic for that purpose. The predicate symbol *bind* taking four arguments will be used as follows: $bind(p, f, q, r)$ holds if r is the environment that maps every symbol the same as the environment p does, except that f is mapped to q. The following rules of inference capture this informal characterization:

Binding 1: $\dfrac{bind(p, f, q, r) \quad p \cdot \langle g \rangle \doteq s}{r \cdot \langle g \rangle \doteq s}$ where $f \neq g$

Binding 2: $\dfrac{bind(p, f, q, r)}{r \cdot \langle f \rangle \doteq q}$

The corrected rule for variable binding is thus

$$E \rightarrow \text{'}let\text{'}\ \omega\ \text{'}=\text{'}\ D\ \text{'}in\text{'}\ B$$
$$\langle E\ env \rangle \doteq \langle D\ env \rangle$$
$$\langle E\ type \rangle \doteq \langle B\ type \rangle$$
$$bind(\langle E\ env \rangle, \omega, \langle D\ type \rangle, \langle B\ env \rangle) \quad .$$

With this rule, the string '$let\ x = id\ in\ let\ x = 3\ in\ id(x)$' would be typed as an integer, as expected. A version of the *let* construct for functions is also easily defined.

$$E \rightarrow \text{'}let\text{'}\ \omega_1\ (\ \omega_2\ )\ \text{'}=\text{'}\ D\ \text{'}in\text{'}\ B$$
$$bind(\langle E\ env \rangle, \omega_2, \langle \omega_2\ type \rangle, \langle D\ env \rangle)$$
$$\langle E\ type \rangle \doteq \langle B\ type \rangle$$
$$\langle \omega_1\ type\ constr \rangle \doteq function$$
$$\langle \omega_1\ type\ result \rangle \doteq \langle D\ type \rangle$$
$$\langle \omega_1\ type\ argument \rangle \doteq \langle \omega_2\ type \rangle$$
$$bind(\langle E\ env \rangle, \omega_1, \langle \omega_1\ type \rangle, \langle B\ env \rangle)$$

This rule allows for the following typings:

- $let\ f(x) = id(x)\ in\ f(3) : INT$

- *let $f = 3$ in let $f(x) = +(3)(f)$ in $f(2)$: INT*
- *let $x(y) = id(y)$ in let $f(x) = +(3)(x)$ in $x(f(3))$: INT*

The potential applications for a constraint logic with the *bind* relation for natural-language description are numerous. The construct is a declarative counterpart to the grossly procedural overwriting operation that has been added to the PATR formalism (Shieber, 1985b), and could well replace that construct in its several uses.

We will not devote further attention to the details of proving the requisite properties of such a logic, preferring instead to move on to exploring a more interesting extension in fuller detail.

Generic Usage of Functions and Subsumption The second of the stumbling blocks in the way of using extant constraint-based formalisms for this purpose is a particular construct in polymorphic computer languages such as ML, which permit declaration of a polymorphic function and subsequent use in *mutually incompatible* but *separately consistent* applications. In the case of ML, any function defined through the '*let... in...*' construct can be employed in this way. Consider, for example, the program fragment '*let $f(x) = x$ in $f(f)(3)$*'. Here f of polymorphic type $\alpha \to \alpha$ has been used separately as a function $(INT \to INT) \to (INT \to INT)$ and $INT \to INT$, each of which is consistent with the defined type, but which are mutually incompatible. The entire expression, of course, is well typed as an *INT* and evaluates to 3.

Using simple equations to describe type information from the three occurrences of the function is clearly too restrictive. Intuitively, we want to require only that the types associated with the uses of the function are individually *subsumed* by (rather than being identical to) the type associated with the function definition. The addition of inequations to $\mathcal{L}_{L,C}$ would allow statement of the required rule. Uses of identifiers would be admitted by the schematic lexical rule

$A \ \to \ \omega$
$\qquad \langle A \ env \ \omega \rangle \leq \langle A \ type \rangle \qquad ,$

requiring that the type of the use be more instantiated than the type given by the identifier's definition.

Adding subsumption inequations to, say, $\mathcal{L}_{L,C}$ as a new type constraint (in addition to identity) turns out to be a relatively straightfor-

ward task, which we will take up in Section 5.4. However, this simple
addition would allow for a precise statement of this aspect of ML type
inference and parsing in a simple constraint grammar, and, by virtue of
the results of Chapter 3, immediate implementation in a type-inference
system.

The addition of subsumption to constraint-based formalisms has application in natural language as well. The syntactic behavior of coordinate structures in English shows a phenomenon remarkably similar to
that described for ML above. In considering coordinate structures, we
need to determine the syntactic properties of the whole in terms of the
syntax of the parts. A naive view might be that identity of all the subconstituents with the constituent as a whole is required. Thus, given the
requirement that the verb 'hire' requires an NP argument, but not an
AP (adjective phrase) or $\overline{S}$ (sentential complement), we would predict
immediately the following grammaticality distributions:[9]

- Pat hired [$_{NP}$ a Republican] and [$_{NP}$ a banker].
- * Pat hired [$_{NP}$ a Republican] and [$_{AP}$ proud of it].
- * Pat hired [$_{NP}$ a Republican] and [$_{PP}$ at the office].

and so forth.

However, certain verbs in English are less selective of their arguments
than 'hire'. The verb 'become' for instance allows either NP or AP
arguments. Similarly, the verb 'be' allows NP, AP, PP, and VP com-
plements. The identity view of conjunction would then allow an argument to 'become' to be either coordinated NPs or APs but not intermixed coordinate structures. Yet such intermixed structures are in fact
grammatical.[10]

- Pat has become [$_{NP}$ a banker] and [$_{AP}$ very conservative].
- Pat is [$_{NP}$ a Republican] and [$_{AP}$ proud of it].
- Pat is either [$_{AP}$ stupid] or [$_{NP}$ a liar].
- Pat is [$_{AP}$ healthy] and [$_{PP}$ of sound mind].
- That was [$_{NP}$ a rude remark] and [$_{PP}$ in very bad taste].

---

[9]We follow the convention of the linguistics literature in marking ungrammatical
example sentences with a preceding asterisk.
[10]The source of the following examples is Sag et al. (1985).

The phenomenon seems quite widespread; similar cases have been described for German (Zaenen and Karttunen, 1984), French (Pullum and Zwicky, 1986), Hungarian (Macken, 1986), Malayalam (Henniss, 1988), Polish (Dyła, 1984), and other languages.

Previous attempts to relax the identity constraint used the dual of unification, generalization (Pereira and Shieber, 1984), possibly together with various other devices (Sag et al., 1985; Kaplan and Maxwell, 1988). Generalization alone tended to be too permissive; augmented systems have not always been rigorously formulated (although the system of Sag et al. (1985) is an exception) and have tended to be cumbersome. Karttunen (1984) alludes to the difficulty of finding a nice formal solution to the problem when he states that "the only obvious alternative is to say that the merge of 'Dozenten' with 'des' and 'der' is done using two identical copies of the noun features. It works technically but it raises many unsettling general questions about unification."

In fact, what seems to be required is the direct analogue of the ML solution, namely, that the subconstituents' types are subsumed by the coordinate constituent's type (at least for a certain subset of the syntactic information, including part of speech). The following coordination rule is intended to give a flavor for the proposal:

$$E \rightarrow C \ Conj \ D$$
$$\langle E \rangle \leq \langle C \rangle$$
$$\langle E \rangle \leq \langle D \rangle$$

Under the standard $\overline{X}$ decomposition of categories, in which the categories NP, AP, VP, and PP and the subcategorization requirements for 'to be' and 'to become' are as depicted in Figure 5.2, the appropriate subsumption relations would hold, allowing the phrases given above. Thus, an extension of this view of language characterization has application to both natural and computer languages.

5.4 Extending $\mathcal{L}_{L,C}$ with Subsumption Constraints

We now turn to a full consideration of adding constraints of inequality, corresponding to subsumption relations in the model.[11] Augmenting

---

[11]I am indebted to Andreas Eisele and Jochen Dörre for pointing out an error in my earlier formulation of the logic described in this section.

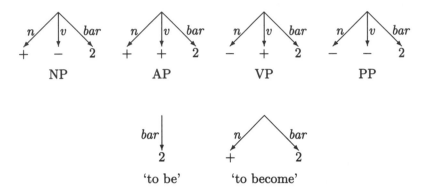

Figure 5.2
$\overline{X}$ decomposition of categories

$\mathcal{L}_{L,C}$ to allow inequations as well as equations is surprisingly simple. We introduce a new relation $\leq$ into the logic obeying the following additional inference rules:

Triviality:

$$\frac{}{\langle\rangle \leq \langle\rangle}$$

Reflexivity:

$$\frac{v \leq p \cdot q}{p \leq p} \qquad \frac{p \cdot q \leq r}{p \leq p}$$

Substitutivity:

$$\frac{q \leq p \quad p \cdot r \leq s}{q \cdot r \leq s} \qquad \frac{v \leq p \cdot r \quad p \leq q}{v \leq q \cdot r}$$

$$\frac{p \leq q \quad p \cdot r \leq p \cdot s}{q \cdot r \leq q \cdot s}$$

Finally, we define equality as mutual inequality.[12]

Equality:

$$\frac{p \leq q \quad q \leq p}{p \doteq q} \qquad \frac{c \leq p}{c \doteq p}$$

In $\mathcal{L}_{L,C}$, the existence of Symmetry allowed a single Reflexivity rule to apply to paths on both sides of an equation. The lack of symmetry

---

[12]The double line is conventionally used to abbreviate several inference rules, one concluding the bottom formula from the top and one each concluding the top formulas from the bottom.

of $\leq$ in the extended logic requires that we explicitly allow Reflexivity to apply to paths on the left and right sides of an equation in order to instantiate the Reflexivity schema of Section 2.7.1 exhaustively.

Similarly, we must explicitly differentiate three roles of Substitutivity, conflated in $\mathcal{L}_{L,C}$ by the availability of Symmetry. Substitution for a path prefix can occur on both the left and right sides of an inequation, as stated in the first two Substitutivity rules, which also capture the contravariant nature of inequations. These rules can be thought of in informational terms. The first, for instance, states that if p contains more information than q, then anything with more information about an aspect of p has more information about that aspect of q. The second makes a similar claim. In short, these two rules state that the set of *properties* true of a path (such as the property of p given by $v \leq p \cdot r$) increases as information does.

It is also necessary to codify that the set of *relations* increases as information does. In particular, if an inequation holds under a path p, it should hold under any more informative path q. This requirement is stated explicitly as the third Substitutivity rule above, as it is not derivable from the first two. In $\mathcal{L}_{L,C}$, of course, its counterpart follows from Symmetry and two uses of Substitutivity.

With these rules, the appropriate instances of the Substitutivity rule schema of Section 2.7.1 follow as well. For example, the instance

$$\frac{q \doteq p \qquad p \cdot r \leq s}{q \cdot r \leq s}$$

can be derived as

$$\frac{\dfrac{q \doteq p}{q \leq p} \qquad p \cdot r \leq s}{q \cdot r \leq s}$$

and the instance

$$\frac{q \doteq p \qquad v \leq q \cdot r}{v \leq p \cdot r}$$

can be derived as

$$\frac{\dfrac{q \doteq p}{q \leq p} \qquad v \leq q \cdot r}{v \leq p \cdot r} \quad .$$

Similarly, the Triviality, Symmetry, Reflexivity, and Substitutivity rules for $\doteq$ also follow from the rules for $\leq$ plus Equality.

Triviality:
$$\frac{\langle\rangle \doteq \langle\rangle}{\langle\rangle \leq \langle\rangle}$$

Symmetry:
$$\frac{p \doteq q \quad p \doteq q}{p \leq q \quad q \leq p}$$
$$q \doteq p$$

Reflexivity:
$$\frac{p \cdot q \doteq v}{\dfrac{v \leq p \cdot q}{\dfrac{p \leq p}{p \doteq p}}}$$

Substitutivity:
$$\frac{q \doteq p \quad p \cdot r \doteq s \quad p \cdot r \doteq s \quad q \doteq p}{\dfrac{q \leq p \quad p \cdot r \leq s \quad s \leq p \cdot r \quad p \leq q}{\dfrac{q \cdot r \leq s \qquad s \leq q \cdot r}{q \cdot r \doteq s}}}$$

$$\frac{p \cdot r \doteq c \quad q \doteq p}{\dfrac{c \leq p \cdot r \quad p \leq q}{\dfrac{c \leq q \cdot r}{q \cdot r \doteq c}}}$$

In summary, the rules for $\leq$ (including Equality) provide a complete basis for a logic with both $\leq$ and $\doteq$. In fact, if we regard equations as being merely abbreviatory forms for inequations, we can remove $\doteq$, and the Equality rule, from the logic completely. In this case, the clash rules defining inconsistency of formulas would need to be revised so that equations were translated into the corresponding inequations they abbreviate.

Constant clash: $a \leq p$ and $b \leq p$ (where $a \neq b$)

Constant/compound clash: $a \leq p$ and either $v \leq p \cdot \langle f \rangle$ or $p \cdot \langle f \rangle \leq q$

We will call this logic $\mathcal{L}_{L,C}^{\leq}$. To summarize, the inference rules for $\mathcal{L}_{L,C}^{\leq}$ are as follows:

Triviality:
$$\frac{}{\langle\rangle \leq \langle\rangle}$$

Reflexivity:
$$\frac{v \leq p \cdot q}{p \leq p} \qquad \frac{p \cdot q \leq r}{p \leq p}$$

Substitutivity:
$$\frac{q \leq p \quad p \cdot r \leq s}{q \cdot r \leq s} \qquad \frac{v \leq p \cdot r \quad p \leq q}{v \leq q \cdot r}$$

$$\frac{p \leq q \quad p \cdot r \leq p \cdot s}{q \cdot r \leq q \cdot s}$$

The close relationship of $\mathcal{L}_{L,C}^{\leq}$ to $\mathcal{L}_{L,C}$ should be apparent. The former merely drops the Symmetry rule and, as a consequence, reverts to the multiple instances of the Reflexivity and Substitutivity schemas that Symmetry made redundant for $\mathcal{L}_{L,C}$. This accords with the intuition that the distinction between an equivalence relation ($\doteq$) and a partial ordering ($\leq$) is symmetry.

5.5   Models for $\mathcal{L}_{L,C}^{\leq}$

Following the evolutionary path pursued in developing models for $\mathcal{L}_{L,C}$ in Chapter 4, we can immediately expect that tree models for $\mathcal{L}_{L,C}^{\leq}$ will suffer from the same lack of a distinction between intensional and extensional constraint satisfaction as was problematic for $\mathcal{L}_{L,C}$. Nonetheless, certain properties of the tree models will be useful later, as trees will form one component of a more comprehensive model class, the potrees, which play the role that the eqtrees played with respect to $\mathcal{L}_{L,C}$.

5.5.1   Infinite-Tree Models

The natural method for using trees as models of $\mathcal{L}_{L,C}^{\leq}$ would define satisfaction as follows: A tree t satisfies the equation $c \leq p$ if and only if t/p is defined and $t/p = c$. A tree t satisfies the equation $p \leq q$ if and only if t/p and t/q are both defined and $t/p \leq t/q$. (Here $\leq$ is the natural tree-subsumption ordering defined in Section 4.1.)

As was the case for $\mathcal{L}_{L,C}$, this definition fails to distinguish intensional from extensional satisfaction of inequalities. The tree models are even less appropriate for $\mathcal{L}_{L,C}^{\leq}$; they are not even logically sound. For instance, the tree in Figure 5.3 satisfies $\langle f \rangle \leq \langle g \rangle$ and $\langle ff \rangle \leq \langle fg \rangle$ but not the consequence (by the third rule of Substitutivity) $\langle gf \rangle \leq \langle gg \rangle$.[13]

---

[13] An alternative formulation of inequations by Dörre and Rounds (1990) does allow

Denotational completeness does hold for infinite trees as a model for the inequational logic, however, and the constructions in the proof will be useful in the development of more intensional models. Therefore, we present the proof of denotational completeness here.

PROPOSITION 79 (DENOTATIONAL COMPLETENESS OF INFINITE TREES FOR $\mathcal{L}_{L,C}^{\leq}$) For all $\Phi \in \mathcal{L}_{L,C}^{\leq}$, if Φ is consistent, then there is a $t \in T_{L,C}^{\infty}$ such that $t \models \Phi$.

Proof   The proof is nearly identical to that for Proposition 62. Define $t = itm(\Phi)$, an *infinite-tree model* of Φ, as follows: $t(p) = v$ if and only if either

1. $v \in C$ and $\Phi \vdash v \leq p$, or

2. $v = \bot$ and $\Phi \vdash p \leq p$, but $\Phi \nvdash c \leq p$ for any $c \in C$.

We must show that t is one of the models for Φ, that is, that it is well defined (a true function), prefix-closed, and satisfies Φ.

t **is a function:**   Suppose t were not a function, that is, the definition of $mm(\Phi)$ assigned two distinct values v and v' to a single path p. If v, $v' \in C$, then $\Phi \vdash v \leq p$ and $\Phi \vdash v' \leq p$, so Φ is inconsistent by a constant clash, contra assumption of consistency. If $v \in C$ and $v' = \bot$, then $\Phi \vdash v \leq p$ and $\Phi \nvdash v \leq p$ for any $v \in C$, here too a contradiction. Thus, t must be a function.

t **is prefix-closed:**   Suppose $t(p \cdot \langle f \rangle)$ is defined. We must show that $t(p) = \bot$ to conclude that t is prefix-closed. Now, by definition of itm, either $\Phi \vdash v \leq p \cdot \langle f \rangle$ or $\Phi \vdash p \cdot \langle f \rangle \leq p \cdot \langle f \rangle$. By Reflexivity, $\Phi \vdash p \leq p$. Since Φ is consistent, $\Phi \nvdash c \leq p$ for any $c \in C$. Thus, $t(p) = \bot$ by definition, and t is prefix-closed. Since $\Phi \vdash \langle \rangle \leq \langle \rangle$, the function t must be defined at $\langle \rangle$, as required.

for trees as a logically sound model. In essence, their system does not require the third rule of substitutivity, replacing it with the weaker

$$\frac{p \leq q \quad p \cdot r \doteq p \cdot s}{q \cdot r \doteq q \cdot s} \quad .$$

The stronger rule is motivated by intuitions about the informational interpretation of subsumption.

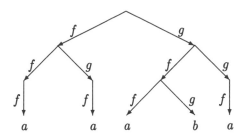

Figure 5.3
A tree model counterexemplifying logical soundness

t satisfies Φ: Finally, we show that t is a model for Φ by proving the stronger result that t is a model for all entailments ϕ of Φ. Any ϕ such that $\Phi \vdash \phi$ is of one of the two forms of atomic formulas. If $\phi = c \leq p$, then $t(p) = c$ by definition, and $t \models \phi$.

If $\phi = p \leq q$, we must show that t/p and t/q are defined and that $t/p \leq t/q$, that is, $t(p \cdot r) \leq t(q \cdot r)$ for all r such that $t(p \cdot r)$ is defined. First, t/p is defined because if $\Phi \vdash p \leq q$, then $\Phi \vdash p \leq p$, so $t(p)$ is defined (by definition of itm); similarly for t/q. Now, suppose $t(p \cdot r)$ is defined. Then either $\Phi \vdash c \leq p \cdot r$ or $\Phi \vdash p \cdot r \leq p \cdot r$ and $\Phi \not\vdash c \leq p \cdot r$ for any $c \in C$. In the former case, we have $\Phi \vdash c \leq q \cdot r$ by Substitutivity, so $t(q \cdot r) = c = t(p \cdot r)$. In the latter case, we can conclude that $\Phi \vdash q \cdot r \leq q \cdot r$ by Substitutivity and Reflexivity. Now it either holds or not that $\Phi \vdash c \leq q \cdot r$ for some $c \in C$ or not. If so, then $t(q \cdot r) = c$; if not, then $t(q \cdot r) = \bot$. Either way, $t(p \cdot r) \leq t(q \cdot r)$. As a consequence, $t/p \leq t/q$ and $t \models p \leq q$. The tree t is therefore a model for ϕ.

Since t is a model for any equation that follows from Φ, it must be a model for Φ itself. We have shown that if Φ is consistent, there exists a model for Φ, namely, that given by $itm(\Phi)$.   □

Having proved denotational completeness for the infinite-tree models, and introducing in the process the notion of a minimal infinite-tree model for a set of inequations, we now turn to an augmented tree model, the potrees.

5.5.2   Potree Models

Just as eqtrees augment trees with an equivalence relation to model intensional identity, *potrees* add a preorder to model a corresponding

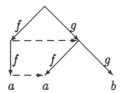

Figure 5.4
An example potree

intensional inequality.[14] A *potree* is a pair $\langle t, R \rangle$, where $t \in T_{L,C}^{\infty}$ is a (possibly infinite) tree and R is a relation over $dom(t)$ (the paths of the tree) such that

1. R is a preorder (a reflexive, transitive relation),

2. If pRp', then $t(p) \leq t(p')$,[15]

3. If pRp' and $p \cdot \langle f \rangle \in dom(t)$, then $p \cdot \langle f \rangle Rp' \cdot \langle f \rangle$, and

4. If pRp' and $p \cdot qRp \cdot s$, then $p' \cdot rRp' \cdot s$.

We will use the notation $T_{L,C}^{\leq}$ for the class of potrees.

Note the close relation of the potrees to the eqtrees (Section 4.3); the key difference is the relaxing of the equivalence relation to a preorder, that is, removal of the requirement that R be symmetric. (As a result, condition 4, stating that R "preserves itself", must be made explicit.) Again this accords with intuition concerning the difference between equality and inequality.

We can notate potrees graphically by drawing the underlying tree, with the overlaid ordering on nodes given by dotted arrows pointing from the subsuming to the subsumed nodes. (Arrows from a node to itself can be omitted for clarity.) For instance, the minimal potree model for the formula $\{a \leq \langle f\ f \rangle, b \leq \langle g\ g \rangle, \langle f \rangle \leq \langle g \rangle\}$ is shown in Figure 5.4.

Properties of Potrees The remainder of this section develops results for potrees that are exactly analogous to those for eqtrees in Section 4.3, namely, Propositions 63 through 70.

---

[14]Even though subsumption is a partial order on trees, the intensional-inequality component of potrees is only a preorder, since it relates *paths*, not trees, and several paths might address identical trees.

[15]Recall that for all $c \in C$, $\perp \leq c$.

First, we demonstrate that the relation component in potrees is a stronger ordering than extensional subsumption.

PROPOSITION 80 For all potrees $\langle t, R \rangle$, if pRp', then $t/p \leq t/p'$.

Proof We must show that $(t/p)(q) \leq (t/p')(q)$ for all q such that $(t/p)(q)$ is defined. Suppose that $(t/p)(q)$ is defined. Then $t(p \cdot q)$ is defined. Now, pRp', so by a simple induction, $p \cdot qRp' \cdot q$ and $t(p \cdot q) \leq t(p' \cdot q) = (t/p')(q)$. By the definition of subsumption on trees, $t/p \leq t/p'$. □

Satisfaction for potrees will follow the definition for eqtrees closely. A potree $\langle t, R \rangle$ satisfies a formula $c \leq p$ just in case $t(p) = c$. The potree satisfies $p \leq q$ if and only if pRq, that is, the subtrees of t at p and q are in an intensional-inequality relationship.

Subsumption on potrees is defined pointwise, as it is for eqtrees.

PROPOSITION 81 (SUBSUMPTION ON POTREES RESPECTS ENTAILMENT)
If whenever $\eta \models \Phi$, $\eta' \models \Phi$ for all $\Phi \in \mathcal{L}^{\leq}_{L,C}$, then $\eta \leq \eta'$.

PROPOSITION 82 (UPWARD CLOSURE OF SUBSUMPTION ON POTREES)
If $\eta \leq \eta'$, then whenever $\eta \models \Phi$, $\eta' \models \Phi$ for all $\Phi \in \mathcal{L}^{\leq}_{L,C}$.

Proof The proofs are only trivially different from those for Propositions 64 and 65, respectively. □

PROPOSITION 83 (LOGICAL SOUNDNESS FOR POTREES) For all potrees $\eta = \langle t, R \rangle \in \mathcal{T}^{\leq}_{L,C}$ and $\Phi \in \mathcal{L}^{\leq}_{L,C}$, if $\eta \models \Phi$ and $\Phi \vdash \phi$, then $\eta \models \phi$.

Proof The proof is by induction on the size of the proof tree for $\Phi \vdash \phi$. The base case occurs when $\Phi \vdash \phi$ is proved either by Triviality or because $\phi \in \Phi$. Clearly, if $\phi \in \Phi$ and $\eta \models \Phi$, then $\eta \models \phi$ by definition of satisfaction for potrees. For Triviality, if $\phi = \langle \rangle \leq \langle \rangle$, then $\eta \models \phi$, since for all trees, $t(\langle \rangle)$ is defined; hence, $\langle \rangle R \langle \rangle$ by reflexivity of R.

The induction step requires that we demonstrate that the other rules of inference preserve modeling. For the Reflexivity rules, assume that $\Phi \vdash v \leq p \cdot q$, so either $vRp \cdot q$ or $t(p \cdot q) = v$ (depending on whether $v \in Path$ or $v \in C$, respectively). In either case, $t/(p \cdot q) = (t/p)/q$ is defined, guaranteeing the definition of t/p. Since R is a preorder—hence reflexive—pRp holds; thus, $\eta \models p \leq p$. A similar argument holds for the second Reflexivity rule under the assumption that $\Phi \vdash p \cdot q \leq r$.

For Substitutivity, we consider only the second and third rules. (The first is verified exactly as the second.) For the second rule, assume that $\Phi \vdash v \leq p \cdot r$ and $\Phi \vdash p \leq q$, yielding $\eta \models v \leq p \cdot r$ and $\eta \models p \leq q$ by the induction hypothesis. From the latter, we can conclude that pRq, and from the former, that either $vRp \cdot r$ or $t(p \cdot r) = v$ (again depending on whether $v \in Path$ or $v \in C$, respectively). If $v \in Path$, then by a simple induction, $p \cdot rRq \cdot r$, whence, by the transitivity of R, $vRq \cdot r$, so $\eta \models v \leq q \cdot r$. If $v \in C$, then $v = (t/p)(r) \leq (t/q)(r) = t(q \cdot r)$. Since v is a constant and $v \leq t(q \cdot r)$, we can conclude that $v = t(q \cdot r)$; again $\eta \models v \leq q \cdot r$.

For the third Substitutivity rule, assume that $\Phi \vdash p \leq q$ and $\Phi \vdash p \cdot r \leq p \cdot s$. Then $\eta \models p \leq q$ and $\eta \models p \cdot r \leq p \cdot s$, so pRq and $p \cdot rRp \cdot s$. By condition 4 on R, $q \cdot rRq \cdot s$, and $\eta \models q \cdot r \leq q \cdot s$.   □

PROPOSITION 84 (DENOTATIONAL SOUNDNESS OF POTREES)   For all formulas $\Phi \in \mathcal{L}_{L,C}^{\leq}$, if there exists a potree $\eta = \langle t, R \rangle \in \mathcal{T}_{L,C}^{\leq}$ such that $\eta \models \Phi$, then Φ is consistent.

Proof   The proof is essentially identical to that for Proposition 61. □

PROPOSITION 85 (MINIMAL-MODEL EXISTENCE FOR POTREES) If $\Phi \in \mathcal{L}_{L,C}^{\leq}$ is consistent, then there is a least $\eta = \langle t, R \rangle \in \mathcal{T}_{L,C}^{\leq}$ such that $\eta \models \Phi$.

Proof   Define $\eta = mptm(\Phi)$, the *minimal potree model* of Φ, as follows: $\eta = \langle t, R \rangle$, where $t = itm(\Phi)$ (see Proposition 79) and pRq if and only if $\Phi \vdash p \leq q$.

We show that η is a well-formed potree, that $\eta \models \Phi$, and that η is the least such potree.

η is a well-formed potree: As proved in Proposition 79, t is a well-formed infinite tree. Now, if pRq, then $\Phi \vdash p \leq q$ and $\Phi \vdash p \leq p$ by Reflexivity. Furthermore, it either holds or not that $\Phi \vdash c \doteq p$ for some $c \in C$. If so, $t(p) = c$; if not, $t(p) = \bot$, according to the *itm* construction. In either case, $p \in dom(t)$, so R is a relation over $dom(t)$.

We turn to the four conditions on the well-formedness of R. First, R is a preorder since it is reflexive (trivially) and transitive (if pRq and qRs, then $\Phi \vdash p \leq q$ and $\Phi \vdash q \leq s$, so by Substitutivity $\Phi \vdash p \leq s$ and pRs).

Second, if pRp', then $\Phi \vdash p \leq p'$. Again we consider two cases as to whether $\Phi \vdash c \leq p$ for some $c \in C$ or not. If so, $t(p) = c$, and by Substitutivity, $\Phi \vdash c \leq p'$, so $t(p') = c$. If not, $t(p) = \perp$. In either case, $t(p) \leq t(p')$, as required.

Third, assume that pRp' and $p \cdot \langle f \rangle \in dom(t)$. Then $\Phi \vdash p \doteq p'$ and, by definition of dom for tree models, $\Phi \vdash p \cdot \langle f \rangle \doteq v$ for some v. By Reflexivity, $\Phi \vdash p \cdot \langle f \rangle \doteq p \cdot \langle f \rangle$, whence, by Substitutivity, $\Phi \vdash p \cdot \langle f \rangle \doteq p' \cdot \langle f \rangle$, so $p \cdot \langle f \rangle Rp' \cdot \langle f \rangle$.

Fourth, assume that pRp' and $p \cdot qRp \cdot s$. Then $\Phi \vdash p \leq p'$ and $\Phi \vdash p \cdot q \leq p \cdot s$. By Substitutivity, $\Phi \vdash p' \cdot q \leq p' \cdot s$, so $p' \cdot qRp' \cdot s$.

This concludes the proof of the well-formedness of R and therefore of η as well.

η is a model for Φ: If $\Phi \vdash p \leq q$, then by construction, pRq and $\eta \models p \leq q$. If $\Phi \vdash c \leq p$, then $t(p) = c$ by the itm construction; hence, $\eta \models c \leq p$. Since η is a model for any equation entailed by Φ, it is a model for Φ itself.

η is the least model for Φ: Consider any model $\eta' = \langle t', R' \rangle$ such that $\eta' \models \Phi$. By logical soundness (Proposition 83), $\eta' \models \Phi'$ for all $\Phi \vdash \Phi'$. In particular, if pRq, then $\Phi \vdash p \leq q$, so $\eta' \models p \leq q$ and $pR'q$. Thus, $R \subseteq R'$. If $t(p) = c$, then $\Phi \vdash c \leq p$, so $\eta' \models c \leq p$ and $t'(p) = c$. Similarly, if $t(p) = \perp$, then $\Phi \vdash p \leq p$, so $\eta' \models p \leq p$ and, by definition of satisfaction, either $t'(p) = \perp$ or $t'(p) = c$ for some $c \in C$. In either case, $t(p) \leq t(p')$, so $t \leq t'$ in general. By definition of subsumption on potrees, $\eta \leq \eta'$.   □

PROPOSITION 86 (CATEGORICITY FOR POTREE MODELS) If $\eta = \langle t, R \rangle$ and $\eta' = \langle t', R' \rangle$ are distinct potrees in $T^{\leq}_{L,C}$, then there exists a formula $\Phi \in \mathcal{L}^{\leq}_{L,C}$ such that $\eta \models \Phi$ and $\eta' \not\models \Phi$ or vice versa.

Proof If η and η' are distinct, they must differ either in t or in R. The possibilities can be divided exhaustively into six cases. The first three cases are as follows:

Case 1: $t(p)$ defined and $t'(p)$ undefined.

Then $\eta \models p \leq p$ but $\eta \not\models p \leq p$.

Case 2: $t(p) = c$ and $t'(p) = \bot$.

Then $\eta \models c \leq p$ but $\eta' \not\models c \leq p$.

Case 3: pRq but not $pR'q$.

Then $\eta \models p \leq q$ but $\eta' \not\models p \leq q$.

The remaining three cases, the symmetric versions of the first three, where t' or R' is more defined, are proved similarly. □

PROPOSITION 87 (LOGICAL COMPLETENESS OF POTREE MODELS) If for all $\eta \in \mathcal{T}_{L,C}^{\leq}$ such that $\eta \models \Phi$, $\eta \models \Phi'$, then $\Phi \vdash \Phi'$.

Proof Without loss of generality, we can restrict ourselves to the case where Φ' is atomic. (For nonatomic formulas, satisfaction holds just in case it holds for the atomic elements, so the problem reduces to the atomic case.) Suppose that for all $\eta \in \mathcal{T}_{L,C}^{\leq}$ such that $\eta \models \Phi$, it is the case that $\eta \models \Phi'$. Then, in particular, $mptm(\Phi) = \langle t, R \rangle \models \Phi'$. We prove that $\Phi \vdash \Phi'$ by cases, depending on the form of Φ'. If Φ' is of the form $p \leq q$, then $\langle t, R \rangle \models p \leq q$ and pRq. By the $mptm$ construction, $\Phi \vdash p \leq q$. If Φ' is of the form $c \leq p$, then $\langle t, R \rangle \models c \doteq p$ and $t(p) = c$. Now, by the itm construction used in the $mptm$ construction, $\Phi \vdash c \leq p$. Thus, in general, $\Phi \vdash \Phi'$. □

The proofs for the model locality properties are similar to those for $\mathcal{L}_{L,C}$, which are contained in the Appendix.

Rational Potrees Of course, potrees, like the eqtrees on which they are based, are not finite objects in general, and, therefore, cannot be used as a basis for computation. We will develop a graph encoding of certain potrees—like the feature-graph models for $\mathcal{L}_{L,C}$—to remedy this problem.

As in Section 4.3.2, we restrict our attention to the *rational* subset of the potrees.

DEFINITION 88 A potree $\langle t, R \rangle$ is *rational* if and only if the maximal cliques of R form a finite set.

In the case where R is actually an equivalence relation, this definition of rationality reduces to that given for eqtrees in Definition 71. Unfortunately, the rational potrees do not possess a closure property analogous to that proved as Proposition 72. Certain formulas in $\mathcal{L}_{L,C}^{\leq}$ have no rational potree model. For instance, the minimal potree model for the

Figure 5.5
An irrational potree

formula $\{\langle\rangle \leq \langle f \rangle\}$ has an infinite set of singleton cliques $\{\langle\rangle\}$, $\{\langle f \rangle\}$, $\{\langle f \ f \rangle\}$, and so on, as can be seen graphically in Figure 5.5. In general, any formula Φ such that $\Phi \vdash p \leq p \cdot q$ but $\Phi \not\vdash p \cdot q \leq p$ for some p and nonempty q has no rational potree model. For the nonce, we will disallow such formulas by fiat, returning in Section 5.5.5 to discuss generalizations of the rational potrees that allow such cyclic formulas to be modeled.[16]

5.5.3 Pograph Models

A pograph is a quintuple $\langle N, n_0, \delta, \pi, \sigma \rangle$ where

- $\langle N, n_0, \delta, \pi \rangle$ is a feature graph, and

- σ is a partial order over N, the *intensional subsumption ordering*, satisfying the following congruence conditions:

1. If $\sigma(n, n')$ and $\delta(n, f)$ is defined, then $\delta(n', f)$ is defined and $\sigma(\delta(n, f), \delta(n', f))$, and

2. If $\sigma(n, n')$ and $\pi(n) - c$, then $\pi(n') = c$, and

3. If $\sigma(n, n')$ and $\sigma(n/p, n/q)$, then $\sigma(n'/p, n'/q)$.

---

[16]Note that cyclic formulas as defined in the comment after Definition 25 are still allowed; they merely engender a single infinite clique, rather than an infinite set of singletons. Thus, none of the expressive power of $\mathcal{L}_{L,C}$ is lost by eliminating the irrational potrees. As mentioned in the text, however, although rational eqtrees are complete for $\mathcal{L}_{L,C}$, rational potrees are not for $\mathcal{L}_{L,C}^{\leq}$. Since the incompleteness is harmless for the applications we have in mind, the problem is not worrisome. The situation is different as regards cyclic equations; these have been proposed for application in several places and would have been unfortunate to give up.

The normal conventions for feature graphs will be used for pographs as well. In particular, the notations n/p and g/p will be employed for traversing pographs (as in the preceding definition of the congruence conditions). We will also require connectedness of pographs, defined in the normal way (see Section 4.4.1).

Satisfaction for Pographs   A pograph $g = \langle N, n_0, \delta, \pi, \sigma \rangle$ satisfies an equation $p \leq q$ if and only if $\sigma(n_0/p, n_0/q)$, and g satisfies $c \leq p$ if and only if $\pi(n_0/p) = c$. As usual, satisfaction for nonatomic formulas is conjunctive.

The important property of pographs that extend feature graphs is the following:

PROPOSITION 89   For all pographs $g = \langle N, n_0, \delta, \pi, \sigma \rangle$ and $n, n' \in N$, if $\sigma(n, n')$, then the subgraph of g rooted at n subsumes the subgraph rooted at n'.

Proof   Suppose $\sigma(n, n')$ and g/n and g/n' are the subgraphs of g rooted at n and n', respectively. We show that any formula satisfied by g/n is also satisfied by g/n'. By Definition 13, $g/n \leq g/n'$.

If $g/n \models p \leq q$, then $\sigma(n/p, n/q)$, which yields $\sigma(n'/p, n'/q)$ by the third congruence property of σ. Thus, $g/n' \models p \leq q$. If $g/n \models c \leq p$, then $\pi(n/p) = c$. The second congruence property of σ guarantees that $\pi(n'/p) = c$ and $g/n' \models c \leq p$. $\square$

Subsumption for Pographs   A syntactic condition on pographs that corresponds to the general semantic notion of subsumption presented as Definition 9 extends the one for graphs presented in Section 4.4.1.

Let $g = \langle N, n_0, \delta, \pi, \sigma \rangle$ and $g' = \langle N', n_0', \delta', \pi', \sigma' \rangle$ be two pographs. Then g subsumes g' by a witness homomorphism $m : N \rightarrow N'$ if and only if the following conditions hold:

1.-3. $\langle N, n_0, \delta, \pi \rangle$ subsumes $\langle N', n_0', \delta', \pi' \rangle$ with witness m (as defined by the three conditions in Section 4.4.1), and

4. If $\sigma(n_1, n_2)$ for $n_1, n_2 \in N$, then $\sigma'(m(n_1), m(n_2))$.

In general, $g \leq g'$ if and only if there exists a witness such that $g \leq g'$ under that witness in accordance with the preceding definition. Proofs of the correctness of this ordering as the subsumption ordering obeying Definition 9 (analogous to Propositions 74, 75, and 76) are straightforward and will be omitted.

5.5.4 Potrees and Pographs

We can extend the results of Section 4.4.2 relating eqtrees to feature graphs, demonstrating that the potrees are isomorphic to the isomorphism classes of the pographs.

PROPOSITION 90 The potrees are isomorphic to the isomorphism classes of the pographs.

The structure of the proof is identical to that for Proposition 77, although we use different mappings τ and γ. We describe the two mappings and prove the requisite properties here. The argument that the existence of these mappings is sufficient is not reiterated.

Given a pograph $g = \langle N, n_0, \delta, \pi, \sigma \rangle$, let $\tau(g) = \langle t, R \rangle$, where

$$t(p) = c \quad \text{if and only if} \quad \pi(g/p) = c$$
$$t(p) = \bot \quad \text{if and only if} \quad g/p \text{ is defined but } \pi(g/p) \text{ is undefined}$$

$$pRp' \qquad \text{if and only if} \quad \sigma(g/p, g/p') \qquad .$$

$\tau(g)$ **is a well-formed potree:** Prefix closure follows as before. We must also show that R obeys the constraints on potree relations.

R is reflexive and transitive because σ is. (R is not necessarily anti-symmetric, since the function mapping p to g/p is not in general one-to-one.) Thus, R is a preorder.

If pRp', then $\sigma(g/p, g/p')$, so if $\pi(g/p) = c$, then $\pi(g/p') = c$ and $t(p') = c$. If $\pi(g/p)$ is undefined, then $t(p) = \bot$. In either case, $t(p) \leq t(p')$.

If pRp' and $p \cdot \langle f \rangle \in dom(t)$, then $\sigma(g/p, g/p')$ and g/p and g/p' are both defined. Furthermore, $g/(p \cdot \langle f \rangle)$ is defined. By the first congruence property of σ, $\sigma(g/(p \cdot \langle f \rangle), g/(p' \cdot \langle f \rangle))$, so $p \cdot \langle f \rangle R p' \cdot \langle f \rangle$.

If pRp' and $p \cdot qRp \cdot s$, then $\sigma(g/p, g/p')$ and $\sigma(g/p \cdot q, g/p \cdot s)$. By the third congruence property of σ, $\sigma(g/p' \cdot r, g/p' \cdot s)$, so $p' \cdot rRp' \cdot s$.

Since t is a well-formed tree and R an appropriate relation, $\tau(g)$ is a well-formed potree.

τ **is total and one-to-one:** This was proved for Proposition 77 by exhibiting a witness m to a subsumption relation between g and g' for any other $g' = \langle N', n_0', \delta', \pi', \sigma' \rangle$ such that $\tau(g) = \tau(g')$. To augment the proof, we need only show that the witness for the feature-graph portions of g and g' extends to the σ portions, that is, that if $\sigma(n_1, n_2)$ for $n_1, n_2 \in N$, then $\sigma'(m(n_1), m(n_2))$.

Suppose $\sigma(n_1, n_2)$. Since g is connected, $n_1 = g/p_1$ and $n_2 = g/p_2$ for some paths p_1 and p_2. By definition of τ, $p_1 R p_2$. Since $\tau(g) = \tau(g')$ by assumption, $\sigma'(g'/p_1, g'/p_2)$ holds, that is, $\sigma'(m(n_1), m(n_2))$.

τ **is satisfaction-preserving:** This follows as directly from the definition of τ as it does in the proof of Proposition 77.

These addenda to the discussion of τ in Proposition 77 suffice to demonstrate the requisite properties of τ as applied to pographs.

We now turn to γ, the inverse mapping from potrees to graphs. We define γ as follows: Given a potree $\eta = \langle t, R \rangle$, let $\gamma(\eta) = \langle N, n_o, \delta, \pi, \sigma \rangle$, where

- N is the set of maximal R-cliques in $dom(t)$ (the notation $[p]$ being used for the clique containing p),

- n_0 is the clique $[\langle \rangle]$,

- δ is exhaustively defined by $\delta([p], f) = [p \cdot \langle f \rangle]$ for all $p \cdot \langle f \rangle \in dom(t)$,

- $\pi([p]) = c$ if and only if $t(p) = c$, and

- $\sigma([p], [q])$ if and only if pRq.

$\gamma(\eta)$ **is a well-formed pograph:** The previous proof in Proposition 77 need only be extended with a demonstration that σ is a partial order. Since R is a preorder, hence reflexive and transitive, so is σ. Suppose $\sigma([p], [q])$ for $[p] \neq [q]$. Then pRq, but not qRp (or else $[p] = [q]$), so $\sigma([q], [p])$ fails to hold and σ is antisymmetric. Thus, σ is a partial order.

γ **is total and one-to-one:** As argued in Proposition 77, we need only show that if $\gamma(\eta) \approx \gamma(\eta')$, then for all atomic formulas $\phi \in \mathcal{L}^{\leq}_{L,C}$, if $\eta \models \phi$, then $\eta' \models \phi$. For ease of reference, let $\eta = \langle t, R \rangle$ and $\eta' = \langle t', R' \rangle$, and let $\gamma(\eta) = \langle N, n_0, \delta, \pi, \sigma \rangle$ and $\gamma(\eta') = \langle N', n'_0, \delta', \pi', \sigma' \rangle$.

If $\eta \models p \leq q$, then pRq, so $\sigma([p], [q])$. Since $\gamma(\eta) \approx \gamma(\eta')$, $\sigma'([p], [q])$ as well, so $pR'q$ and $\eta' \models p \leq q$.

Similarly, if $\eta \models c \leq p$, then $t(p) = c$, so $\pi([p]) = c$ and $t'(p) = c$. Thus, $\eta' \models c \leq p$.

γ **is satisfaction-preserving:**   We must show that $\eta \models \Phi$ if and only if $\gamma(\eta) \models \Phi$. Since satisfaction for nonatomic formulas is defined identically for the two model classes, we can consider only the atomic cases. By definition of satisfaction for potrees, $\eta \models p \leq q$ if and only if pRq if and only if $\sigma([p], [q])$ by definition of γ. Since in general $[r] = [\langle\rangle]/r = n_0/r = \gamma(\eta)/r$, we can conclude that $\sigma(\gamma(\eta)/p, \gamma(\eta)/q)$, so, by definition of satisfaction for pographs, $\gamma(\eta) \models p \leq q$.

For formulas of the form $c \leq p$, $\eta \models c \leq p$ if and only if $t(p) = c$ if and only if $\pi([p]) = c$ by definition of γ. Replacing $[p]$ with the equivalent $\gamma(\eta)/p$ as before, we have that $\pi(\gamma(\eta)/p) = c$, so that $\gamma(\eta) \models c \leq p$.

This concludes the extensions of the proof of Proposition 77 to demonstrate the relationship between potrees and pographs. $\square$

5.5.5   Computing with Pographs

To accrue the benefits of Chapter 3, we must finally provide algorithms for the various operations $(/, \backslash, \upharpoonright, \sqcup)$ on pographs, as we did for their counterparts for feature graphs. All but the last of these operations are straightforward, and require little discussion. For instance, to embed a pograph underneath a path, we merely add a chain of features for the path, each pointing to the next, the last pointing to the embedded pograph; the process is identical to that for feature graphs. Similar methods work for extraction and restriction. Informational union is slightly more complex, and makes use of the corresponding operation on graphs.

A simple, but not particularly efficient, method for computing the informational union of two pographs is the following. Given two pographs $g = \langle N, n_0, \delta, \pi, \sigma \rangle$ and $g' = \langle N', n_0', \delta', \pi', \sigma' \rangle$, we form the feature graph $g^{\sqcup} = \langle N^{\sqcup}, n_0^{\sqcup}, \delta^{\sqcup}, \pi^{\sqcup} \rangle = \langle N, n_0, \delta, \pi \rangle \sqcup \langle N', n_0', \delta', \pi' \rangle$, as described in Section 4.4.4. Note that the congruence $\equiv$ is defined and used in that procedure. Now construct the ordering $\sigma^{\sqcup} = (\sigma \cup \sigma')/ \equiv$. The structure $\langle g^{\sqcup}, \sigma^{\sqcup} \rangle$ may not be a pograph, either because $\sigma^{\sqcup}$ may not be antisymmetric or because $g^{\sqcup}$ may not satisfy the subsumption relations given by $\sigma^{\sqcup}$. Consequently, we repeatedly correct such deficiencies in the structure until these conditions are satisfied.

In particular, if $n_i \sigma^{\sqcup} n_j$ and $n_j \sigma^{\sqcup} n_i$ for distinct $n_i, n_j \in N^{\sqcup}$, we form a new structure $\langle g^{\sqcup}, \sigma^{\sqcup} \rangle$ as before but with the congruence strengthened to include $n_i \equiv n_j$. (This can be performed efficiently by merely smashing n_i and n_j to the same node and propagating the change down $\delta^{\sqcup}$. In effect, we build $g^{\sqcup} \sqcup mm(\{p_i \doteq p_j\})$, where p_i and p_j are paths to n_i and n_j, respectively, and modify $\sigma^{\sqcup}$ according to the congruence used in this operation.)

Also, if $n_i \sigma^{\sqcup} n_j$ but $g^{\sqcup}/p_i \nleq g^{\sqcup}/p_j$ (with p_i and p_j defined as before), we form the new $g^{\sqcup}$ given by $g^{\sqcup} \sqcup g^{\sqcup}/p_i \backslash p_j$ and again modify $\sigma^{\sqcup}$ according to the congruence used in this operation.

These two operations are repeated until their preconditions are no longer met.

We will not provide a formal proof of correctness corresponding to Proposition 78 for feature graphs. Informally, though, it should be clear that if this process terminates, the structure $\langle g^{\sqcup}, \sigma^{\sqcup} \rangle$ will be a well-formed pograph that satisfies all of the constraints of g and g'. That it is a least such pograph can be seen, intuitively at least, by noting that all of the operations were forced, in the sense that without them, the resultant structure was not a pograph, and each operation was the minimum one for correcting the structure thus far built. Finally, that it is the least such pograph could be shown by proving a kind of confluence property of the two operations just described.

The question of termination of the algorithm is not an idle one, however. As mentioned in Section 5.5.2, the pographs do not close correctly under $\sqcup$ because they are defined only in correspondence with rational potrees, and the rational potrees are not closed under $\sqcup$; irrational potrees may result. In those cases in which two rational potrees generate an irrational one, the algorithm operating on the corresponding graphs will fail to terminate. (It is the second type of corrective operation that recurs. The first type possesses a simple well-foundedness criterion as it decreases the number of nodes at each step.)

More sophisticated graph-like models may be explored that can correspond to irrational potrees as well. Observe that in the case of an irrational potree (say, one satisfying $p \leq p \cdot q$), we have an infinite descending chain of subsumption relations $p \leq p \cdot q \leq p \cdot q \cdot q \leq p \cdot q \cdot q \cdot q \leq \cdots$, each subgraph potentially larger than the next. However, starting with a finite formula, we can have only a finite amount of information about each of these subgraphs, so that at a certain depth in this iteration, all of the subgraphs will be described by the same set of constraints. Thus, a kind of "lazy evaluation" approach to modeling such equations may be possible in which the graph descends only as far as is necessary to capture the currently manifest inequalities. The bottom of the chain would be marked in such a way that another unfolding could occur if information that differentiated it from the next subgraph were encountered. Nonetheless, as will be discussed in the next section, no technique of this or any other nature can guarantee termination of the algorithm.

5.5.6   Decidability and a Weaker System

Informational union in a system with inequations of this sort corresponds to the problem of semiunification. Unfortunately, as shown by Kfoury, Tiuryn, and Urzyczyn (1989) and Dörre and Rounds (1990), the problem of semiunification is undecidable in general.[17] It appears, then, that the "solution" to the problem of characterizing *let*-polymorphism and coordination phenomena is not practical. We will not be able to guarantee termination of the informational union algorithm presupposed.

As it turns out, this problem presents an excellent opportunity to make use of the close analogy between parsing of natural language and type inference of computer languages in such a way as to enable an efficient solution to the problem. Leiß (1990), noting the ramifications of Dörre and Rounds's results for the analysis of coordination presented here, pursues the analogy between coordination and *let*-polymorphism further. The particular subcases of polymorphic type inference that appear in ML do allow for effective inference of types, even in *let* contexts. The ML restriction of generic polymorphism to syntactic contexts in which the base type is known (i.e., only *let* contexts) allows for this effectiveness. By analogy, we might restrict "polymorphic" coordination to contexts in which the polymorphism is allowed as well. By means of a detailed explicit proposal for the relationship between the *let* construct in ML and coordination of unlike categories in natural language, Leiß makes just that restriction, and in so doing, allows for handling of the phenomenon in a restricted system that allows for decidable type inference (or, in the natural-language case, parsing). Thus, the analogy of parsing as type inference has led directly to a discovery of a more effective handling of coordination phenomena in natural language through use of a result in computer-language type inference. In essence, Leiß's result perfectly exemplifies the new rapprochement of natural and computer languages.

---

[17]Actually, Dörre and Rounds (1990) use a slightly different kind of system (see Footnote 13). Nonetheless, the decidability results should be applicable to the system given in this chapter.

6 Conclusion

Building on our own recent work and that of others on the semantics of particular constraint logics, models for the logics, and grammar formalisms, we have attempted to develop a uniform mathematical and computational approach to grammar formalisms based on systems of declarative constraints. A series of novel results in the field of computational linguistics has been presented:

- We have developed an abstract characterization of the notion of constraint-based grammar formalism in general, rather than a particular formalism. To our knowledge, this is the first such general characterization.

- We have developed and proved correct an abstract parsing algorithm, abstract both in that it applies to all formalisms in the constraint-based class and in that the specifics of control are eliminated. The control abstraction allows applications in general natural-language parsing (by mimicking Earley's algorithm) and psycholinguistic modeling (by mimicking shift-reduce parsing). The proof of correctness constitutes the first such proof for a single constraint-based grammar formalism, let alone for a class thereof. It provides a demonstration of the correctness of several general techniques that have been used in implementations of practical grammar-interpretation systems — the subsumption check for chart parsing and the use of a weakening operator ρ to limit top-down prediction, for instance.

- We have pinpointed the need for the use of graphs as models for $\mathcal{L}_{L,C}$, as opposed to tree models of various sorts.

- We have developed a constraint-based formalism that allows inequational as well as equational constraints, and have shown its applications both to natural and to computer languages.

- We have initiated a rapprochement between the techniques in use for stating well-formedness conditions of natural and computer languages, bringing back together these two areas that diverged shortly after the application of context-free grammars to both. The enabling conception for this enterprise is the analogy of natural-language grammar with computer-language typing, and hence, that of natural-language parsing with computer-language type inference.

Evidence for the practical application of the results presented here is provided by the CL-PATR grammar development system. This system was developed by the author as an implementation of the algorithm of Chapter 3 as applied to the PATR formalism based on $\mathcal{L}_{L,C}$. The system incorporates parameters for specifying the control regime used in parsing, thereby taking advantage of the control-independence of the abstract algorithm and enabling the system to be used in modes mimicking a variety of more traditional parsing algorithms including Earley's and shift-reduce parsers. Furthermore, the abstract algorithm as instantiated in CL-PATR has been applied to the task of natural-language generation as well, a topic beyond the scope of the present work but discussed elsewhere (Shieber, 1988b). Besides its use as a development system for constraint-based grammars, the CL-PATR system has been incorporated as a natural-language front- and back-end in various projects at SRI International, including an utterance-planning system (GENESYS) and a mobile robot (Flakey).

More generally, however, the present work serves as an initial effort toward a new approach to designing grammar formalisms. The vast bulk of research endeavors developing and applying constraint-based grammar formalisms to the problem of describing and analyzing natural languages have proceeded by first designing the data structures to be used for capturing information about linguistic expressions, then constructing a language for talking about and manipulating these structures. Every previous initiative in the semantics of constraint-based formalisms—from Pereira and Shieber's and (1984), to that of Rounds and his colleagues (Kasper and Rounds, 1986; Rounds and Kasper, 1986; Moshier and Rounds, 1987), and Johnson (1988)—shares this modus operandi.

Here, we have taken a different approach, choosing to look first at the kinds of information that we would like to capture, embodying the properties that this information possesses—partiality, modularity, equationality—in a class of logical languages, only then developing appropriate data structures (models) on the basis of these prior desiderata.[1] Such an approach is a first step toward a more abstract characterization of a class of grammar formalisms for describing natural languages.

---

[1] The methodology described in this volume is just a beginning, however; there is much room for improvement in the abstractness of the approach. In particular, we believe that a more algebraic rather than syntactic flavor to characterizing the models would significantly simplify the system.

The generality of the approach allows the development of constraint systems and formalisms that are applicable to computer languages as well. The problems of describing aspects of binding and polymorphism in typed programming languages motivate extensions of the kind of informational constraints prevalent in natural languages. Closing the loop, we discover that these extensions are applicable to certain outstanding problems in natural-language description, the cases at hand concerning the areas of nonmonotonic constraints and coordination phenomena.

By proceeding from model to logic, as previous work has, the question of appropriateness of model is ruled out a priori; in the abstract approach begun here, the question of appropriateness of model is paramount. Thus, we have shown in this work *why* graph models are correct and useful models for the equational logic, instead of mandating these models and finding a logic that uses such structures as models. As the utility of a formalism is contingent on whether it can express what needs to be expressed, the language of expression, rather than its models, seems more apt for serving as the independent variable.

Finally, we have seen that by aiming for such an abstract approach to formalisms, we do not necessarily forego computational results. On the contrary, the results that are obtained, such as the abstract parsing algorithm for constraint-based formalisms, increase in utility, as they can be applied generally to any constraint-based formalism, whether extant or yet to be designed.

Appendix: Proofs of Properties of $\mathcal{L}_{L,C}$

This appendix comprises the proofs for the properties that must be demonstrated of an individual logic independent of the class of models chosen for it (i.e., Properties 1, 2, 11, 28, 29, 30, and 31). The proofs are carried out for the simple equational logic $\mathcal{L}_{L,C}$. Corresponding proofs for the extended logic including explicit subsumption constraints, $\mathcal{L}^{\leq}_{L,C}$, are similar.

Logical Locality and Transparency

PROPOSITION 91 (LOGICAL LOCALITY FOR $\mathcal{L}_{L,C}$) If Φ is a formula of $\mathcal{L}_{L,C}$ all of whose paths have some member of $\{p_i\}$ as a prefix and $\Phi \vdash \phi$, then all paths in ϕ are prefixes or extensions of some member of $\{p_i\}$.

Proof Proved as Proposition 3 in Section 2.7.3. □

PROPOSITION 92 (LOGICAL TRANSPARENCY FOR $\mathcal{L}_{L,C}$) If $\Phi \vdash \phi$ for nonempty $\Phi \in \mathcal{L}_{L,C}$, then for any prefixed homomorphism m_s, $m_s(\Phi) \vdash m_s(\phi)$ where $m_s(\Phi)$ is the result of replacing all paths q in Φ by $m_s(q)$.

Proof Suppose we are given a prefixed homomorphism $m_s : Path \rightarrow Path$. We must show that m_s applied to each inference rule maintains soundness. We consider the inference rules individually.

Triviality: For any homomorphism m, $m(q) = m(\langle\rangle \cdot q) = m(\langle\rangle) \cdot m(q)$, so $m(\langle\rangle) = \langle\rangle$. Thus, m_s applied to an instance of Triviality yields the consequent $s \doteq s$. Now since Φ is nonempty, there must be some path q in Φ, so we can construct the proof

$$\frac{\dfrac{m_s(\Phi)}{m_s(q) \doteq m_s(q)}}{0 \doteq 0}$$

using Reflexivity twice. Thus, $m_s(\Phi) \vdash m_s(\langle\rangle \doteq \langle\rangle)$.

Symmetry: The prefixed homomorphism m_s applied to the Symmetry rule yields

$$\frac{m_s(p) \doteq m_s(q)}{m_s(q) \doteq m_s(p)} ,$$

which is sound because it is itself an instance of Symmetry.

Reflexivity: The prefixed homomorphism m_s applied to Reflexivity yields

$$\frac{m_s(p \cdot q) \doteq m_s(v) \text{ (respectively, } v)}{m_s(p) \doteq m_s(p)}$$

(depending on whether $v \in Path$ or $v \in C$, respectively); that is,

$$\frac{s \cdot m(p) \cdot m(q) \doteq s \cdot m(v) \text{ (respectively, } v)}{s \cdot m(p) \doteq s \cdot m(p)} \quad ,$$

which is sound because it is itself an instance of Reflexivity.

Substitutivity: The prefixed homomorphism m_s applied to Substitutivity yields

$$\frac{m_s(q) \doteq m_s(p) \quad m_s(p \cdot r) \doteq m_s(v) \text{ (respectively, } v)}{m_s(q \cdot r) \doteq m_s(v) \text{ (respectively, } v)}$$

(depending on whether $v \in Path$ or $v \in C$, respectively); that is,

$$\frac{s \cdot m(q) \doteq s \cdot m(p) \quad s \cdot m(p) \cdot m(r) \doteq s \cdot m(v) \text{ (respectively, } v)}{s \cdot m(q) \cdot m(r) \doteq s \cdot m(v) \text{ (respectively, } v)} \quad ,$$

which is sound because it is itself an instance of Substitutivity.

Thus, all inference rules maintain soundness under prefixed homomorphic images. Consequently, proofs do as well.   □

Compactness and Model Locality

Before proving the model locality properties for $\mathcal{L}_{L,C}$, we develop a useful lemma concerning the equivalence classes of paths defined by a formula. In the lemma, the notation $[p]_\Phi$ denotes an equivalence class of paths defined as those paths q such that $\Phi \vdash p \doteq q$. The set of equivalence classes for Φ will be written $[\ ]_\Phi$. Similarly, we will use the notation $[\ ]_M$ for the equivalence classes over paths for which M is defined given by $[p]_M = [q]_M$ if and only if $M \models p \doteq q$. The set of paths for which a model is defined will be called its *path domain* and notated $pdom(M)$.

LEMMA 93 Given a formula Φ such that paths p and q are in the domain of Φ, the equivalence classes defined by $\Phi \cup \{p \doteq q\}$ are a collapsing of those defined by Φ such that $[r]_\Phi$ and $[s]_\Phi$ are collapsed in $[\ ]_{\Phi \cup \{p \doteq q\}}$ just in case there is a t for which $r = p \cdot t$ and $s = q \cdot t$.

Proof The proof for Proposition 72 shows that there is at most one equivalence class in $[\ ]_\Phi$ for each prefix of a path in Φ. Since p and q are paths in Φ, the set of classes $[\ ]_{\Phi \cup \{p \doteq q\}}$ is bound by that limit as well. Since $\Phi \vdash r \doteq s$ entails $\Phi \cup \{p \doteq q\} \vdash r \doteq s$, the equivalence classes for $\Phi \cup \{p \doteq q\}$ are stronger.

All that remains to be shown, therefore, is that if $\Phi \cup \{p \doteq q\} \vdash r \doteq s$ and $\Phi \not\vdash r \doteq s$, then $[r]_{\Phi \cup \{p \doteq q\}} = [p \cdot t]_{\Phi \cup \{p \doteq q\}}$ and $[s]_{\Phi \cup \{p \doteq q\}} = [q \cdot t]_{\Phi \cup \{p \doteq q\}}$ for some t, which we argue as follows. Consider the proof for $\Phi \cup \{p \doteq q\} \vdash r \doteq s$. It must use the equation $p \doteq q$ or else the conclusion would follow from Φ alone. We can normalize the proof to remove all uses of Triviality and Reflexivity, since they are not the final steps in the proof (as the conclusion would follow from Φ alone) and they do not help to feed any other rule (as should be obvious). Thus, the proof contains only uses of Symmetry and Substitutivity.

Now, we will say that a path r is $p+t$ if $[r]_{\Phi \cup \{p \doteq q\}} = [p \cdot t]_{\Phi \cup \{p \doteq q\}}$. We show that if one of the antecedents of Symmetry or Substitutivity has paths that are $p + x$ and $q + x$ for some x, then the consequent's paths are $p + y$ and $q + y$ for some y. First consider Symmetry; if we start with $r \doteq s$ where one of the paths is $p + x$ and the other is $q + x$, then the conclusion, having the same paths as the antecedent, also equates a $p + x$ and a $q + x$. For Substitutivity, examine an instance of the rule given by

$$\frac{r \doteq s \quad s \cdot t \doteq u}{r \cdot t \doteq u} \ .$$

There are two cases to consider, depending on whether the first or the second antecedent has paths that are $p + x$ and $q + x$. In case it is the first antecedent, then r is $p + x$ and s is $q + x$ (or vice versa, but we will assume this without loss of generality). Then $s \cdot t$ is $q + (x \cdot t)$, and u is as well (since $s \cdot t \doteq u$, that is, $[s \cdot t]_{\Phi \cup \{p \doteq q\}} = [u]_{\Phi \cup \{p \doteq q\}}$). Similarly, $r \cdot t$ is $p + (x \cdot t)$, so that the conclusion has paths that are $p + y$ and $q + y$ (y being $x \cdot t$ in particular). In case the second antecedent is the crucial one, then $s \cdot t$ is $p + x$ and u is $q + x$. Now, from $r \doteq s$ and $s \cdot t \doteq u$ we can prove that $r \cdot t \doteq s \cdot t$, so since $s \cdot t$ is $p + x$, $r \cdot t$ is as well. Thus, the consequent of Substitutivity has paths that are, respectively, $p + x$ and $q + x$.

Since the proof for $\Phi \cup \{p \doteq q\} \vdash r \doteq s$ contains only uses of Symmetry and Substitutivity, and since at least one of its leaves has paths that are $p+x$ and $q+x$ for some x (namely, $p \doteq q$), then, by an obvious induction, its conclusion must have paths that are $p + y$ and $q + y$ as well. That is, $[r]_{\Phi \cup \{p \doteq q\}} = [p \cdot t]_{\Phi \cup \{p \doteq q\}}$ and $[s]_{\Phi \cup \{p \doteq q\}} = [q \cdot t]_{\Phi \cup \{p \doteq q\}}$ for some t. □

Compactness

We now demonstrate that the logic $\mathcal{L}_{L,C}$ is compact in the sense of Property 11.

PROPOSITION 94 (COMPACTNESS OF $\mathcal{L}_{L,C}$) Given a consistent (possibly infinite) set of atomic formulas S from $\mathcal{L}_{L,C}$, if all models M such that $M \models \phi_i$ for all $\phi_i \in S$ are such that $M \models \Psi$, then $\Phi \vdash \Psi$ for Φ a finite subset of S.

Proof   We can restrict our attention to the case where Ψ is an atomic formula for the usual reasons. Further, we can ignore the case where S is finite, since in that case taking $S = \Phi$ (together with logical completeness) is sufficient to show the proposition.

Suppose that all models M such that $M \models S$ (that is, $M \models \phi_i$ for all $\phi_i \in S$) have the property that $M \models \psi$ for ψ an atomic formula. We can choose an enumeration of the atomic formulas in S, $s_1, s_2, \ldots$ and build an increasing infinite series of formulas Φ_i defined by

$$\Phi_i = \{s_1, s_2, \ldots, s_i\} \qquad .$$

We will demonstrate that there is an i such that $\Phi_i \models \psi$. By logical completeness, then, $\Phi_i \vdash \psi$, from which the theorem follows.

To show that $\Phi_i \models \psi$, it suffices to demonstrate that $[\,]_{\Phi_i}$ is at least as strong an equivalence relation as $[\,]_\psi$ and that the equivalence classes in $[\,]_{\Phi_i}$ are labeled at least as strongly as those in $[\,]_\psi$. We show that there is such a Φ_i for which these two criteria hold, considering each criterion in turn.

The equivalence relation for S, $[\,]_S$ is just the infinite union of the relations $[\,]_{\Phi_i}$. That is, for all paths p in the path domain of S,

$$[p]_S = \bigcup_{i=1}^{\infty} [p]_{\Phi_i} \quad .$$

Since all models of S are models of ψ, it follows that

$$[p]_\psi \subseteq \bigcup_{i=1}^{\infty} [p]_{\Phi_i}$$

for all paths p in the path domain of ψ. We want to show that this subset relation still holds even if ∞ is replaced by a suitably large integer.

It follows from the argument in the proof of Proposition 72 that $[\,]_\psi$ contains only a finite number of equivalence classes. Suppose each of these equivalence classes is itself finite. The equivalence relations $[p]_{\Phi_i}$ are increasingly strong (by Lemma 93) so that for any given equivalence class $[p]_\psi$, there must be an index i such that $[p]_{\Phi_i}$ contains it. Taking the maximum of the indices needed for each of the finite number of equivalence classes yields an i such that $[\,]_\psi \subseteq [\,]_{\Phi_i}$.

However, it might be the case that some equivalence class is not finite. This occurs just in case ψ is cyclic, that is, of the form $p \doteq p \cdot q$ for nonempty q (or $p \cdot q \doteq p$; without loss of generality, we will assume the former). In this case, the infinite equivalence classes are of the form $[p^n \cdot q']_\psi$ for q' a prefix of p or q. For such an equivalence class, we might imagine the possibility that only in the limit is this infinite class constructed, each of the equivalence relations $[\,]_{\Phi_i}$ containing only an approximation of it. However, this is not the case. Consider the pair of paths $p \cdot q'$ and $p \cdot p \cdot q'$. This pair, as it is in the equivalence relation $[p \cdot q']_\psi$, must be in one of the $[p \cdot q']_{\Phi_i}$. But, by virtue of the constraints on the equivalence relations (they are congruence-closed, recall), $[p \cdot q']_{\Phi_i}$ must also include all paths of the form $p^n \cdot q'$. Again, for each of the finite number of (now possibly infinite) equivalence classes, there is such an index. Taking the maximum of the indices yields an i such that $[\,]_\psi \subseteq [\,]_{\Phi_i}$.

That the labeling on the equivalence classes $[\,]_\psi$ is generated by some $[\,]_{\Phi_i}$ follows from similar reasoning, namely, that since the equivalence class is labeled in the infinite union, it must be so labeled in one of the components $[\,]_{\Phi_i}$ and there are only a finite number of equivalence classes, hence labels, that are pertinent, so that we can again take the maximum of the finite number of indices to choose a $[\,]_{\Phi_i}$ that labels equivalence classes at least as strongly as $[\,]_\psi$. $\qquad \square$

Model Locality

PROPOSITION 95 (MODEL LOCALITY 1 FOR $\mathcal{L}_{L,C}$) For $\mathcal{L}_{L,C}$, given a model M in the range of mm such that $p \in pdom(M)$ and $q \in pdom(M)$, then $M \sqcup mm(\{p \doteq q\})$ is defined if and only if $M/p \sqcup M/q$ is defined.

Proof If $M \sqcup mm(\{p \doteq q\})$ is undefined, then by Lemma 50, there exist Φ and Φ' such that $M \models \Phi$ and $mm(\{p \doteq q\}) \models \Phi'$ and $\Phi \cup \Phi'$ is inconsistent. By Lemma 16, $\{p \doteq q\} \vdash \Phi'$, so $\Phi \cup \{p \doteq q\}$ is inconsistent as well.

Now consider the equivalence classes over paths defined by $[\,]_{\Phi \cup \{p \doteq q\}}$. By Lemma 93, just proved above, these classes are merely a collapsing of the classes defined by Φ alone, where the classes $[p \cdot t]_\Phi$ and $[q \cdot t]_\Phi$ are collapsed for all t. The formula Φ is itself consistent; thus, its equivalence classes can be felicitously labeled with elements of C, assigning a unique constant to some of the classes corresponding to terminals. Since the formula $\Phi \cup \{p \doteq q\}$ is inconsistent, it must not be able to be so labeled. This must be because a collapsing of two classes—say $[p \cdot t]_\Phi$ and $[q \cdot t]_\Phi$— has made it impossible to appropriately label an equivalence class with a member of C. This could be either because $\Phi \vdash p \cdot t \doteq a$ and $\Phi \vdash q \cdot t \doteq b$ or because $\Phi \vdash p \cdot t \doteq a$ and $\Phi \vdash q \cdot t \cdot \langle f \rangle \doteq v$ for some label f. In the former case, $M/p \models s \doteq a$ and $M/q \models s \doteq b$, so $M/p \sqcup M/q$ is undefined. In the latter case, $M/p \models s \doteq a$ and $M/q \models s \cdot \langle f \rangle \doteq v$, and $M/p \sqcup M/q$ is again undefined.

Proving the other direction is much simpler. If $M/p \sqcup M/q$ is undefined but each is separately defined, then the individual submodels must satisfy clashing formulas. Assume that $M/p \models s \doteq a$ and $M/q \models s \doteq b$. (The other possibilities for clashes are proved similarly.) Then $M \models p \cdot s \doteq a$ and $M \models q \cdot s \doteq b$. The union $M \sqcup mm(\{p \doteq q\})$, if defined, would then have to satisfy both $p \cdot s \doteq a$ and $p \cdot s \doteq b$, which clash. Thus, the union is not well defined.   □

PROPOSITION 96 (MODEL LOCALITY 2 FOR $\mathcal{L}_{L,C}$)   Given models M and N with disjoint domains such that $p \in pdom(M)$ and $q \in pdom(N)$, then

$$(M \sqcup N \sqcup mm(\{p \doteq q\})) \upharpoonright dom(M) = M \sqcup N/q \backslash p \quad .$$

Proof We prove the proposition by demonstrating that the models on either side of the equals sign generate the same equivalence classes identically labeled. By categoricity, the two sides must then be equal.

Consider the equivalence classes over the path domain of $N/q\backslash p$ given by $[r]_{N/q\backslash p} = [s]_{N/q\backslash p}$ if and only if $N/q\backslash p \models r \doteq s$. These equivalence classes are generable from those for N itself, by replacing any paths $q \cdot s$ with $p \cdot s$, dropping all paths that do not have q as a prefix, and adding classes for each improper prefix p' of p. Consequently, there is a mapping $m_1 : [\ ]_{N/q\backslash p} \to [\ ]_N \cup [\ ]_{\{p \doteq q\}}$, where $[p \cdot s]_{N/q\backslash p} \mapsto [q \cdot s]_N$ and $[p']_{N/q\backslash p} \mapsto [p']_{\{p \doteq q\}}$ for p' a prefix of p. Now, the equivalence classes of paths N in the image of this mapping can themselves be mapped onto those for $N \sqcup mm(\{p \doteq q\})$. We will define this mapping m_2 to take $[q \cdot s]_N$ onto $[p \cdot s]_{N \sqcup mm(\{p \doteq q\})}$. (The path $p \cdot s$ is guaranteed to be in the path domain for $N \sqcup mm(\{p \doteq q\})$ if $q \cdot s$ is, because if $N \models q \cdot s \doteq q \cdot s$, then some formula satisfied by N entails it and that formula, together with $p \doteq q$, will prove $p \cdot s \doteq p \cdot s$ by Substitutivity. Thus, $p \cdot s$ will be in the path domain of $N \sqcup mm(\{p \doteq q\})$.) Finally, we define m_3 mapping from the portion of the image of m_1 concerning the path prefixes of p into the corresponding equivalence classes in $[\ ]_{N \sqcup mm(\{p \doteq q\})}$; that is, m_3 takes $[p']_{mm(\{p \doteq q\})}$ onto $[p']_{N \sqcup mm(\{p \doteq q\})}$. Taken together, we can compose the separate portions of m_1 with m_2 and m_3, respectively, yielding a mapping m from $N/q\backslash p$ to $N \sqcup mm(\{p \doteq q\})$, where $[p \cdot s]_{N/q\backslash p} \mapsto [p \cdot s]_{N \sqcup mm(\{p \doteq q\})}$ and $[p']_{N/q\backslash p} \mapsto [p']_{N \sqcup mm(\{p \doteq q\})}$ for p' a prefix of p.

It will be useful to examine the paths that occur in $[\ ]_{N/q\backslash p}$ and $[\ ]_{N \sqcup mm(\{p \doteq q\})}$. Recall that the path domain of N is disjoint from that of M. Now adding $mm(\{p \doteq q\})$ closes the path set under substitutions of ps for qs and adds path prefixes of p. All of these new paths (that is, the set of paths $\{p \cdot s \mid q \cdot s \in pdom(N)\} \cup \{p' \mid p'$ a prefix of $p\}$) are in the path domain of M, but these are also exactly the paths in the path domain for $N/q\backslash p$. Thus, the difference of the path domains of $N \sqcup mm(\{p \doteq q\})$ and $N/q\backslash p$ is comprised only of paths in the path domain of N and therefore outside the path domain of M.

We will now demonstrate that the classes for the left-hand-side and right-hand-side models have the same structure. We start by showing the structural similarity of $[\ ]_{N/q\backslash p}$ and $[\ ]_{N \sqcup mm(\{p \doteq q\})}$. For two distinct classes c_1 and c_2 in $[\ ]_{N/q\backslash p}$, their images under m in $[\ ]_{N \sqcup mm(\{p \doteq q\})}$ are also distinct, because both are generated from the equivalence classes of N under transformations that collapse no equivalence classes. (Forming

$N \sqcup mm(\{p \doteq q\})$ collapses no equivalence classes of N, because p is not even in the path domain of N; hence, there are no classes $[p \cdot s]_N$ to collapse with.)

So far we have shown that there is a one-to-one mapping m from $[\ ]_{N/q \backslash p}$ to $[\ ]_{N \sqcup mm(\{p \doteq q\})}$, where the classes not in the image of the mapping consist only of paths outside the path domain of M and where $m(c) - c$ for any class c in $[\ ]_{N/q \backslash p}$ also contains only paths outside the path domain of M. Taking the respective informational unions with M, namely, $M \sqcup (N \sqcup mm(\{p \doteq q\}))$ and $M \sqcup N/q \backslash p$, the engendered equivalence class structures are still parallel in this way. We argue this by showing that two equivalence classes in the latter are collapsed if and only if their images in the former are. Suppose we have a class $c_1 \in [\ ]_{N/q \backslash p}$ and another class $c_2 \in [\ ]_{N \sqcup mm(\{p \doteq q\})}$ that collapse in the classes of the informational union $M \sqcup N/q \backslash p$, that is, they share some element. Since $c_1 \subseteq m(c_1)$, then $m(c_1)$ also shares a path with c_2; hence, they collapse in the union $M \sqcup (N \sqcup mm(\{p \doteq q\}))$. Suppose c_1 and c_2 do not collapse. Then, since $m(c_1) - c_1$ contains only paths outside the path domain of M, and c_2 contains paths in the path domain of M, the classes $m(c_1)$ and c_2 do not collapse either.

In summary, the equivalence class structures for $M \sqcup N \sqcup mm(\{p \doteq q\})$ and $M \sqcup N/q \backslash p$ are the same except that the former contains extra classes and extra paths all of which are outside the path domain of M. Thus, the restricted class $(M \sqcup N \sqcup mm(\{p \doteq q\})) \backslash dom(M)$ and $M \sqcup N/q \backslash p$ have identical equivalence classes.

Similar arguments show that the labeling of the classes is shared as well. Thus, the two models must be equal. $\square$

PROPOSITION 97 (MODEL LOCALITY 3 FOR $\mathcal{L}_{L,C}$) If $dom(M)$ is disjoint from $dom(N)$ and M and N are not top-cyclic, then $(M \sqcup N) \backslash dom(M) = M$.

Proof By Lemma 39, $M \leq M \sqcup N$. Monotonicity yields $M \backslash dom(M) \leq (M \sqcup N) \backslash dom(M)$, so $M \leq (M \sqcup N) \backslash dom(M)$ by Lemma 48.

We must show, then, that $(M \sqcup N) \backslash dom(M) \leq M$. By definition of restriction along with compactness, $(M \sqcup N) \backslash dom(M) \models \phi$ if and only if $\Psi \vdash \phi$ and $M \sqcup N \models \Psi$ for some Ψ such that all paths in Ψ are either trivial or start with an element of $dom(M)$. We will show that for all such cases, there is a proof of $\Psi \vdash \phi$ using only atomic formulas in Ψ

satisfied by M. Therefore, there is a subset of Ψ—say Ψ'—such that $M \models \Psi'$ and $\Psi' \vdash \phi$. Thus, $M \models \phi$, and $(M \sqcup N)|\!\!\upharpoonright dom(M) \leq M$.

Consider the proof for $\Psi \vdash \phi$, and divide Ψ into Ψ_M, those atomic formulas that M satisfies, and Ψ_N, those that M does not satisfy (but N does). There are three cases: only Ψ_M is used in the proof, only Ψ_N is used in the proof, or both are. First, we will reduce the third case to the first two.

Suppose the proof uses some formulas in Ψ that are satisfied only by N (i.e., elements of Ψ_N) and some satisfied by M (i.e., elements of Ψ_M). Then there must be a step in the proof that uses antecedents ϕ_M and ϕ_N, where $M \models \phi_M$ and $N \models \phi_N$, but $M \not\models \phi_N$; schematically, the proof looks like this:

$$
\begin{array}{cc}
\underline{\Psi_M} & \underline{\Psi_N} \\
\cdot & \cdot \\
\cdot & \cdot \\
\cdot & \cdot \\
\underline{\phi_M} & \underline{\phi_N} \\
\underline{\phi_{MN}} & \qquad \Psi \\
& \cdot \\
& \cdot \\
& \cdot \\
\phi & \cdot
\end{array}
$$

The crucial step in the proof (from ϕ_M and ϕ_N to ϕ_{MN}) must be Substitutivity, so either $\phi_M = q \doteq p$ and $\phi_N = p \cdot r \doteq v$ or $\phi_N = q \doteq p$ and $\phi_M = p \cdot r \doteq v$. We will assume the former for the moment, returning to the latter case below. Now if p is nontrivial, we have the two proofs

$$
\begin{array}{cc}
\underline{\Psi_M} & \underline{\Psi_N} \\
\cdot & \cdot \\
\cdot & \cdot \\
\cdot & \cdot \\
\underline{q \doteq p} & \underline{p \cdot r \doteq v} \\
\underline{p \doteq p} & \underline{p \doteq p} \\
\langle f \rangle \doteq \langle f \rangle & \langle f \rangle \doteq \langle f \rangle
\end{array}
$$

from which it follows that $M \models \langle f \rangle \doteq \langle f \rangle$ and $N \models \langle f \rangle \doteq \langle f \rangle$. Thus, the domains of M and N are not disjoint; p must be trivial.

But if p is trivial, and M and N are not top-cyclic, then q must be trivial as well. Thus, the proof must be of the form

$$
\begin{array}{ccc}
\dfrac{\Psi_M}{\vdots} & \dfrac{\Psi_N}{\vdots} & \\[4pt]
\overline{\langle\rangle \doteq \langle\rangle} \quad r \doteq v & & \\
\overline{\qquad r \doteq v \qquad} & \Psi & \\
\vdots & & \\
\phi & &
\end{array}
$$

in which case the proof can be simplified to

$$
\begin{array}{cc}
\dfrac{\Psi_N}{\vdots} & \\[4pt]
\overline{r \doteq v} & \Psi \\
\vdots & \\
\phi &
\end{array}
$$

thereby eliminating this dependence on Ψ_M. Returning to the earlier assumption that $\phi_M = q \doteq p$ and $\phi_N = p \cdot r \doteq v$, if we assume the alternative, namely, that $\phi_N = q \doteq p$ and $\phi_M = p \cdot r \doteq v$, the proof goes through as before but eliminates dependence on Ψ_N. Since all such separating steps can be eliminated, the entire proof can be normalized to use only one of Ψ_M or Ψ_N.

If the proof uses only Ψ_N (i.e., $N \models \phi$), then all paths in ϕ must be prefixes or extensions of paths in $dom(N)$ (by logical locality). Since the domains of M and N are disjoint, $\phi = \langle\rangle \doteq \langle\rangle$. But this can be proved from Ψ_M alone. Thus, in every case, a proof can be found using only Ψ_M. As argued above, this entails that $(M \sqcup N)|\backslash dom(M) \leq M$. By categoricity, we can conclude that $(M \sqcup N)|\backslash dom(M) = M$. $\square$

PROPOSITION 98 (MODEL LOCALITY 4 FOR $\mathcal{L}_{L,C}$) Given models M and N and a set of features F, if $dom(N) \subseteq F$ and M and N are not top-cyclic, then $(M \sqcup N)|\backslash F = M|\backslash F \sqcup N$.

Proof   We must show that $M|\backslash F \sqcup N \leq (M \sqcup N)|\backslash F$ and $(M \sqcup N)|\backslash F \leq M|\backslash F \sqcup N$. Then, by categoricity, the equality holds.

By Lemma 39, $M{\restriction}F \leq M{\restriction}F \sqcup N$. Since $M{\restriction}F$ and N are not top-cyclic, all paths in $M{\restriction}F{\sqcup}N$ start with F, so $M{\restriction}F{\sqcup}N = (M{\restriction}F{\sqcup}N){\restriction}F$. Thus, $M{\restriction}F \leq (M{\restriction}F \sqcup N){\restriction}F$, whence by monotonicity, $M{\restriction}F \leq (M \sqcup N){\restriction}F$. Similarly, $N \leq (M \sqcup N){\restriction}F$. Thus, $M{\restriction}F \sqcup N \leq (M \sqcup N){\restriction}F$ by definition of $\sqcup$.

The other direction of subsumption is argued as follows. By definition of restriction, along with compactness, $(M \sqcup N){\restriction}F \models \phi$ if and only if $\Psi \vdash \phi$ and $M \sqcup N \models \Psi$ for some Ψ such that all paths in Ψ are either trivial or start with an element of F. We will show that $M{\restriction}F{\sqcup}N \models \Psi$. Thus, $M{\restriction}F \sqcup N \models \phi$ and $(M \sqcup N){\restriction}F \leq M{\restriction}F \sqcup N$.

To show that $M{\restriction}F \sqcup N \models \Psi$, consider any atomic formula $\psi \in \Psi$. Since $M \sqcup N \models \psi$, by compactness, there is a Ψ' such that $M \sqcup N \models \Psi'$ and $\Psi' \vdash \psi$. Consider the proof of ψ from Ψ', and recall that the paths in ψ either are trivial or start with an element of F. If the last step in the proof of ψ is Triviality, Reflexivity, or Symmetry, the antecedents have the same path prefixes as ψ; thus, their paths also either are trivial or start with an element of F. In the case of a Substitutivity step

$$\frac{q \doteq p \quad p \cdot r \doteq v}{\psi}$$

this is also true unless q is trivial but p is not. In this case, however, $M \sqcup N$ is top-cyclic, contra assumption. (It is easy to see that if $M \sqcup N$ is top-cyclic, then either M or N or both are.) Thus, the immediate antecedents of ψ, and by a simple induction all antecedents including the elements of Ψ, have paths that either are trivial or start with elements of F. Thus, $M{\restriction}F{\sqcup}N{\restriction}F \models \Psi'$. Since $N = N{\restriction}F$, we have that $M{\restriction}F{\sqcup}N \models \Psi'$ and $M{\restriction}F \sqcup N \models \phi$. $\qquad\square$

Glossary

$mm(\Phi)$	minimal model of a formula Φ, 36
$metm(\Phi)$	minimal eqtree model of a formula Φ, 99
$mptm(\Phi)$	minimal potree model of a formula Φ, 142
m_p	prefixed homomorphism, 28
NP	noun phrase, 8
num	number feature, 9
$p + t$	the property of being equivalent (according to a particular model) to the path $p \cdot t$, 159
P	productions of a grammar, 52
p_0	start production of a grammar, 52
$Path$	set of paths (label sequences), 25
$pdom(M)$	path domain of a model M, the set of paths for which a model is defined; cf. dom, 158
per	person feature, 9
ϕ	atomic formula, 26
Φ	nonatomic formula, 26
$\Phi\langle p \to q \rangle$	substitution of $q \cdot r$ for a single occurrence of $p \cdot r$ in Φ, 27
$\Phi[p \to q]$	substitution of $q \cdot r$ for all paths in Φ, which are all of the form $p \cdot r$, 27
π	π, 101
Π	the set of parse trees, 54
Π_i	the set of parse trees of depth i, 55
ρ	monotonic weakening function used in prediction step of the abstract algorithm, 59
$R(\vec{v})$	arbitrary atomic formula, 27
S	sentence, 8
$\overline{S}$	sentential complement, 132
Σ	vocabulary of a grammar, 52
τ	mapping from graphs to corresponding eqtrees; inverse of γ, 108
$terminals(s)$	the terminal nodes of a frame s, 104
$\mathcal{T}_{L,C}$	class of finite feature trees, 88
$\mathcal{T}_{L,C}^{\infty}$	class of infinite trees, 92
$\mathcal{T}_{L,C}^{=}$	class of eqtrees, 97
$\mathcal{T}_{L,C}^{\leq}$	class of potrees, 140
$type$	type feature, 17
V	value descriptors (constants and paths), 26
VP	verb phrase, 8

Bibliography

Aho, Al V. and Jeffrey D. Ullman. 1972. *Theory of Parsing, Translation and Compiling*, volume 1. Prentice-Hall, Englewood Cliffs, New Jersey.

Aït-Kaci, Hassan. 1985. *A New Model of Computation Based on a Calculus of Type Subsumption*. Ph.D. thesis, University of Pennsylvania, Philadelphia, Pennsylvania.

Barwise, Jon. 1988. Paper presented at the Mathematical Theories of Language Workshop at the 1988 Linguistic Institute, Stanford University, Stanford, California.

Boyer, Robert S. and J Strother Moore. 1972. The sharing of structure in theorem-proving programs. In B. Meltzer and D. Michie, editors, *Machine Intelligence*, volume 7. John Wiley and Sons, New York, New York, pages 101–116.

Bresnan, Joan, editor. 1982. *The Mental Representation of Grammatical Relations*. MIT Press, Cambridge, Massachusetts.

Cardelli, Luca. 1984. A semantics of multiple inheritance. Technical report, Bell Laboratories, Murray Hill, New Jersey.

Chomsky, Noam and M. P. Schutzenberger. 1963. The algebraic theory of context-free languages. In P. Braffort and D. Hirschberg, editors, *Computer Programming and Formal Systems*. North Holland, Amsterdam, Holland.

Colmerauer, Alain. 1970. Les systèmes-q ou un formalisme pour analyser et synthétiser des phrases sur ordinateur. Internal Publication 43, Département d'Informatique, Université de Montréal, Canada.

Colmerauer, Alain. 1978. Metamorphosis grammars. In L. Bolc, editor, *Natural Language Communication with Computers*. Springer-Verlag, Berlin, West Germany.

Courcelle, Bruno. 1983. Fundamental properties of infinite trees. *Theoretical Computer Science*, 25(2):95–169, March.

Crain, Stephen and Mark Steedman. 1985. On not being led up the garden path: The use of context by the psychological syntax processor. In David R. Dowty, Lauri Karttunen, and Arnold M. Zwicky, editors, *Natural Language Parsing: Psychological, Computational, and Theoretical Perspectives*. Cambridge University Press, Cambridge, England, pages 320–358.

Dahl, Veronica and Harvey Abramson. 1984. On gapping grammars. In Sten-Åke Tärnlund, editor, *Proceedings of the Second International Logic Programming Conference*, pages 77–88, Uppsala, Sweden, 2–6 July.

Dahl, Veronica and Michael C. McCord. 1983. Treating coordination in logic grammars. *American Journal of Computational Linguistics*, 9(2):69–91, April–June.

Dawar, Anuj and K. Vijay-Shanker. 1990. An interpretation of negation in feature structures. *Computational Linguistics*, 16(1):11–21, March.

Dörre, Jochen and William Rounds. 1990. On subsumption and semiunification in feature algebras. In *Proceedings of the Fifth Annual IEEE Symposium on Logic in Computer Science*, pages 300–310, Philadelphia, Pennsylvania, 4–7 June.

Dyla, Stefan. 1984. Across-the-board dependencies and case in Polish. *Linguistic Inquiry*, 15(4):701–705.

Earley, Jay. 1970. An efficient context-free parsing algorithm. *Communications of the ACM*, 13(2):94–102, February.

Ford, Marilyn, Joan Bresnan, and Ronald M. Kaplan. 1982. A competence-based theory of syntactic closure. In Joan Bresnan, editor, *The Mental Representation of Grammatical Relations*. MIT Press, Cambridge, Massachusetts.

Frazier, Lyn and Janet D. Fodor. 1978. The sausage machine: A new two-stage parsing model. *Cognition*, 6:291–325.

Gazdar, Gerald. 1981. Unbounded dependencies and coordinate structure. *Linguistic Inquiry*, 12(2):155–184.

Gazdar, Gerald. 1982. Phrase structure grammar. In Pauline Jacobson and Geoffrey K. Pullum, editors, *The Nature of Syntactic Representation*. D. Reidel, Dordrecht, Holland, pages 131–186.

Gazdar, Gerald, Ewan Klein, Geoffrey K. Pullum, and Ivan A. Sag. 1985. *Generalized Phrase Structure Grammar*. Blackwell Publishing, Oxford, England, and Harvard University Press, Cambridge, Massachusetts.

Gazdar, Gerald, Geoffrey K. Pullum, and Ivan A. Sag. 1982. Auxiliaries and related phenomena in a restrictive theory of grammar. *Language*, 58(3):591–638, September.

Graham, Susan L., Michael A. Harrison, and Walter L. Ruzzo. 1980. An improved context-free recognizer. *ACM Transactions on Programming Languages and Systems*, 2(3):415–462.

Haas, Andrew. 1989. A parsing algorithm for unification grammar. *Computational Linguistics*, 15(4):219–232, December.

Henniss, Kathryn. 1988. Control, coordination, and subjects in Malayalam. Unpublished manuscript.

Hindley, Roger. 1969. The principal type-scheme of an object in combinatory logic. *Transactions of the American Mathematical Society*, 146, December.

Hirsh, Susan B. 1986. P-PATR: A compiler for unification-based grammars. Master's thesis, Stanford University, Stanford, California.

Jaffar, Joxan and Jean-Louis Lassez. 1987. Constraint logic programming. In *Proceedings of the Fourteenth Annual ACM Symposium on Principles of Programming Languages*, Munich, West Germany, 21–23 January.

Johnson, Mark. 1988. *Attribute-Value Logic and the Theory of Grammar*, volume 16 of *CSLI Lecture Notes*. Center for the Study of Language and Information, Stanford, California.

Kahn, Gilles. 1987. Natural semantics. Rapport de recherche no. 102, INRIA, Sophia-Antipolis, France.

Kaplan, Ronald M. 1973. A general syntactic processor. In R. Rustin, editor, *Natural Language Processing*. Algorithmics Press, New York, New York.

Kaplan, Ronald M. and Joan Bresnan. 1982. Lexical-functional grammar: A formal system for grammatical representation. In Joan Bresnan, editor, *The Mental Representation of Grammatical Relations*. MIT Press, Cambridge, Massachusetts.

Kaplan, Ronald M. and John Maxwell. 1988. Coordination in LFG. Talk presented to the Foundations of Grammar project, Center for the Study of Language and Information, Stanford, California.

Karttunen, Lauri. 1984. Features and values. In *Proceedings of the Tenth International Conference on Computational Linguistics*, pages 28–33, Stanford University, Stanford, California, 2–6 July.

Karttunen, Lauri. 1986. Radical lexicalism. Technical Report CSLI–86–68, Center for the Study of Language and Information, Stanford, California, December.

Karttunen, Lauri and Martin Kay. 1985. Structure sharing with binary trees. In *Proceedings of the 23rd Annual Meeting of the Association for Computational Linguistics*, University of Chicago, Chicago, Illinois, 8–12 July.

Kasper, Robert. 1987. *Feature Structures: A Logical Theory with Application to Language Analysis*. Ph.D. thesis, University of Michigan, Ann Arbor, Michigan.

Kasper, Robert and William Rounds. 1986. A logical semantics for feature structures. In *Proceedings of the 24th Annual Meeting of the Association for Computational Linguistics*, pages 257–266, Columbia University, New York, New York, 10–13 June.

Kay, Martin. 1980. Algorithm schemata and data structures in syntactic processing. Technical report, Xerox Palo Alto Research Center, Palo Alto, California.

Kay, Martin. 1983. Unification grammar. Technical report, Xerox Palo Alto Research Center, Palo Alto, California.

Kay, Martin. 1985. Parsing in functional unification grammar. In David R. Dowty, Lauri Karttunen, and Arnold M. Zwicky, editors, *Natural Language Parsing: Psychological, Computational, and Theoretical Perspectives*. Cambridge University Press, Cambridge, England, pages 251–278.

Kfoury, A. J., J. Tiuryn, and P. Urzyczyn. 1989. Computational consequences and partial solutions of a generalized unification problem. In *Proceedings of the Fourth Annual IEEE Symposium on Logic in Computer Science*, pages 98–105, Asilomar, California, 5–8 June.

Kimball, John P. 1973. Seven principles of surface structure parsing in natural language. *Cognition*, 2(1):15–47.

Knuth, Donald E. 1965. On the translation of languages from left to right. *Information and Control*, 8(6):607–639.

Kowalski, Robert A. 1979. Algorithm = logic + control. *Communications of the ACM*, 22(7):424–436, July.

Leiß, Hans. 1990. Polymorphic constructs in natural and programming languages. In Jan van Eijck, editor, *Logics in AI: European Workshop JELIA '90*. Springer-Verlag, Berlin, West Germany, pages 348–365.

Macken, Marlys A. 1986. Agreement, rule interaction and the phonology-syntax interface. In Joshua A. Fishman *et al.*, editor, *The Fergusonian Impact, Volume 1: From Phonology to Society*. Mouton de Gruyter, Berlin, West Germany.

Marcus, Mitchell. 1980. *A Theory of Syntactic Recognition for Natural Language*. MIT Press, Cambridge, Massachusetts.

McCord, Michael C. 1980. Slot grammars. *American Journal of Computational Linguistics*, 6(1):255–286, January–March.

Milner, Robin. 1978. A theory of type polymorphism in programming. *Journal of Computer and System Sciences*, 17:348–375.

Moshier, M. Drew. 1988a. Paper presented at the Mathematical Theories of Language Workshop at the 1988 Linguistic Institute.

Moshier, M. Drew. 1988b. *Extensions to Unification Grammar for the Description of Programming Languages*. Ph.D. thesis, University of Michigan, Ann Arbor, Michigan, March.

Moshier, M. Drew and William C. Rounds. 1987. A logic for partially specified data structures. In *Proceedings of the Fourteenth Annual ACM Symposium on Principles of Programming Languages*, pages 156–167, Munich, West Germany, 21–23 January.

Nelson, Greg and Derek C. Oppen. 1978. Fast decision algorithms based on congruence closure. Technical Report AIM-309, Stanford Artificial Intelligence Laboratory, Stanford University, Stanford, California, February. Also in *Proceedings of the 18th Annual Symposium on Foundations of Computer Science*, Providence, Rhode Island, October, 1977.

Pereira, Fernando C. N. 1981. Extraposition grammars. *American Journal of Computational Linguistics*, 7(4):243–256, October-December.

Pereira, Fernando C. N. 1983. Logic for natural language analysis. Technical Note 275, Artificial Intelligence Center, SRI International, Menlo Park, California.

Pereira, Fernando C. N. 1985a. A new characterization of attachment preferences. In David R. Dowty, Lauri Karttunen, and Arnold M. Zwicky, editors, *Natural Language Parsing: Psychological, Computational, and Theoretical Perspectives*. Cambridge University Press, Cambridge, England, pages 307–319.

Pereira, Fernando C. N. 1985b. A structure-sharing representation for unification-based grammar formalisms. In *Proceedings of the 23rd Annual Meeting of the Association for Computational Linguistics*, University of Chicago, Chicago, Illinois, 8–12 July.

Pereira, Fernando C. N. and Stuart M. Shieber. 1984. The semantics of grammar formalisms seen as computer languages. In *Proceedings of the Tenth International Conference on Computational Linguistics*, Stanford University, Stanford, California, 2–6 July.

Pereira, Fernando C. N. and David H. D. Warren. 1983. Parsing as deduction. In *Proceedings of the 21st Annual Meeting of the Association for Computational Linguistics*, pages 137–144, Massachusetts Institute of Technology, Cambridge, Massachusetts, 15–17 June.

Peters, Jr., P. Stanley and Robert W. Ritchie. 1973. Context-sensitive immediate constituent analysis: Context-free languages revisited. *Mathematical Systems Theory*, 6(4):324–333, January.

Pollard, Carl. 1985a. Lecture notes on head-driven phrase-structure grammar. Center for the Study of Language and Information, Stanford, California, February.

Pollard, Carl. 1985b. Phrase structure grammar without metarules. In Jeff Goldberg, Marcy Macken, and Michael Wescoat, editors, *Proceedings of the Fourth West Coast Conference on Formal Linguistics*, University of Southern California, Los Angeles, California.

Pollard, Carl and Ivan A. Sag. 1987. *Information-Based Syntax and Semantics*, volume 13 of *CSLI Lecture Notes*. Center for the Study of Language and Information, Stanford, California.

Pullum, Geoffrey K. and Arnold M. Zwicky. 1986. Phonological resolution of syntactic feature conflict. *Language*, 62(4):751–773, December.

Robinson, J. A. 1965. A machine-oriented logic based on the resolution principle. *Journal of the ACM*, 12(1):23–44, January.

Robinson, Jane J. 1982. DIAGRAM: A grammar for dialogues. *Communications of the ACM*, 25(1):27–47, January.

Rosenschein, Stanley J. and Stuart M. Shieber. 1982. Translating English into logical form. In *Proceedings of the 20th Annual Meeting of the Association for Computational Linguistics*, pages 1–8, University of Toronto, Toronto, Ontario, Canada, 16–18 June.

Rounds, William C. and Robert Kasper. 1986. A complete logical calculus for record structures representing linguistic information. In *Proceedings of the Symposium on Logic in Computer Science*, pages 34–43, 16–18 June.

Sag, Ivan A., Gerald Gazdar, Thomas Wasow, and Steven Weisler. 1985. Coordination and how to distinguish categories. *Natural Language and Linguistic Theory*, 3(2):117–171, May.

Sato, Taisuke and Hisao Tamaki. 1984. Enumeration of success patterns in logic programs. *Theoretical Computer Science*, 34(1–2):227–240, November.

Shieber, Stuart M. 1983. Sentence disambiguation by a shift-reduce parsing technique. In *Proceedings of the 21st Annual Meeting of the Association for Computational Linguistics*, pages 113–118, Massachusetts Institute of Technology, Cambridge, Massachusetts, 15–17 June.

Shieber, Stuart M. 1984. The design of a computer language for linguistic information. In *Proceedings of the Tenth International Conference on Computational Linguistics*, pages 362–366, Stanford University, Stanford, California, 2–6 July.

Shieber, Stuart M. 1985a. Criteria for designing computer facilities for linguistic analysis. *Linguistics*, 23:189–211.

Shieber, Stuart M. 1985b. *An Introduction to Unification-Based Approaches to Grammar*, volume 4 of *CSLI Lecture Notes*. Center for the Study of Language and Information, Stanford, California.

Shieber, Stuart M. 1985c. Using restriction to extend parsing algorithms for complex-feature-based formalisms. In *Proceedings of the 23nd Annual Meeting of the Association for Computational Linguistics*, pages 145–152, University of Chicago, Chicago, Illinois, 8–12 July.

Shieber, Stuart M. 1986. A simple reconstruction of GPSG. In *Proceedings of the Eleventh International Conference on Computational Linguistics*, pages 211–215, University of Bonn, Bonn, West Germany, 25–29 August.

Shieber, Stuart M. 1988a. Separating linguistic analyses from linguistic theories. In Uwe Reyle and Christian Rohrer, editors, *Natural Language Parsing and Linguistic Theories*. D. Reidel, Dordrecht, Holland, pages 33–68.

Shieber, Stuart M. 1988b. A uniform architecture for parsing and generation. In *Proceedings of the Twelfth International Conference on Computational Linguistics*, pages 614–619, Karl Marx University of Economics, Budapest, Hungary, 22–27 August.

Shieber, Stuart M., Lauri Karttunen, and Fernando C. N. Pereira. 1984. Notes from the unification underground: A compilation of papers on unification-based grammar formalisms. Technical Report 327, Artificial Intelligence Center, SRI International, Menlo Park, California, June.

Shieber, Stuart M., Hans Uszkoreit, Fernando C. N. Pereira, Jane J. Robinson, and Mabry Tyson. 1983. The formalism and implementation of PATR-II. In Barbara Grosz and Mark Stickel, editors, *Research on Interactive Acquisition and Use of Knowledge*, volume SRI Final Report 1894. Artificial Intelligence Center, SRI International, Menlo Park, California.

Smolka, Gert. 1988. A feature logic with subsorts. LILOG Report 33, IBM Deutschland, Stuttgart, West Germany.

Thompson, Henry. 1981. Chart parsing and rule schemata in GPSG. In *Proceedings of the 19th Annual Meeting of the Association for Computational Linguistics*, pages 167–172, Stanford University, Stanford, California, 29 June–1 July.

Uszkoreit, Hans. 1986. Categorial unification grammars. Technical Report CSLI–86–66, Center for the Study of Language and Information, Stanford, California, December.

Warren, David H. D. and Fernando C. N. Pereira. 1982. An efficient easily adaptable system for interpreting natural language queries. *American Journal of Computational Linguistics*, 8(3-4):110–122, July.

Winograd, Terry. 1983. *Language as a Cognitive Process—Volume 1: Syntax*. Addison-Wesley, Reading, Massachusetts.

Wittenburg, Kent Barrows. 1986. *Natural Language Parsing with Combinatory Categorial Grammar in a Graph-Unification-Based Formalism*. Ph.D. thesis, University of Texas, Austin, Texas, August.

Woods, William. 1970. Transition network grammars for natural language analysis. *Communications of the ACM*, 13(10), October.

Wroblewski, David A. 1987. Nondestructive graph unification. In *Proceedings of the Sixth National Conference on Artificial Intelligence*, pages 582–587, Seattle, Washington, 13–17 July.

Zaenen, Annie and Lauri Karttunen. 1984. Morphological non-distinctiveness and coordination. In *Eastern States Conference on Linguistics 1*, The Ohio State University, Columbus, Ohio.

Zeevat, Henk. 1988. Combining categorial grammar and unification. In Uwe Reyle and Christian Rohrer, editors, *Natural Language Parsing and Linguistic Theories*. D. Reidel, Dordrecht, Holland, pages 202–229.

Index